BEYOND BUREAUCRACY

BEYOND BUREAUCRACY

essays on the development and evolution of human organization

WARREN BENNIS

McGraw-Hill Book Company

New York • St. Louis • San Francisco • London • Düsseldorf
Kuala Lumpur • Mexico • Montreal • Panama • São Paulo
Sydney • Toronto • Johannesburg • New Delhi • Singapore

BEYOND BUREAUCRACY

Formerly titled **Changing Organizations**

Library of Congress Catalog Card Number 65–25915

07-004760-X

First McGraw-Hill Paperback Edition, 1973

123456789   MUMU   79876543

To Clurie and Katie:
my living links with evolution

preface to the Paperback Edition

It is sometimes the fate of a book to appear a decade or more before its point of greatest timeliness.

One thinks, for example, of William Vogt's *The Road to Survival* which in 1949 sounded the warning of man's ecological suicide long before the word "ecology" was in common use; it was not heeded until the mid-1960s, only after Rachel Carson's *Silent Spring*. My own *The Temporary Society*, co-authored with Philip Slater in 1967, found its maximum impact after Alvin Toffler in 1971 dramatized some of its findings in *Future Shock*. Both Scott Nearing and Louis Bromfield were preaching and practicing organic farming in the 1940s; Nearing, now in his late eighties, still raising and eating organic food on a farm in Vermont, finds his reissued book *Living the Good Life* (co-authored with his wife) a best seller among youngsters who were not even born when it was first published three decades ago.

This book *Beyond Bureaucracy* first appeared in 1966 as *Changing Organizations*. Some of its earlier readers have suggested that it is even timelier for the America of 1973 than it was for the America of 1966, or for the America of 1961 when I began the essays that comprise it.

The subject of the book is Change—by 1966 already so swift and so profound that in the original preface I wrote "no exaggeration, no hyperbole, no outrage can realistically" describe its pace and extent, much less (in Robert Oppenheimer's words) "the changing scale and scope of change itself . . . so that the world alters even as we walk on it." In the seven years since that preface was written the exponential acceleration of change, the concatenation and tragedy of unforeseeable events—assassinations, bloody and unpopular war, campus upheavals, ghetto uprisings—would require a modern-day Homer even to begin to tell the story.

In India, while on a special academic mission, I put these essays together. It was like being in one of H. G. Wells' time machines to be able to observe the world's most technologized society from one just beginning to break out of the feudal past. Such a society can, in a sense, "see" the future before it happens—it can see the alternative future expressed in the great industrialized states. The simultaneous existence of societies at markedly different stages of economic, political and social development and the mass media which transmit images of these societies to all nations at any stage of development, from primitive villages to urban complexes, make this phenomenon possible. The potential exists to *seize* the future through the examination and evaluation of the social and moral consequences of change before they occur. I was able to watch America while in India from this vast distance of both physical miles and technological time. In those years of the tremendous growth of technology and the efflorescence of multinational corporations, it seemed not too wild a dream to hope that all problems of organization and society could be solved by technology, and that even the problems created by these solutions could in turn be eliminated by higher technology.

The biggest single problem of technology, it seemed to me at the time of writing this book, was not merely to accept the inevitability of bewildering, upheaving change (like Emerson's supposed retort to Margaret Fuller's "I accept the Universe"—"By God, she'd better"), but rather to manage and control it. The supreme question was whether man must forever, as in the past, be tossed and blown by change, or whether he can, by rational foresight, conscious effort and plan, become "pro-active" enough to control, at least in substantial part, his own evolution. My thesis, therefore, is how those organizations—in which nine-tenths of all Americans find their livelihood—can be reformed and reshaped in a life-enhancing and spiritually summoning way. And to do so before that predictable time, whether a quarter or half century away, when bureaucracy as the prevailing and dominant system of organization comes to an inevitable end. Hence, *Beyond Bureaucracy.*

Both the military and ecclesiastical models, from which all modern bureaucratic systems have been drawn, are in serious turmoil and disarray. It is not the Jesuit father, Daniel Berrigan, who cries his order's motto, "Ad majorem Dei gloriam," to comfort some errant parishioner; it is the Catholic FBI agent who cries it while collaring the fugitive Berrigan as an enemy of organized authority. Berrigan himself cries: "I burned files, not babies." As for the military, the carrier *Constellation* is immobilized by the refusal of black seamen to serve. David Halberstam's exhaustive search for a cause of bureaucracy's ultimate failure can find little more than the fact that (as one reviewer writes) "generals and cabinet officers and lesser bureaucrats are all 'players' in the game of bureaucratic politics where their primary loyalty is to the team, and what's good for the team may not necessarily be good for the country." Shifting to business, there is the spectacle of IT&T shredding its own documents and the Penn Central merger, which seemed to integrate the most rational, efficient transportation system ever devised, blowing up in a way that almost ruined unsuspecting bankers and came within a whisper of shattering the whole economy.

I am not quite as optimistic as I was seven years ago about some of my assumptions. I am less confident that (to quote the title of Chapter 2) "Democracy Is Inevitable." But I am more convinced that our future depends upon making it so.

A year's trials as President of a large university make me even more certain that a viable managerial strategy does not lie in consensus. In caring, surely; in civility, definitely; in comity, especially—but not in consensus. At a time when perhaps two-thirds of our ablest students seek, for a purposeful life, to apply themselves to some meaningful area of health, welfare or another social service; at a time when our great cities are torn by drug addiction, crime and alienation for lack of these services—I am convinced that we can adequately deal with our crises only through managers who can devise strategies that will carry us "beyond bureaucracy" into control of our own evolution.

Warren Bennis
President, University of Cincinnati
March 1973

preface

It so happens that the world is undergoing a transformation to which no change that has yet occurred can be compared.

Charles de Gaulle

One thing that is new is the prevalence of newness, the changing scale and scope of change itself, so that the world alters as we walk on it, so that the years of man's life measure not some small growth or rearrangement or moderation of what he learned in childhood, but a great upheaval.

Robert Oppenheimer

"Everything nailed down is coming loose," a historian said recently, and it seems that no exaggeration, no hyperbole, no outrage can realistically describe the extent and pace of change which modernization involves. In fact, only the exaggerations appear to be true. And it is to our credit that the pseudo horror stories and futuristic fantasies about *increases* in the rate of change (rate of obsolescence of workers, growth of technology and science, and the number of "vanishing stories"—the vanishing salesman, the vanishing host, the vanishing adolescent, the vanishing village, etc.) fail to deter our compulsive desire to invent, to overthrow, to upset inherited patterns. As Ecclesiastes glumly observes, men persist in disordering their settled ways and beliefs by seeking out many inventions.

This book of essays approaches the problem of change from many different angles, all of which focus on the cause and consequences of change in *organizational* behavior. In a way, I suppose, these essays reveal my favorite intellectual preoccupations: (1) the problems of change, (2) how they affect human organizations, and (3) what the behavioral sciences can do about directing the rate, shape, and consequences of change. Man's fate today, as never before, is to understand this "prevalence of newness" so that we can welcome and even predict the force of change without a guarded frozenness or a heightened susceptibility. Justice Holmes's remark that "science has made major contributions to minor needs" no longer holds in my view. It seems to me that the behavioral sciences can contribute a good deal to an understanding of our contemporary crises.

The book is divided into two parts. Part 1 identifies some important evolutionary trends in organizational development. Part 2 focuses on the ways behavioral scientists can illuminate and direct processes of change. In other words, Part 1 discusses some developments and certain "natural" tendencies, for example, toward democracy and science. Part 2, on the other hand, shows how action based on knowledge and self-determination can change the nature of organizational life.

To use the language of child psychology, evolutionary tendencies are basic regularities of growth in certain directions, toward *maturation,* while planned change involves human or cultural interventions, toward *acculturation.* Of course, it is sometimes difficult or even meaningless to distinguish between the two. Illness, for example, can slow down the growth of long bones and delay the appearance of ossification centers, so that the natural process is retarded. At the same time, recent progress on bone and cartilage surgery has affected significantly the natural process of bone maturation. I would wager that as science progresses, the relationship between *evolutionary* and *directed* change will blur, just as so-called natural childbirth is damned unnatural for most.

In any case, while I forecast the structure and value coordinates for organizations of the future and contend that they are inevitable, it should not bar any of us from giving a little push here and there to that inevitability. And while the French moralist may be right when he says that there are no delightful marriages, just good ones, it is possible that if practitioners and students of organizations get their heads together, they will develop delightful organizations—just possibly.

If there is a strain of optimism in these essays, I hope it is not of the Pollyanna or ostrich kind. While I am by nature a "yea-sayer" (and this trait may become more pronounced as I work in India, where malaria has been wiped out in five years, where family planning is expected to curb the birthrate within five years and the absolute growth within twenty years, and where even the Himalayas are growing 2 inches a year), I do not think I am a "nature faker." Of course, I have tried to prophesy, and that is always risky. This reminds me of the story of the Polish visionary who claimed that he could see the synagogue burning to the ground in the town of Lwów (45 miles away). Late the next day, a visitor from Lwów appeared on the scene and discounted the whole story. The local villagers were still proud of their visionary: *so what* if he was wrong. Look how far he could see!

WARREN BENNIS

contents

part one

evolutionary trends in organizational development

Man is the animal that can direct and control his own evolution. Our species is probably a million years old. Homo sapiens emerged with twice the cortical capacity only 100,000 years ago. With cortical development came the ability to symbolize which enables us to transmit information from generation to generation. Agriculture was invented roughly 10,000 years ago and city-states about 5,000 years ago. Science, only recently institutionalized (say within the past 75 to 100 years), has accelerated the psycho-cultural evolution a thousand times faster than biological evolution has.

All the essays in Part One reflect a particular bias which is a belief that certain ideas, generated and maintained by institutions, are not only more appropriate for our times but irresistible to them. Henry Murray has coined the word "idene" to relate to social evolution as gene does to biological evolution. Some idenes accelerate evolution; others, like Nazism or apartheid or slavery, may be as dangerous as hemophilia.

The idenes revived in the following essays are inevitable, within plus or minus 50 years, and they are captivating as well. They have been enshrined, idolized, and monotonously enunciated at least since the American Revolution was exported via France. They are the values of (1) choice and freedom, (2) collaboration, and (3) science, i.e., an ethic of testing and predicting reality. Although these concepts are familiar, their radical and accelerating effects can probably only be recognized in historical perspective. The first value is called by the political term "democracy" and is codified under certain constitutional guarantees of individual rights. The third dimly emerged about 300 years ago; ours is really the first and only "scientific age," and 90 per cent of the people who call themselves scientists are alive today. The second, collaboration, is the most recent value and the most ancient necessity, and it must surely preempt Darwin's emphasis on "competition." The price of competition, seen in Herman Kahn's Doomsday Machine and "Dr. Strangelove," is costly; we are committed to living together.

I see democracy, collaboration, and science as three broad streams moving steadily toward a confluence in the twentieth century. When I wrote Chapter 3 in 1961 I was convinced that democracy is a political twin of science and that their moral life is parallel. Collaboration is more implicit in science where there is an ethic of cooperation than in democracy which is fixated on independence rather than interdependence.

In any case, these essays suggest that when the true content of these three idenes surfaces and invades the institutional juglars we shall have not only coped with the tasks of our time but progressed further along the course of social evolution.

If these ideas sound ethnocentric and absolute, I must confess to a current revulsion from my collegiate belief in political and cultural relativism. I do believe that the values and moral imperatives of science and democracy are appropriate and necessary everywhere today. I do believe that they are the most civilized and advanced systems available. I do feel impatient with their visible alternatives: unskeptical and unquestioning faith in authority and totalitarianism.

Man, before Darwin, was elevated as the "darling of the gods." This Victorian fiction has been dissolved by too many wars, too much poverty, and too many diseased. But we remain a moral and ethical animal; our survival and security depend on the exploitation of moral and ethical systems.

1

*the decline of bureaucracy and organizations of the future**

Most of us spend all of our working day and a great deal of our non-working day in a unique and extremely durable social arrangement called "bureaucracy." I use the term "bureaucracy" descriptively, not as an epithet about "those guys in Washington" or as a metaphor *à la* Kafka's *Castle*, which conjures up an image of red tape, faceless masses standing in endless lines, and despair. Bureaucracy, as I shall use the term here, is a social invention, perfected during the Industrial Revolution to organize and direct the activities of the firm. To paraphrase Churchill's ironic remark about democracy, we can say of bureaucracy that it is the worst possible theory of organization—apart from all the others that have so far been tried.

* Adapted from an Invited Address presented to the Division of Industrial and Business Psychology at the American Psychological Association meeting, Los Angeles, Calif., Sept. 5, 1964. Reprinted by permission from *Transaction*, where it was originally published in July, 1965.

The burden of this book rests upon the premise that this form of organization is becoming less and less effective, that it is hopelessly out of joint with contemporary realities, and that new shapes, patterns, and models—currently recessive—are emerging which promise drastic changes in the conduct of the corporation and in managerial practices in general. So within the next twenty-five to fifty years, we should all be witness to, and participate in, the end of bureaucracy and the rise of new social systems better able to cope with twentieth-century demands.*

The argument will be presented in the following sequence:

1   A quick look at bureaucracy: what it is and what its problems are;
2   A brief survey of how behavioral scientists and practitioners have attempted to modify and alter the bureaucratic mechanism so that it would respond more appropriately to changing times (in this section I shall show how these emergency remedies have been only stopgap measures and how more basic changes are required);
3   A general forecast of how most organizations of the future will operate.

BUREAUCRACY AND ITS DISCONTENTS

Corsica, according to Gibbon, is much easier to deplore than to describe. The same holds true for bureaucracy. Basically, though, it is simple: bureaucracy is a social invention which relies exclusively on the power to influence through reason and law. Max Weber, the German sociologist who conceptualized the idea of bureaucracy around the turn of the century, once likened the bureaucratic mechanism to a judge qua computer: "Bureaucracy is like a modern judge who is a vending machine into which the pleadings are inserted together with the fee and which then disgorges the judgment together with its reasons mechanically derived from the code."[1]

The bureaucratic "machine model" Weber outlined was devel-

---

* The number of years necessary for this transition is, of course estimated from forecasts for the prospects of industrialization. Sociological evolutionists are substantially agreed that within a twenty-five- to fifty-year period, most of the people in the world will be living in industrialized societies. And it is this type of society that concerns me here, not the so-called underadvanced, semiadvanced, or partially advanced societies.

oped as a reaction against the personal subjugation, nepotism, cruelty, emotional vicissitudes, and subjective judgment which passed for managerial practices in the early days of the Industrial Revolution. Man's true hope, it was thought, was his ability to rationalize and calculate—to use his head as well as his hands and heart. Thus, in this system roles are institutionalized and reinforced by legal tradition rather than by the "cult of personality"; rationality and predictability were sought for in order to eliminate chaos and unanticipated consequences; technical competence rather than arbitrary or "iron" whims was emphasized. These are oversimplifications, to be sure, but contemporary students of organizations would tend to agree with them. In fact, there is a general consensus that bureaucracy can be dimensionalized in the following way:

1   A division of labor based on functional specialization
2   A well-defined hierarchy of authority
3   A system of rules covering the rights and duties of employees
4   A system of procedures for dealing with work situations
5   Impersonality of interpersonal relations
6   Promotion and selection based on technical competence[2]

These six dimensions describe the basic underpinnings of bureaucracy, the pyramidal organization which dominates so much of our thinking and planning related to organizational behavior.

It does not take a great critical imagination to detect the flaws and problems in the bureaucratic model. We have all *experienced* them: bosses without technical competence and underlings with it; arbitrary and zany rules; an underworld (or informal) organization which subverts or even replaces the formal apparatus; confusion and conflict among roles; and cruel treatment of subordinates, based not upon rational or legal grounds, but upon inhumane grounds. Unanticipated consequences abound and provide a mine of material for those comics, like Chaplin or Tati, who can capture with a smile or a shrug the absurdity of authority systems based on pseudologic and inappropriate rules.

Almost everybody, including many students of organizational behavior, approaches bureaucracy with a chip on his shoulder. It has been criticized for its theoretical confusion and contradictions, for moral and ethical reasons, on practical grounds such as its inefficiency, for its methodological weaknesses, and for containing too many implicit values or for containing too few. I have recently cataloged the criticisms of bureaucracy, and they outnumber and outdo the Ninety-five Theses tacked on the church door at Wittenberg in attacking another bureaucracy.[3] For example:

1 Bureaucracy does not adequately allow for personal growth and the development of mature personalities.
2 It develops conformity and "group-think."
3 It does not take into account the "informal organization" and the emergent and unanticipated problems.
4 Its systems of control and authority are hopelessly outdated.
5 It has no adequate juridical process.
6 It does not possess adequate means for resolving differences and conflicts among ranks and, most particularly, among functional groups.
7 Communication (and innovative ideas) are thwarted or distorted because of hierarchical divisions.
8 The full human resources of bureaucracy are not being utilized because of mistrust, fear of reprisals, etc.
9 It cannot assimilate the influx of new technology or scientists entering the organization.
10 It will modify the personality structure such that man will become and reflect the dull, gray, conditioned "organization man."

Max Weber himself, the developer of the theory of bureaucracy, came around to condemning the apparatus he helped immortalize. While he felt that bureaucracy was inescapable, he also thought it might strangle the spirit of capitalism or the enterprenuerial attitude, a theme which Schumpeter later on developed. And in a debate on bureaucracy he once said, more in sorrow than in anger:

> It is horrible to think that the world could one day be filled with nothing but those little cogs, little men clinging to little jobs and striving towards bigger ones—a state of affairs which is to be seen once more, as in the Egyptian records, playing an ever-increasing part in the spirit of our present administrative system, and especially of its offspring, the students. This passion for bureaucracy . . . is enough to drive one to despair. It is as if in politics . . . we were deliberately to become men who need "order" and nothing but order, who become nervous and cowardly if for one moment this order wavers, and helpless if they are torn away from their total incorporation in it. That the world should know no men but these: it is such an evolution

that we are already caught up in, and the great question is therefore not how we can promote and hasten it, but what can we oppose to this machinery in order to keep a portion of mankind free from this parcelling-out of the soul from this supreme mastery of the bureaucratic way of life.[4]

I think it would be fair to say that a good deal of the work on organizational behavior over the past two decades has been a footnote to the bureaucratic "backlash" which aroused Weber's passion: saving mankind's soul "from the supreme mastery of the bureaucratic way of life." At least, very few of us have been indifferent to the fact that the bureaucratic mechanism is a social instrument in the service of repression; that it treats man's ego and social needs as a constant, or as nonexistent or inert; that these confined and constricted needs insinuate themselves into the social processes of organizations in strange, unintended ways; and that those very matters which Weber claimed escaped calculation—love, power, hate—not only are calculable and powerful in their effects but must be reckoned with.

MODIFICATIONS OF BUREAUCRACY

In what ways has the system of bureaucracy been modified in order that it may cope more successfully with the problems that beset it? Before answering that, we have to say something about the nature of organizations, *all* organizations, from mass-production leviathans all the way to service industries such as the university or hospital. Organizations are primarily complex goal-seeking units. In order to survive, they must also accomplish the secondary tasks of (1) maintaining the internal system and coordinating the "human side of enterprise" —a process of mutual compliance here called "reciprocity"—and (2) adapting to and shaping the external environment—here called "adaptability." These two organizational dilemmas can help us organize the pivotal ways the bureaucratic mechanism has been altered—and found wanting.

Resolutions of the Reciprocity Dilemma

Reciprocity has to do primarily with the processes which can mediate conflict between the goals of management and the individual goals of the workers. Over the past several decades, a number of interesting theoretical and practical resolutions have been made which truly allow for conflict and mediation of interest. They revise, if not transform, the very nature of the bureaucratic mechanism by explicit recognition of the inescapable tension between individual and organizational goals. These theories can be called, variously, "exchange," "group," "value," "structural," or "situational," depending on what variable of the situation one wishes to modify.

The exchange theories postulate that wages, incomes, and services are given to the individual for an equal payment to the organization in work. If the inducements are not adequate, the individual may withdraw and work elsewhere.[5] This concept may be elaborated by increasing the payments to include motivational units. That is to say, the organization provides a psychological anchor in times of rapid social change and a hedge against personal loss, as well as position, growth and mastery, success experience, and so forth, in exchange for energy, work, and commitment.[6]

I shall discuss this idea of payment in motivational units further, as it is a rather recent one to gain acceptance. Management tends to interpret motivation by economic theory. Man is logical; man acts in the manner which serves his self-interest; man is competitive. Elton Mayo and his associates were among the first to see human affiliation as a motivating force, to consider industrial organization a social system as well as an economic-technical system. They judge a manager in terms of his ability to sustain cooperation.[7] In fact, once a cohesive, primary work group is seen as a motivating force, a managerial elite may become obsolete, and the work group itself become the decision maker. This allows decisions to be made at the most relevant point of the organizational social space, where the data are most available.[8]

Before this is possible, some believe that the impersonal value system of bureaucracy must be modified.[9] In this case the manager plays an important role as the instrument of change, as an interpersonal specialist. He must instill values which permit and reinforce expression of feeling, experimentalism and norms of individuality, trust, and concern. Management, according to Blake,[10] is successful as it maximizes "concern for people"—along with "concern for production."

Others[11,12] believe that a new conception of the structure of bureaucracy will create more relevant attitudes toward the function of management than formal role specifications do. If the systems are seen as organic rather than mechanistic, as adapting spontaneously to the needs of the system, then decisions will be made at the critical point, and roles and jobs will devolve to the "natural" incumbent. The shift would probably be from the individual to cooperative group effort, from delegated to shared responsibility, from centralized to decentralized authority, from obedience to confidence, and from antagonistic arbitration to problem solving.[13] Management which is centered around problem solving, which assumes or relaxes authority according to task demands, has most concerned some theorists. They are as concerned with organizational success and productivity as with the social system.[14,15,16,17]

However, on all sides we find a growing belief that the effectiveness of bureaucracy should be evaluated on human as well as economic criteria. Social satisfaction and personal growth of employees must be considered, as well as the productivity and profit of the organization.

The criticisms and revisions of the *status quo* tend to concentrate on the internal system and its human components. But although it appears on the surface that the case against bureaucracy has to do with its ethical-moral posture and the social fabric, the real *coup de grâce* has come from the environment. While various proponents of "good human relations" have been fighting bureaucracy on humanistic grounds and for Christian values, bureaucracy seems most likely to founder on its inability to adapt to rapid change in the environment.

The Problem of Adaptability

Bureaucracy thrives in a highly competitive, undifferentiated, and stable environment, such as the climate of its youth, the Industrial Revolution. A pyramidal structure of authority, with power concentrated in the hands of few with the knowledge and resources to control an entire enterprise was, and is, an eminently suitable social arrangement for routinized tasks.

However, the environment has changed in just those ways which make the mechanism most problematical. Stability has vanished. As Ellis Johnson said: ". . . the once-reliable constants have now become 'galloping' variables. . . ."[18] One factor accelerating change is the growth of science, research and development activities, and intellectual technology. Another is the increase of transactions with social institutions and the importance of the latter in conducting the enterprise—including government, distributors and consumers, shareholders, competitors, raw-material and power suppliers, sources of employees (particularly managers), trade unions, and groups within the firms.[19] There is, as well, more interdependence between the economic and other facets of society, resulting in complications of legislation and public regulation. Thirdly, and significantly, competition between firms diminishes as their fates intertwine and become positively correlated.[20]

My argument so far, to summarize quickly, is that the first assault on bureaucracy arose from its incapacity to manage the tension between individual and management goals. However, this conflict is somewhat mediated by the growth of an ethic of productivity which includes personal growth and/or satisfaction. The second and more major shock to bureaucracy has been caused by the scientific and technological revolution. It is the requirement of adaptability to the environment which leads to the predicted demise of bureaucracy and to the collapse of management as we know it now.

A Forecast for the Future

A forecast falls somewhere between a prediction and a prophecy. It lacks the divine guidance of the latter and the empirical foundation of the former. On thin empirical ice, I want to set forth some of the conditions that will dictate organizational life in the next twenty-five to fifty years.

1 **The environment** Those factors already mentioned will continue in force and will increase. That is, rapid technological change and diversification will lead to interpenetration of the government and legal and economic policies in business. Partnerships between industry and government (like Telstar) will be typical, and because of the immensity and expense of the projects, there will be fewer identical units competing for the same buyers and sellers. Or, in reverse, imperfect competition leads to an oligopolistic and government-business-controlled economy. The three main features of the environment will be interdependence rather than competition, turbulence rather than stability, and large rather than small enterprises.

2 **Aggregate population characteristics** We are living in what Peter Drucker calls the "educated society," and I think this is the most distinctive characteristic of our times. Within fifteen years, two-thirds of our population (living in metropolitan areas) will attend

college. Adult education programs, especially the management development courses of such universities as M.I.T., Harvard, and Stanford, are expanding and adding intellectual breadth. All this, of course, is not just "nice," but necessary. As Secretary of Labor Wirtz recently pointed out, computers can do the work of most high school graduates—more cheaply and effectively. Fifty years ago, education was called "nonwork," and intellectuals on the payroll (and many staff) were considered "overhead." Today, the survival of the firm depends, more than ever before, on the proper exploitation of brainpower.

One other characteristic of the population which will aid our understanding of organizations of the future is increasing job mobility. The lowered expense and ease of transportation, coupled with the real needs of a dynamic environment, will change drastically the idea of "owning" a job— and of "having roots," for that matter. Participants will be shifted from job to job even from employer to employer with much less fuss than we are accustomed to.

3 Work-relevant values The increased level of education and mobility will change the values we hold vis-à-vis work. People will be more intellectually committed to their jobs and will probably require more involvement, participation, and autonomy in their work. [This turn of events is due to a composite of the following factors: (1) There is a positive correlation between education and need for autonomy; (2) job mobility places workers in a position of greater influence in the system; and (3) job requirements call for more responsibility and discretion.]

Also, people will tend to be more "other-directed" in their dealings with others. McClelland's data suggest that as industrialization increases, other-directedness increases;[21] so we will tend to rely more heavily than we do even now on temporary social arrangements, on our immediate and constantly changing colleagues.

4 Tasks and goals of the firm The tasks of the firm will be more technical, complicated, and unprogrammed. They will rely more on intellect than on muscles. And they will be too complicated for one person to handle or for individual supervision. Essentially, they will call for the collaboration of specialists in a project form of organization.

Similarly there will be a complication of goals. "Increased profits" and "raised productivity" will sound like oversimplifications and clichés. Business will concern itself with its adaptive or innovative-creative capacity. In addition, *meta*-goals will have to be articulated and developed; that is, supra-goals which shape and provide the foundation for the goal structure. For example, one *meta*-goal might be a system for detecting new and changing goals; another could be a system for deciding priorities among goals.

Finally, there will be more conflict, more contradiction among effectiveness criteria, just as in hospitals and universities today there is conflict between teaching and research. The reason for this is the number of professionals involved, who tend to identify as much with the supra-goals of their profession as with those of their immediate employer. University professors are a case in point. More and more of their income comes from outside sources, such as private or public foundations and consultant work. They tend not to make good "company men" because they are divided in their loyalty to professional values and organizational demands. Role conflict and ambiguity are both causes and consequences of goal conflict.

5 *Organizational structure*   The social structure in organizations of the future will have some unique characteristics. The key word will be "temporary"; there will be adaptive, rapidly changing *temporary systems*.[22] These will be organized around *problems-to-be-solved*. The problems will be solved by groups of relative *strangers* who represent a set of diverse professional skills. The groups will be conducted on *organic* rather than mechanical models; they will evolve in response to the problem rather than programmed role expectations. The function of the "executive" thus becomes *coordinator,* or "linking pin" between various project groups. He must be a man who can speak the diverse languages of research and who can relay information and mediate among the groups. *People will be differentiated not vertically according to rank and role but flexibly according to skill and professional training.*

Adaptive, temporary systems of diverse specialists, solving problems, linked together by coordinating and task-evaluative specialists, in organic flux, will gradually replace bureaucracy as we know it. As no catchy phrase comes to mind, let us call this an "organic-adaptive" structure.

As an aside, what will happen to the rest of society, to the manual laborers, to the less educated, to those who desire to work in conditions of high authority, and so forth? Many such jobs will disappear; automatic jobs will be automated. However, there will be a corresponding growth in the service-type of occupation, such as the "War on Poverty" and the Peace Corps programs. In times of change, where there is a discrepancy between cultures, industrialization, and especially urbanization, society becomes the client for skill in human interaction. Let us hypothesize that approximately 40 per cent of the population would be involved in jobs of this nature and 40 per cent in technological jobs, making an *organic-adaptive* majority, with, say, a 20 per cent bureaucratic minority.

6 *Motivation in organic-adaptive structures* The section of this chapter on reciprocity stated the shortcomings of bureaucracy in maximizing employee effectiveness. The organic-adaptive structure should increase motivation and thereby effectiveness because of the satisfactions intrinsic to the task. There is a congruence between the educated individual's need for meaningful, satisfactory, and creative tasks and flexible structure or autonomy.

Of course, where the reciprocity issue is ameliorated, there are corresponding stresses between professional identification and high task involvement. Professionals are notoriously disloyal to organizational demands. For example, during the Oppenheimer hearing, Boris Pash of the FBI reported: "It is believed that the only undivided loyalty that he [Oppenheimer] can give is to science and it is strongly felt that if in his position the Soviet government could offer more for the advancement of scientific cause he would select that government as the one to which he would express his loyalty."[23]

There will be, as well, reduced commitment to work groups. These groups, as I have already mentioned, will be transient and changing. While skills in human interaction will become more important because of the necessity of collaboration in complex tasks, there will be a concomitant reduction in group cohesiveness. I would predict that in the organic-adaptive system, people will have to learn to develop quick and intense relationships on the job and to endure their loss.

In general I do not agree with the emphasis of Kerr et al.[24] on the "new bohemianism," whereby leisure—not work—becomes the emotional-creative sphere of life, or with Leavitt,[25] who holds similar views. They assume a technological slowdown and leveling off and a stabilizing of social mobility. This may be a society of the future, but long before then we will have the challenge of creating that push-button society and a corresponding need for service-type organizations with the organic-adaptive structure.

Jobs in the next century should become *more*, rather than less, involving; man is a problem-solving animal, and the tasks of the future guarantee a full agenda of problems. In addition, the adaptive process itself may become captivating to many. At the same time, I think the future I describe is far from a utopian or a necessarily "happy" one. Coping with rapid change, living in temporary systems, and setting up (in quickstep time) meaningful relations—and then breaking them—all augur strains and tensions. Learning how to live with ambiguity and to be self-directing will be the task of education and the goal of maturity.

NEW STRUCTURES OF FREEDOM

In these new organizations, participants will be called on to use their minds more than at any other time in history. Fantasy and imagination will be legitimized in ways that today seem strange. Social structures will no longer be instruments of repression (see Marcuse,[26] who says that the necessity of repression and the suffering derived from it decreases with the maturity of the civilization) but will exist to promote play and freedom on behalf of curiosity and thought.

Not only will the problem of adaptability be overcome through the organic-adaptive structure, but the problem we started with, reciprocity, will be resolved. Bureaucracy, with its "surplus repression," was a monumental discovery for harnessing muscle power via guilt and instinctual renunciation. In today's world, it is a prosthetic device, no longer useful. For we now require organic-adaptive systems as structures of freedom to permit the expression of play and imagination and to exploit the new pleasure of work.

NOTES

1. Bendix, R., *Max Weber: An Intellectual Portrait*, Doubleday & Company, Inc., Garden City, N.Y., 1960, p. 421.
2. Hall, R. H., "The Concept of Bureaucracy: An Empirical Assessment," *The American Journal of Sociology*, vol. 69, p. 33, 1963.
3. Bennis, W. G., "Theory and Method in Applying Behavioral Science to Planned Organizational Change," MIT Paper presented at the International Operational Research Conference, Cambridge University, Cambridge, Sept. 14, 1964.
4. Bendix, *op. cit.*, pp. 455–456.
5. March, J. G., and H. A. Simon, *Organizations*, John Wiley & Sons, Inc., New York, 1958.

6. Levinson, H., "Reciprocation: The Relationship between Man and Organization," Invited Address presented to the Division of Industrial and Business Psychology, Washington, D.C., Sept. 3, 1963.

7. Mayo, E., *The Social Problems of an Industrial Civilization*, Harvard University Press, Cambridge, Mass., 1945, p. 122.

8. Likert, R., *New Patterns of Management*, McGraw-Hill Book Company, New York, 1961.

9. Argyris, C., *Interpersonal Competence and Organizational Effectiveness*, Dorsey Press, Homewood, Ill., 1962.

10. Blake, R. R., and J. S. Mouton, *The Managerial Grid*, Gulf Publishing Company, Houston, 1964.

11. Shepard, H. A., "Changing Interpersonal and Intergroup Relationships in Organizations," in J. March (ed.), *Handbook of Organization*, Rand McNally & Company, Chicago, 1965.

12. Burns, T., and G. M. Stalker, *The Management of Innovation*, Quadrangle, Chicago, 1961.

13. Shepard, *op. cit.*

14. McGregor, D., *The Human Side of Enterprise*, McGraw-Hill Book Company, New York, 1960.

15. Leavitt, H. J., "Unhuman Organizations," in H. J. Leavitt and L. Pondy (eds.), *Readings in Managerial Psychology*, The University of Chicago Press, Chicago, 1964, pp. 542–556.

16. Leavitt, H. J., and T. L. Whisler, "Management in the 1980's," in Leavitt and Pondy, *ibid.*

17. Thompson, J. D., and A. Tuden, "Strategies, and Processes of Organizational Decision," in J. D. Thompson, P. B. Hammond, R. W. Hawkes, B. H. Junker, and A. Tuden (eds.), *Comparative Studies in Administration*, The University of Pittsburgh Press, Pittsburgh, Pa., 1959, pp. 195–216.

18. Johnson, E. A., "Introduction," in McClosky and Trefethen (eds.), *Operations Research for Management*, The Johns Hopkins Press, Baltimore, 1954, p. xii.

19. Wilson, A. T. M., "The Manager and His World," *Industrial Management Review*, Fall, 1961.

20. Emery, F. E., and E. L. Trist, "The Causal Texture of Organizational Environments," Paper read at the International Congress of Psychology, Washington, September, 1963.

21. McClelland, D., *The Achieving Society*, D. Van Nostrand Company, Inc., Princeton, N.J., 1961.

22. Miles, M. B., "On Temporary Systems," in M. B. Miles (ed.), *Innovation in Education*, Bureau of Publications, Teachers College, Columbia University, New York, 1964, pp. 437–490.

23. Jungk, R., *Brighter than a Thousand Suns*, Grove Press, Inc., New York, 1958, p. 147.

24. Kerr, C., J. T. Dunlop, F. Harbison, and C. Myers, *Industrialism and Industrial Man*, Harvard University Press, Cambridge, Mass., 1960.

25. Leavitt, *op. cit.*

26. Marcuse, H., *Eros and Civilization*, Beacon Press, Boston, 1955.

2

*democracy is inevitable**

Cynical observers have always been fond of pointing out that business leaders who extol the virtues of democracy on ceremonial occasions would be the last to think of applying them to their own organizations. To the extent that this is true, however, it reflects a state of mind which by no means is peculiar to businessmen but which characterizes all Americans, if not perhaps all citizens of democracies.

This attitude, briefly, is that democracy is a nice way of life for nice people, despite its manifold inconveniences—a kind of expensive and inefficient luxury, like owning a large medieval castle. Feelings about it are for the most part affectionate, even respectful, but a little impatient. There are probably few men of affairs in America who have not at some time nourished in their hearts the blasphemous

* Reprinted by permission of the coauthor and the publisher from *Harvard Business Review*, pp. 51–59, March–April, 1964. Written in collaboration with Philip E. Slater, of Brandeis University.

thought that life would go much more smoothly if democracy could be relegated to some kind of Sunday morning devotion.

The bluff practicality of the "nice-but-inefficient" stereotype masks a hidden idealism, however, for it implies that institutions can survive in a competitive environment through the sheer good-heartedness of those who maintain them. We would like to challenge this notion and suggest that even if all those benign sentiments were eradicated today, we would awaken tomorrow to find democracy still firmly entrenched, buttressed by a set of economic, social, and political forces as practical as they are uncontrollable.

We shall argue that democracy has been so widely embraced not because of some vague yearning for human rights but because *under certain conditions* it is a more "efficient" form of social organization. (Our concept of efficiency includes the ability to survive and prosper.) We do not regard it as accidental that those nations of the world which have endured longest under conditions of relative wealth and stability are democratic, while authoritarian regimes have, with few exceptions, either crumbled or eked out a precarious and backward existence.

Despite this evidence, even so acute a statesman as Adlai Stevenson argued in a *New York Times* article on November 4, 1962, that the goals of the Communists are different from ours. "They are interested in power," he said, "we in community. With such fundamentally different aims, how is it possible to compare communism and democracy in terms of efficiency? You might as well ask whether a locomotive is more efficient than a symphony orchestra."

Is this not simply the speech of an articulate man who believes that democracy is inefficient but who does not like to say so? Actually, we are concerned with locomotives and symphony orchestras, with power and community. The challenges of communism and democracy are, in fact, identical: to compete successfully for the world's resources and imagination.

Our position is, in brief, that democracy (whether capitalistic or socialistic is not at issue here) is the only system which can successfully cope with the changing demands of contemporary civilization. We are not necessarily endorsing democracy as such; one might reasonably argue that industrial civilization is pernicious and should be abolished. We suggest merely that given a desire to survive in this civilization, democracy is the most effective means to achieve this end.

DEMOCRACY TAKES OVER

There are signs, in fact, that our business community is becoming aware of this law. Several of the newest and most rapidly blooming companies in the United States boast unusually democratic organizations. Even more surprising is the fact that some of the largest of the established corporations have been moving steadily, if accidentally, toward democratization. Frequently they began by feeling that administrative vitality and creativity were lacking in the older systems of organization. In increasing numbers, therefore, they enlisted the support of social scientists and of outside programs, the net *effect* of which has been to democratize their organizations. Executives and even entire management staffs have been sent to participate in human relations and organizational laboratories to learn skills and attitudes which ten years ago would have been denounced as anarchic and revolutionary. At these meetings, status prerogatives and traditional concepts of authority are severely challenged.

Many social scientists have played an important role in this development toward humanizing and democratizing large-scale bureaucracies. The contemporary theories of McGregor, Likert, Argyris, and Blake have paved the way to a new social architecture. Research and training centers at the National Training Laboratories, Tavistock Institute, Massachusetts Institute of Technology, Harvard Business School, Boston University, the University of California at Los Angeles, Case Institute of Technology, and others have pioneered in the application of social science knowledge to the improvement of organizational effectiveness. So far, the data are not all in; conclusive evidence is missing, but the forecast seems to hold genuine promise: that it is possible to bring about greater organizational effectiveness through the utilization of valid social knowledge.*

System of Values

What we have in mind when we use the term "democracy" is not permissiveness or laissez faire, but a system of values—a "climate

---

* For a complete review of this work, see W. G. Bennis, "Effecting Organizational Change: A New Role for the Behavioral Scientist," *Administrative Science Quarterly*, September, 1963. See also C. Argyris, "T-groups for Organizational Effectiveness," *Harvard Business Review*, March–April, 1964.

of beliefs" governing behavior—which people are internally compelled to affirm by deeds as well as words. These values include:

1 Full and free communication, regardless of rank and power
2 A reliance on consensus, rather than on the more customary forms of coercion or compromise, to manage conflict
3 The idea that influence is based on technical competence and knowledge rather than on the vagaries of personal whims or prerogatives of power
4 An atmosphere that permits and even encourages emotional expression as well as task-oriented acts
5 A basically human bias, one which accepts the inevitability of conflict between the organization and the individual but which is willing to cope with and mediate this conflict on rational grounds

Changes along these dimensions are being promoted widely in American industry. Most important, for our analysis, is what we believe to be the reason for these changes: *Democracy becomes a functional necessity whenever a social system is competing for survival under conditions of chronic change.*

Adaptability to Change

The most familiar variety of such change to the inhabitants of the modern world is technological innovation. This has been characterized most dramatically by J. Robert Oppenheimer: "One thing that is new is the prevalence of newness, the changing scale and scope of change itself, so that the world alters as we walk on it, so that the years of a man's life measure not some small growth or rearrangement or moderation of what he learned in childhood but a great upheaval."[1]

But if change has now become a permanent and accelerating factor in American life, then adaptability to change becomes increasingly the most important single determinant of survival. The profit, the saving, the efficiency, and the morale of the moment become secondary to keeping the door open for rapid readjustment to changing conditions.

Organization and communications research at the Massachusetts Institute of Technology reveals quite dramatically what type of organization is best suited for which kind of environment. Specifically, for simple tasks under static conditions, an autocratic centralized structure, such as has characterized most industrial organizations in the past, is quicker, neater, and more efficient. But for adaptability to changing conditions, for "rapid acceptance of a new idea," for "flexibility in dealing with novel problems, generally high morale and loyalty . . . the more egalitarian or decentralized type seems to work better." One of the reasons for this is that the centralized decision maker is "apt to discard an idea on the grounds that he is too busy or the idea too impractical."[2]

Our argument for democracy rests on an additional factor, one that is fairly complicated but profoundly important in shaping our ideas. First of all, it is interesting to note that modern industrial organization has been based roughly on the antiquated system of the military. Relics of the military system of thought can still be found in the clumsy terminology used, such as "line and staff," "standard operating procedure," "table of organization," and so on. Other remnants can be seen in the emotional and mental assumptions regarding work and motivation held today by some managers and industrial consultants. By and large these conceptions are changing, and even the military is moving away from the oversimplified and questionable assumptions on which its organization was originally based. Even more striking, as we have mentioned, are developments taking place in industry, no less profound than a fundamental change away from the autocratic and arbitrary vagaries of the past and toward democratic decision making.

This change has been coming about because of the palpable inadequacy of the military-bureaucratic model, particularly its response to rapid change, and also because the institution of science is now emerging as a more suitable model.

Scientific Attitude

But why is science gaining acceptance as a model? Most certainly not because we teach and conduct research within research-oriented universities. Curiously enough, universities have been stubbornly resistant to democratization, far more so than most other institutions.

We believe that science is winning out because the challenges facing modern enterprises are, at base, *knowledge*-gathering, *truth*-requiring dilemmas. Managers are not scientists, nor do we expect them to be. But the processes of problem solving, conflict resolution, and recognition of dilemmas have great kinship with the academic pursuit of truth. The institution of science is the only institution based on, and geared for, change. It is built not only to adapt to change but to overthrow and create change. So it is—and will be—with modern industrial enterprises.

And here we come to the point. In order for the "spirit of inquiry," the foundation of science, to grow and flourish, there is a necessity for a democratic environment. Science encourages a political view which is egalitarian, pluralistic, and liberal. It accentuates freedom of opinion and dissent. It is against all forms of totalitarianism, dogma, mechanization, and blind obedience. As a prominent social psychologist has pointed out: "Men have asked for freedom, justice and respect precisely as science has spread among them."* In short, we believe that the only way in which organizations can ensure a scientific *attitude* is by providing conditions where it can flourish. Very simply, this means democratic social conditions.

In other words, democracy in industry is not an idealistic conception but a hard necessity in those areas in which change is ever present and in which creative scientific enterprise must be nourished. For democracy is the only system of organization which is compatible with perpetual change.

RETARDING FACTORS

It might be objected here that we have been living in an era of rapid technological change for 100 years, without any noticeable change in the nature of the average industrial firm. True, there are many restrictions on the power of the executive over his subordinates now compared with those prevailing at the end of the nineteenth century. But this hardly constitutes industrial democracy; the decision-making function is still an exclusive and jealously guarded prerogative of the top echelons. If democracy is an inevitable consequence of perpetual change, why then have we not seen more dramatic changes in the structure of industrial organizations? The answer is twofold.

Obsolete Individuals

First, the rate of technological change is rapidly accelerating. Take advance in scientific knowledge as one criterion: it shows a

* N. Sanford, "Social Science and Social Reform," Presidential Address presented to the Society for the Psychological Study of Social Issues at the annual meeting of the American Psychological Association, Washington, Aug. 28, 1958.

doubling every ten years. Casamir calculated that if the *Physical Review* continued to grow as rapidly as it did between 1945 and 1960, it would weigh more than the earth during the next century.[3] Prior to World War I, a businessman might live a productive and successful life and find himself outmoded at the end of it. By the end of World War II, a similar man could find that his training, skills, outlook, and ways of thinking were obsolescent in the middle of his career. James R. Killian, Jr., chairman of the Corporation of Massachusetts Institute of Technology, estimates that already several hundred thousand engineers are obsolete.[4] This is undoubtedly matched by an equal number of managers.

We are now beginning an era when a man's knowledge and approach can become obsolete before he has even begun the career for which he was trained. The value of what one learns is always slipping away, like the value of money in a runaway inflation. We are living in an era which could be characterized as a runaway inflation of knowledge and skill, and it is this which is perhaps responsible for the feelings of futility, alienation, and lack of individual worth which are said to characterize our time.

Under such conditions, the individual is of relatively little significance. No matter how imaginative, energetic, and brilliant he may be, time will soon catch up with him to the point where he can be profitably replaced by someone who is equally imaginative, energetic, and brilliant but who has a more up-to-date viewpoint and fewer obsolete preconceptions. As Martin Gardner says, with regard to the difficulty some physicists have in grasping Einstein's theory of relativity: "If you are young, you have a great advantage over these scientists. Your mind has not yet developed those deep furrows along which thoughts so often are forced to travel."[5] This situation is just beginning to be felt as an immediate reality in American industry, and it is this kind of uncontrollably rapid change which generates democratization.

Powers of Resistance

The second reason is that the mere existence of a dysfunctional tendency, such as the relatively slow adaptability of authoritarian structures, does not automatically bring about its disappearance. This drawback must first either be recognized for what it is or become so severe as to destroy the structures in which it is embedded. Both these conditions are only now beginning to make themselves felt, primarily through the peculiar nature of modern technological competition.

The crucial change has been that the threat of technological defeat no longer comes necessarily from rivals within the industry, who usually can be imitated quickly without too great a loss, but often from outside—from new industries using new materials in new ways. One can therefore make no intelligent prediction about "what the next likely development in our industry will be." The blow may come from anywhere. Correspondingly, a viable corporation cannot merely develop and advance in the usual ways. In order to survive and grow, it must be prepared to go anywhere—to develop new products or techniques even if they are irrelevant to the present activities of the organizations.* It is perhaps for this reason that the beginnings of democratization have appeared most often in industries (such as electronics) which depend heavily on invention. It is undoubtedly for this reason that more and more sprawling behemoths are planning consequential changes in their organizational structures and climates toward releasing democratic potentiality.

FAREWELL TO "GREAT MEN"

The passing of years has also given the *coup de grâce* to another force that retarded democratization—the "great man," who with brilliance and farsightedness could preside with dictatorial powers at the head of a growing organization and keep it at the vanguard of American business. In the past he was usually a man with a single idea, or a constellation of related ideas, which he developed brilliantly. This is no longer enough.

Today, just as he begins to reap the harvest of his imagination, he finds that someone else (perhaps even one of his stodgier competitors, aroused by desperation) has suddenly carried the innovation a step further or found an entirely new and superior approach to it, and he is suddenly outmoded. How easily can he abandon his idea, which contains all his hopes, his ambitions, his very heart? His aggressiveness now begins to turn in on his own organization, and the absolutism of his position begins to be a liability, a dead hand, an

* For a fuller discussion of this trend, see Theodore Levitt, "Marketing Myopia," *Harvard Business Review*, p. 45, July–August, 1960.

iron shackle upon the flexibility and growth of the company. But he cannot be removed—in the short run the firm would even be hurt by his loss, since its prestige derives to such an extent from his reputation. And by the time he has left, the organization will have receded into a secondary position within the industry. It may even decay further when his personal touch is lost.

The cult of personality still exists, of course, but it is rapidly fading. More and more large corporations (General Motors, for one) predicate their growth not on "heroes" but on solid management teams.

"Organization Men"

Taking the place of the great man, we are often told, is the organization man. A good many tears have been shed over this transition by liberals and conservatives alike. The liberals, of course, have in mind, as the "individual," some sort of creative deviant—an intellectual, artist, or radical politician. The conservatives are thinking of the old captains of industry and perhaps of some great generals. (In the Soviet Union they think of Stalin.)

Neither is at all unhappy to lose the individuals mourned by the other, dismissing them contemptuously as Communists and rabble-rousers, on the one hand, and as criminals and Fascists, on the other. What is particularly confusing in terms of the present issue is a tendency to equate conformity with autocracy—to see the new industrial organization as one in which all individualism is lost except in the case of a few villainous individualistic manipulators at the top.

But this, of course, is absurd in the long run. The trend toward the organization man is also a trend toward a looser and more flexible organization in which the roles are to some extent interchangeable and in which no one is indispensable. To many people this trend is a monstrous nightmare, but one should at least not confuse it with the nightmares of the past. It may mean anonymity and homogeneity, but it does not and cannot mean authoritarianism in the long run, despite the bizarre anomalies and hybrids that may arise in a period of transition.

The reason it cannot is that it arises out of a need for flexibility and adaptability. Democracy and the dubious trend toward the organization man alike (for this trend is a part of democratization, whether we like this aspect of democracy or not) arise from the need to maximize the availability of appropriate knowledge, skill, and insight under conditions of great variability.

Rise of the Professional

While the organization-man idea has titillated the imagination of the American public, it has masked a far more fundamental change now taking place: the rise of the "professional man." Professional specialists, holding advanced degrees in such abstruse sciences as cryogenics or computer logic as well as the more mundane business disciplines, are entering all types of organizations at a higher rate than any other sector of the labor market.

And these men can hardly be called "organization men." They seemingly derive their rewards from inward standards of excellence, from their professional societies, and from the intrinsic satisfaction of their task. In fact, they are committed to the task, not the job; to their standards, not their boss. And because they have degrees, they travel. They are not good "company men"; they are uncommitted except to the challenging environments where they can "play with problems."

These new professional men are remarkably compatible with our conception of a democratic system. For like these new men, democracy seeks no new stability, no end point; it is purposeless, save that it purports to ensure perpetual transition, constant alteration, and ceaseless instability. It attempts to upset nothing, but only to facilitate the potential upset of anything. Democracy and our new professional men identify primarily with the adaptive process, not the "establishment."

Yet it must also be remembered that all democratic systems are not entirely so—there are always limits to the degree of fluidity which can be borne. Thus, it is not a contradiction to the theory of democracy to find that a particular democratic society or organization may be more "conservative" than some autocratic one. Indeed, the most dramatic, violent, and drastic changes have always taken place under autocratic regimes, for such changes usually require prolonged self-denial, while democracy rarely lends itself to such voluntary asceticism. But these changes have been viewed as finite and temporary, aimed at a specific set of reforms, and moving toward a new state of nonchange. It is only when the society reaches a level of technological development in which survival is dependent on the institutionalization of perpetual change that democracy becomes necessary.

REINFORCING FACTORS

The Soviet Union is rapidly approaching this level and is beginning to show the effects, as we shall see. The United States has already reached it. Yet democratic institutions existed in the United States when it was still an agrarian nation. Indeed, democracy has existed in many places and at many times, long before the advent of modern technology. How can we account for these facts?

Expanding Conditions

In the first place, it must be remembered that modern technology is not the only factor which could give rise to conditions of necessary perpetual change. Any situation involving rapid and unplanned expansion, sustained over a sufficient period of time, will tend to produce great pressure for democratization. Second, when we speak of democracy, we are referring not only or even primarily to a particular political format. Indeed, American egalitarianism has perhaps its most important manifestation not in the Constitution but in the family.

Historians are fond of pointing out that Americans have always lived under expanding conditions—first the frontier, then the successive waves of immigration, and now a runaway technology. The social effects of these kinds of expansion are, of course, profoundly different in many ways, but they share one impact in common: all have made it impossible for an authoritarian family system to develop on a large scale. Every foreign observer of American mores since the seventeenth century has commented that American children "have no respect for their parents," and every generation of Americans since 1650 has produced forgetful native moralists who complain about the decline in filial obedience and deference.

Descriptions of family life in colonial times make it quite clear that American parents were as easygoing, permissive, and child-oriented then as they are now and that the children were as independent and "disrespectful." This "lack of respect" is, of course, not for the "parents" as individuals but for the concept of parental authority as such.

The basis for this loss of respect has been outlined quite

dramatically by historian Oscar Handlin, who points out that in each generation of early settlers, the children were more at home in their new environment than their parents—they had less fear of the wilderness and fewer inhibiting European preconceptions and habits.[6] Furthermore, their parents were heavily dependent on them physically and economically. This was less true of the older families after the East became settled. But as one moved nearer to the frontier, the conditions for familial democracy became again strikingly marked, so that the cultural norm was ever protected from serious decay.

Further reinforcement came later from new immigrants, who similarly found their children better adapted to the world than themselves because of their better command of the language, better knowledge of the culture, better occupational opportunities, and so forth. It was the children who were expected to improve the social position of the family and who, through their exposure to peer groups and the school system, could act as intermediaries between their parents and the New World. It was not so much "American ways" that shook up the old family patterns, but the demands and requirements of a new situation. How could the young look to the old as the ultimate fount of wisdom and knowledge when, in fact, that knowledge was irrelevant—when, indeed, the children had a better practical grasp of the realities of American life than their elders?

The New Generation

These sources of reinforcement have now disappeared. But a third has only begun. Rapid technological change again means that the wisdom of elders is largely obsolete and that the young are better adapted to their culture than their parents. How many of the latter can keep up with their children in knowledge of the sciences, for example? Santayana put it beautifully when he said: "No specific hope about distant issues is ever likely to be realized. The ground shifts, the will of mankind deviates, and what the father dreamt of the children neither fulfill nor desire."[7]

It is this fact that reveals the basis for the association between democracy and change. The old, the learned, the powerful, the wealthy, those in authority—these are the ones who are committed. They have learned a pattern and have succeeded in it. But when change comes, it is often the uncommitted who can best realize it, take advantage of it. This is why primogeniture has always lent itself so easily to social change in general and to industrialization in particular. The uncommitted younger sons, barred from success in the older system, are always ready to exploit new opportunities. In Japan, these younger sons were treated more indulgently by the parents and were given more freedom to choose an occupation, since ". . . in Japanese folk wisdom, it is the younger sons who are the innovators."[8]

Democracy is a superior technique for making more available to the uncommitted. The price it extracts is the price of uninvolvement, alienation, and skepticism. The benefits that it gives are flexibility and the joy of confronting new dilemmas.

DOUBTS AND FEARS

Indeed, we may even in this way account for the poor opinion which democracy has of itself. We underrate the strength of democracy because it creates a general attitude of doubt, of skepticism, and of modesty. It is only among the authoritarian that we find the dogmatic confidence, the self-righteousness, the intolerance, and the cruelty that permit one never to doubt oneself and one's beliefs. The looseness, the sloppiness, and the untidiness of democratic structures express the feeling that what has been arrived at today is probably only a partial solution and may well have to be changed tomorrow.

In other words, one cannot believe that change is in itself a good thing and still believe implicitly in the rightness of the present. Judging from the report of history, democracy has always underrated itself—one cannot find a democracy anywhere without also discovering (side by side with expressions of outrageous chauvinism) an endless pile of contemptuous and exasperated denunciations of it. (One of the key issues in our national politics today, as in the presidential campaign in 1960, is our "national prestige.") And perhaps this is only appropriate. For when a democracy ceases finding fault with itself, it has probably ceased to be a democracy.

Overestimating Autocracy

But feeling doubt about our own social system need not lead us to overestimate the virtues and efficiency of others. We can find this kind of overestimation in the exaggerated fear of the "Red menace"—mere exposure to which is seen as leading to automatic conversion. Few authoritarians can conceive of the possibility that an individual could encounter an authoritarian ideology and not be swept away by it.

Of a similar nature, but more widespread, is the "better dead than Red" mode of thinking. Here again we find an underlying assumption that communism is socially, economically, and ideologically inevitable—that once the military struggle is lost, all is lost. It is interesting that in all our gloomy war speculations, there is never any mention of an American underground movement. It is everywhere assumed that if a war were fought in which anyone survived and the Soviet Union won, then:

1 All Americans would immediately become Communists.
2 The Soviet Union would set up an exact replica of itself in this country.
3 It would work.
4 The Soviet system would remain unchanged.
5 The Soviets in America would be uninfluenced by what they found here.

Not only are these assumptions patently ridiculous, but they also reveal a profound misconception about the nature of social systems. The structure of a society is not determined merely by a belief. It cannot be maintained if it does not work—that is, if no one, not even those in power, is benefiting from it. How many times in history have less civilized nations conquered more civilized ones only to be entirely transformed by the cultural influence of their victims? Do we then feel ourselves to be less civilized than the Soviet Union? Is our system so brittle and theirs so enduring?

Actually, quite the contrary seems to be the case. For while democracy seems to be on a fairly sturdy basis in the United States (despite the efforts of self-appointed vigilantes to subvert it), there is considerable evidence that autocracy is beginning to decay in the Soviet Union.

SOVIET DRIFT

Most Americans have great difficulty in evaluating the facts when they are confronted with evidence of decentralization in the Soviet Union, of relaxation of repressive controls, or of greater tolerance for criticism. We seem bewildered. And we do not seem to sense the contradiction when we say that these changes were made in response to public discontent. For have we not also believed deeply that an authoritarian regime, if efficiently run, can get away with ignoring the public's clamor?

There is a secret belief among us that Khrushchev must have been mad to relax his grip in this way, or a contradictory suspicion that it is all part of a secret plot to throw the West off guard: a plot which is too clever for naïve Americans to fathom. It is seldom suggested that "de-Stalinization" took place because the rigid, repressive authoritarianism of the Stalin era was inefficient and that many additional relaxations will be forced upon the Soviet Union by the necessity of remaining amenable to technological innovation.

But the inevitable Soviet drift toward a more democratic structure is not dependent on the realism of leaders. Leaders come from communities and families, and their patterns of thought are shaped by their experiences with authority in early life as well as by their sense of what the traffic will bear. We saw that the roots of American democracy were to be found in the nature of the American family. What does the Russian family tell us in this respect?

Pessimism regarding the ultimate destiny of Soviet political life has always been based on the seemingly fathomless capacity of the Russian people for authoritarian submission. Their tolerance for autocratic rulers was matched only by their autocratic family system, which was equal to that of Germany, China, or many Latin countries in its demand for filial obedience. On this early experience in the family the acceptance of authoritarian rule was based.

Role of the Family

But modern revolutionary movements, both Fascist and Communist, have tended to regard the family with some suspicion, as the preserver of old ways and as a possible refuge from the state. Fascist dictators have extolled its conservatism but tended at times to set up competitive loyalties for the young. Communist revolutionaries, on the other hand, have more unambivalently attacked family loyalty as reactionary and have deliberately undermined familiar allegiances, partly to increase loyalty to the state and partly to facilitate industrialization and modernization by discrediting traditional mores.

Such destruction of authoritarian family patterns is a two-edged sword, which eventually cuts away political autocracy as well as the familial variety. The state may attempt to teach submission in its own youth organizations, but so long as the family remains as an institution, this earlier and more enduring experience will outweigh all others. And if the family has been forced by the state to be less authoritarian, the result is obvious.

In creating a youth which has a knowledge, a familiarity, and a set of attitudes more appropriate for successful living in the changing culture than those of its parents, the autocratic state has created a Frankenstein monster which will eventually sweep away the authoritarianism in which it is founded. Russian attempts during the late 1930s to reverse their stand on the family perhaps reflect some realization of this fact. Krushchev's denunciations of certain Soviet artists and intellectuals also reflect fear of a process going beyond what was originally intended.

A similar ambivalence has appeared in Communist China, where the slogan "all for the children" recently produced the unforeseen consequence of a rash of articles stressing filial obligations. As Goode points out: ". . . the propaganda campaign against the power of the elders may lead to misunderstanding on the part of the young, who may at times abandon their filial responsibilities to the State."[9]

Further, what the derogation of parental wisdom and authority has begun, the fierce drive for technological modernization will finish. Each generation of youth will be better adapted to the changing society than its parents. And each generation of parents will feel increasingly modest and doubtful about overvaluing its wisdom and superiority as it recognizes the brevity of its usefulness.[*]

CONCLUSION

We cannot, of course, predict what forms democratization might take in any nation of the world, nor should we become unduly optimistic about its impact on international relations. Although our thesis predicts the ultimate democratization of the entire globe, this is a view

[*] See, for example, O. Handlin, *The Uprooted*, Little, Brown and Company, Boston, 1951, pp. 252–253; and Kent Geiger, "Changing Political Attitudes in Totalitarian Society: A Case Study of the Role of the Family," *World Politics*, pp. 187–205, January, 1956.

so long-range as to be academic. There are infinite opportunities for global extermination before any such stage of development can be achieved.

We should expect that, in the earlier stages of industrialization, dictatorial regimes will prevail in all the less developed nations, and as we well know, autocracy is still highly compatible with a lethal if short-run military efficiency. We may expect many political grotesques, some of them dangerous in the extreme, to emerge during this long period of transition, as one society after another attempts to crowd the most momentous social changes into a generation or two, working from the most varied structural base lines.

But barring some sudden decline in the rate of technological change, and on the (outrageous) assumption that war will somehow be eliminated during the next half century, it is possible to predict that after this time democracy will be universal. Each revolutionary autocracy, as it reshuffles the family structure and pushes toward industrialization, will sow the seeds of its own destruction, and democratization will gradually engulf it. Lord Acton once remarked about Christianity that it is not that people have tried it and found it wanting; it is that they have been afraid to try it and found it impossible. The same comment may have once applied to democracy, but the outlook has changed to the point where people may *have* to try it.

We may, of course, rue the day. A world of mass democracies may well prove homogenized and ugly. It is perhaps beyond human social capacity to maximize both equality and understanding, on the one hand, and diversity, on the other. Faced with this dilemma, however, many people are willing to sacrifice quaintness to social justice, and we might conclude by remarking that just as Marx, in proclaiming the inevitability of communism, did not hesitate to give some assistance to the wheels of fate, so our thesis that democracy represents the social system of the electronic era should not bar these persons from giving a little push here and there to the inevitable.

NOTES

1. Oppenheimer, J. Robert, "Prospects in the Arts and Sciences," *Perspectives USA*, pp. 10–11, Spring, 1955.
2. Bennis, W. G., "Towards a 'Truly' Scientific Management: The Concept of Organization Health," *General Systems Yearbook*, p. 273, December, 1962. A similar version of this article appears as Chap. 3 of this book.

3. Oppenheimer, J. Robert, "On Science and Culture," *Encounter*, p. 5, October, 1962.

4. Killian, J. R., Jr., "The Crisis in Research," *The Atlantic Monthly*, p. 71, March, 1963.

5. Gardner, M., *Relativity for the Millions*, The Macmillan Company, New York 1962, p. 11.

6. Handlin, O., *The Uprooted*, Little, Brown and Company, Boston, 1951.

7. Edman, I. (ed.), *The Philosophy of Santayana*, Modern Library, Inc., New York, 1936.

8. Goode, W. J., *World Revolution and Family Patterns*, The Free Press of Glencoe, New York, 1963, p. 355.

9. *Ibid.*, pp. 313–315.

3

toward a "truly" scientific management: the concept of organization health*

MUGGERIDGE: Now, Charles, you, because you're a scientist . . . you have this idea, as I understand from your writings, that one of the failings of our sort of society, is that the people who exercise authority, we'll say Parliament and so on, are singularly unversed in scientific matters.

SNOW: Yes, I think this is a terrible weakness of the whole of Western society, and one that we're not going to get out of without immense trouble and pain.

MUGGERIDGE: Do you mean by that, for instance, an M.P. would be a better M.P. if he knew a bit about science?

SNOW: I think some M.P.'s ought to know a bit about science. They'd be better M.P.'s in the area where scientific insight becomes important. And there are quite a number of such areas.[1]

* A similar version of this paper appears in *General Systems Yearbook*, p. 273, December, 1962.

Extolling science has become something of a national and international pastime which typically stops short of the truly radical reforms in social organization that scientific revolution implies. Knowing "a bit about science" is a familiar and increasingly popular example of that which C. P. Snow treats in his *Two Cultures and the Scientific Revolution*.[2] But if culture is anything it is a way of life, the way real people live and grow, the way ideals and moral imperatives are transmitted and infused. Culture is more *value* than knowledge. Dr. Bronowski, who shares with Snow the view that "humanists" tend to be ignorant of and removed from science, understands better than Snow seems to that a fundamental unification of cultural outlook is what is required.[3] The connective tissue required, then, is cultural, social, and institutional, not grafted-on evening courses in science.

In this connection, and closer to some of the general aims of this paper, Nevitt Sanford has said:

> The ethical systems of other professions, such as business or the military, have become models for whole societies. Why should not the practice of science become such a model? After we have shown, as we can, that joy and beauty have their places in this system? At any rate, anyone who takes it upon himself to be a scientist, and succeeds in living up to its requirements, may be willing for his behavior to become a universal norm.[4]

This foreshadows the general theme of this chapter: the recognition that the *institution* of science can and should provide a viable model for other institutions not solely concerned with developing knowledge. To demonstrate this proposition, this chapter first discusses the criterion problem in relation to organizations.* An attempt is made to show that the usual criteria for evaluating organizational effectiveness, "enhancement of satisfaction on the part of industry's participants and improvement of effectiveness of performance,"[5] are inadequate, incorrect, or both, as valid indicators of organizational "health." (For the moment let us use the term "health" in the same vague way as "effectiveness." Organizational health is defined later in the chapter.) Next it is suggested that an alternative set of criteria, extracted from the normative and value processes of science, provides

---

* For the purposes of this discussion, organization is defined as any institution from which one receives cash for services rendered. This chapter deals with all such supra-individual entities, although reference is made mostly to industrial organizations.

a more realistic basis for evaluating organizational performance. These criteria are related to those of positive mental health, for it will be argued that there is a profound kinship between the mores of science and the criteria of health for an individual. From this confluence is fashioned a set of psychologically based criteria for examining organizational health. Finally, a discussion is presented of some of the consequences of these effectiveness criteria for organizational theory and practice.

THE SEARCH FOR EFFECTIVENESS CRITERIA

> There is hardly a term in current psychological thought as vague, elusive and ambiguous as the term "mental health." That it means many things to many people is bad enough. That many people use it without even attempting to specify the idiosyncratic meaning the term has for them makes the situation worse . . . for those who wish to introduce concern with mental health into systematic psychological theory and research.[6]

> No one can say with any degree of certainty by what standards an executive ought to appraise the performance of his organization. And it is questionable whether the time will ever arrive when there will be any pattern answers to such a question—so much does the setting of an organization and its own goal orientation affect the whole process of appraisal.[7]

Raising the problem of criteria, the standards for judging the "goodness" of an organization seldom fail to generate controversy and despair. Establishing criteria for an organization (or, for that matter, for education, marriage, psychotherapy, etc.) accentuates questions of value, choice, and normality and all the hidden assumptions that are used to form judgments of operations. Often, as Jahoda has said in relation to mental-health criteria, the problem ". . . seems so difficult that one is almost tempted to claim the privilege of ignorance."[8]

However, as tempting as ignorance can be, researchers on organizations—particularly industrial organizations—have struggled heroically to identify and measure a number of dimensions associated with organizational effectiveness.[9] Generally, these dimensions have been of two kinds: those dealing with some index of organizational performance, such as profit, cost, rates of productivity, or individual output, and those associated with the human resources, such as morale, motivation, mental health, job commitment, cohesiveness, or

TABLE 1 Major variables employed in the study of organizational behavior

		Criteria Variables	
		Organizational efficiency	Satisfaction or health
Independent Variables	Technology (rationalized procedures)	Management science: systems research, operations research, decision processes, etc.	Human engineering
	Human factors	Personnel psychology, training, and other personnel functions	Industrial social psychology and sociology

attitudes toward employer or company. In short, as Katzell pointed out in his 1957 review of industrial psychology, investigations in this area typically employ measures of *performance* and *satisfaction*.[10] In fact, it is possible to construct a simple table that adequately accounts for most of the research on organizations that has been undertaken to date, as shown in Table 1. On one axis are located the criteria variables: organizational efficiency (the ethic of work performance) and member satisfaction (the ethic of "health"). On the other axis are located the two main independent variables employed: human factors and rationalized procedures. In other words, it is possible to summarize most of the research literature in the organizational area by locating the major independent variables (technological and human) on one axis and the dependent variables (efficiency and health) on the other.

This classification is necessarily crude and perhaps a little puzzling, principally because research on organizations lacks sufficient information concerning the empirical correlation between the two dependent variables, organizational efficiency and health factors. For a time it seemed (or was hoped) that personal satisfaction and efficiency were positively related, that as satisfaction increased so did performance. This alleged correlation allowed the "human relations" school and the industrial engineers (Taylorism being one example)*

* For a recent historical review, see Aitken.[11]

to proceed coterminously without necessarily recognizing the tension between "happy workers" and "high performance."

As Likert put it: "It is not sufficient merely to measure morale and the attitudes of employees toward the organization, their supervision, and their work. Favorable attitudes and excellent morale do not necessarily assure high motivation, high performance, and an effective human organization. A good deal of research indicates that this relationship is much too simple."[12]

Indeed, today we are not clear about the relation of performance to satisfaction, or even whether there is any interdependence between them. Likert and his associates have found organizations with all the logical possibilities—high morale with low productivity, low productivity with low morale, etc. Argyris's work,[13,14] with a popular assist from William H. Whyte, Jr.,[15] clouds the picture even further by postulating the inevitability of conflict between human need-satisfaction and organizational performance (as formal organizations are presently conceived). This creates, as Mason Haire has recognized,[16] a calculus of values: How much satisfaction or health is to be yielded for how many units of performance?

Generally speaking, this is the state of affairs: two criteria, crudely measured, ambiguous in meaning, questionable in utility, and fraught with value connotations.[17] In view of these difficulties, a number of other, more promising approaches have been suggested. The most notable of these are the criterion of multiple goals, the criterion of the situation, and the criterion of system characteristics.

The Criterion of Multiple Goals

This approach rests on the assumption that ". . . organizations have more than a single goal and that the interaction of goals will produce a different value framework in different organizations."[18] Likert, who is a proponent of the multiple-criteria approach, claims that very few organizations, if any, obtain measurements that clearly reflect the quality and capacity of their human resources. This situation is due primarily to (1) the shadow of traditional theory, which tends to overlook the human and motivational variables, and (2) the relatively new developments in social science that only now permit measurements of this type. Likert goes on to enumerate twelve criteria, covering such dimensions as loyalty and identification with the institution and its objectives, degree of confidence and trust, adequacy and efficiency of communication, amount and quality of teamwork, etc.[19] By and large, Likert's criteria are psychologically based, and they substantially enrich the impoverished state of effectiveness criteria. *

The Criterion of the Situation

This approach is based on the reasoning that organizations differ with respect to goals and that they can be analytically distinguished in terms of goal orientation. As Parsons pointed out: "As a formal analytical point of reference, *primacy of orientation to the attainment of a specific goal is used as the defining characteristic of an organization* which distinguishes it from other types of social systems."[21]

In an earlier paper by Bennis,[22] a framework was presented for characterizing four different types of organizations based on a specific criterion variable. These "pure" types are rarely observed empirically, but they serve to sharpen the differences among formally organized activities. Table 2 represents an example of developing effectiveness variables on the basis of organizational parameters.

The Criterion of System Characteristics

This approach, most cogently advanced by sociologists, is based on a "structural-functional" analysis. Selznick, one of its chief proponents, characterizes the approach in the following way: "Structural-functional analysis relates contemporary and variable behavior to a presumptively stable system of needs and mechanisms. This means that a given empirical system is deemed to have basic needs, essentially related to self-maintenance; the system develops repetitive. means of self-defense, and day-to-day activity is interpreted in terms of the function served by that activity for the maintenance and defense of the system."[23]

Derivable from this system model are basic needs or institutional imperatives that have to be met if the organism is to survive and "grow." Selznick, for example, lists five: (1) the security of the organization as a whole in relation to social forces in its environment, (2) the stability of the lines of authority and communication, (3) the stability of informal relations within the organization, (4) the continuity

---

* See also Kahn et al.[20] for other suggestions for criteria.

TABLE 2   Typology of organization*

Type of organization	Major function	Examples	Effectiveness criterion
Habit	Replicating standard and uniform products	Highly mechanized factories, etc.	Number of products
Problem-solving	Creating new ideas	Research organizations, design and engineering divisions, consulting organizations, etc.	Number of ideas
Indoctrination	Changing people's habits, attitudes, intellect, behavior (physical and mental)	Universities, prisons, hospitals, etc.	Number of "clients" leaving
Service	Distributing services either directly to consumer or to above types	Military, government, advertising, taxi companies, etc.	Extent of services performed

* From W. G. Bennis, "Leadership Theory and Administrative Behavior: The Problem of Authority," *Administrative Science Quarterly*, vol. 4, no. 3, p. 299, December, 1959.

of policy and of the sources of its determination, and (5) a homogeneity of outlook with respect to the meaning and role of the organization.[24]

Caplow, starting from the fundamental postulate that organizations tend to maintain themselves in continuous operation, identifies three criteria of organizational success: (1) the performance of objective functions, (2) the minimization of spontaneous conflict, and (3) the maximization of satisfaction for individuals.[25] Obviously, with the exception of the second criterion, these resemble the old favorites, performance and satisfaction.

The preceding summaries do not do full justice to the nuances of these three approaches or the enormous creative effort that went into their development, nor do they include the ideas of many thoughtful practitioners.* Despite these limitations, the discussion of multiple criteria, situational parameters, and system characteristics represents the main attempts to solve the criterion problem.†

INADEQUACY OF CRITERION VARIABLES FOR THE MODERN ORGANIZATION

> The history of other animal species shows that the most successful in the struggle for survival have been those which were most adaptable to change in their world.[28]

The present ways of thinking about and measuring organizational effectiveness are seriously inadequate and often misleading. These criteria are insensitive to the important needs of the organization and are out of joint with the emerging view of contemporary organization that is held by many organizational theorists and practitioners. The present techniques of evaluation provide static indicators of certain output characteristics (i.e., performance and satisfaction) without illuminating the processes by which the organization searches for, adapts to, and solves its changing goals.[29] However, it is these dynamic processes of problem solving that provide the critical dimensions of organizational health, and without knowledge of them, output measurements are woefully inadequate.‡

This rather severe charge is based upon the belief that the main challenge confronting the modern organization (and society) is that of coping with external stress and change. This point hardly needs elaboration or defense. The recent work in the field of organizational behavior reflects this need and interest; it is virtually a catalog of the problems of organizational change.§ In a 1961 monograph on managing major change in organizations, Mann and Neff stated the

---

* See, for example, Urwick.[26]

† Another approach, advocated by A. L. Comrey, is the deliberate (and often wise) avoidance of a definition of effectiveness or health by obtaining judgments of knowledgeable observers. "This method of defining 'effectiveness' seems to be the only feasible course of action in view of the tremendous number of meanings involved in a conceptual definition of this term and the obvious impossibility of providing a criterion which would reflect all or most of those meanings."[27]

‡ See Ridgway[30] for other criticisms of the use of performance measurements.

§ See, for example, March and Simon;[31] Argyris;[32] Shepard[33]; Gibb and Lippitt;[34] Lippitt et al.;[35] Bennis et al.;[36] and Walker.[37]

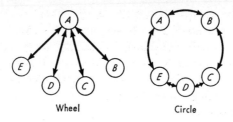

Wheel   Circle

FIG. 1 Two types of communication networks for problem solving by a group of five persons

issue this way: "Among the most conspicuous values in American culture of the twentieth century are progress, efficiency, science and rationality, achievement and success. These values have helped to produce a highly dynamic society—a society in which the predominant characteristic is *change*."[38] Kahn, Mann, and Seashore, when discussing a criterion variable, the "ability of the organization to change appropriately in response to some objective requirement for change," remarked: "Although we are convinced of the theoretical importance of this criterion, which we have called organizational flexibility, we have thus far been unable to solve the operational problems involved in its use."[39]

The basic flaw in the present effectiveness criteria is their inattention to the problem of adapting to change. To illuminate some of the consequences of this omission, let us turn to one rather simple example. The example is drawn from an area of research, started at the Massachusetts Institute of Technology about 1949, on the effects of certain organizational patterns (communication networks) on problem solving by groups.[40] Two of these networks, the Wheel and the Circle, are shown in Fig. 1.

The results of these experiments showed that an organization with a structure like the Wheel can solve simple tasks (e.g., identification of the color of a marble that is common to all five group members) more rapidly, more clearly, and more efficiently than an organization with a structure like the Circle. Thus the Wheel arrangement is plainly superior in terms of the usual criteria employed to evaluate effectiveness. However, if we consider two other criteria of organizational effectiveness that are relevant to the concern with change flexibility and creativity, we discover two interesting phenomena. First, the rapid acceptance of a new idea is more likely in the Circle than in the Wheel. The man in the middle of the Wheel is apt to discard an idea on the grounds that he is too busy or the idea is impractical. Second, when the task is changed, for example, by going from "pure-color" marbles to unusually colored marbles (such as ginger-ale color or blue-green), the Circle organization is better able to adapt to this change by developing a new code.[41]

As Leavitt pointed out:

> By certain industrial engineering-type (speed, clarity of organization and job descriptions, parsimonious use of paper, etc.), the highly structured, highly routinized, non-involving centralized net seems to work best. But if our criteria of effectiveness are more ephemeral, more general (like acceptance of creativity, flexibility in dealing with novel problems, general high morale and loyalty), then the moral egalitarian or decentralized type net seems to work better.[42]

If we view organizations as adaptive, problem-solving, organic structures, then inferences about effectiveness have to be made, not from static measures of output, though these may be helpful, but on the basis of the processes through which the organization approaches problems. In other words, no single measurement of organizational efficiency or satisfaction—no single time-slice of organizational performance—can provide valid indicators of organizational health. An organization may be essentially healthy despite measurements that reveal that its performance and satisfaction measurements are lower than last month's; it can be unhealthy even if its performance and efficiency figures are higher than last month's—unhealthy or healthy, that is, in relation to the ability to cope with change, with the future. Discussing the neurotic processes, Kubie makes the same point:

> There is not a single thing which a human being can do or feel, or think, whether it is eating or sleeping or drinking or fighting or killing or hating or loving or grieving or exulting or working or playing or painting or inventing, which cannot be either sick or well. . . . The measure of health is flexibility, the freedom to learn through experience, the freedom to change with changing internal and external circumstances, to be influenced by reasonable argument, admonitions, exhortations, and the appeal to emotions; the freedom to respond appropriately to the stimulus of reward and punishment, and especially the freedom to cease when sated. The essence of normality is flexibility in all of these vital ways.[43]

Any moment of behavior is unhealthy if the processes that set it in motion predetermine its automatic repetition, regardless of the environmental stimuli or consequences of the act. For example, it is plausible that lowering efficiency in order to adjust to some product change may be quite appropriate when market demands are considered. It is equally plausible that morale, or whatever measure is used to gauge the human factor, may also plummet during this period. In fact, maintaining the same level of efficiency and morale under new circumstances may be dysfunctional for the health of the organization.

Let me review the argument thus far. The main challenge confronting today's organization, whether it is a hospital or a business enterprise, is that of responding to changing conditions and adapting to external stress. The salience of change is forced on organizations because of the growing interdependence between their changing boundary conditions and society (a point that will be elaborated later) and the increasing reliance on scientific knowledge. The traditional ways that are employed to measure organizational effectiveness do not adequately reflect the true determinants of organizational health and success. Rather, these criteria yield static time-slices of performance and satisfaction, which may be irrelevant or misleading. These static, discrete measurements do not provide viable measures of health, for they tell us nothing about the processes by which the organization copes with its problems. Therefore, different effectiveness criteria have to be identified, criteria that reveal the processes of problem solving. This point is corroborated by some recent works on organizational theory. Consider, for example, these remarks by Wilfred Brown, chairman and managing director of the Glacier Metal Company:

> Effective organization is a function of the work to be done and the resources and techniques available to do it. The changes in methods of production bring about changes in the number of work roles, in the distribution of work between roles and in their relationship to one another. Failure to make explicit acknowledgement of this relationship between work and organization gives rise to non-valid assumptions (e.g., that optimum organization is a function of the personalities involved, that it is a matter connected with the personal style and arbitrary decision of the chief executive, that there are choices between centralized and decentralized types of organization, etc.). Our observations lead us to accept that optimum organization must be derived from an analysis of the work to be done and the techniques and resources available[44]

The work of Emery and Trist, which has influenced the thinking of Brown, stressed the "socio-technical system," based on Bertalanffy's "open system" theorizing.[45] They conclude that ". . . the primary task of managing an enterprise as a whole is to relate the total system to its environment, and not internal regulation per se."[46] They further conclude that:

> If management is to control internal growth and development it must in the first instance control the "boundary conditions"—the forms of exchange between the enterprise and the environment. . . . The strategic objective should be to place the enterprise in a position in its environment where it has some assured conditions for growth—unlike war the best position is not necessarily that of unchallenged monopoly. Achieving this position would be the primary task or overriding mission of the enterprise.[47]

In reference to management development, A. T. M. Wilson, former director of Tavistock Institute, pointed out:

> One general point of high relevance can be seen in these discussions of the firm as an institution. The tasks of the higher level managers center on problems in which there is a continuously high level of uncertainity; complex value decisions are inevitably involved; and this has a direct bearing on the requirements of personality for top level management. . . .[48]

And H. J. Leavitt said on the same subject:

> Management development programs need, I submit, to be oriented much more toward the future, toward change, toward differences from current forms of practice and behavior. . . . We ought to allocate more of the effort of our programs to making our student a more competent analyst. We ought, in other words, to try to teach them to think a little more like scientists, and indeed to know a good deal more about the culture and methods of scientists.[49]

What relevance have these quotations* to the main theme of this chapter? Note, first of all, that these theorists all view the organization (or institution) as an adaptive structure actively encountering many different environments, both internal and external, in its productive efforts. Note also the key terms: "change," "uncertainty," "future," "task," "mission," "work to be done," "available resources," "exchange between the enterprise and environment." There is no dialogue here on the relation between productivity and satisfaction, no fruitless

* Although not quoted here, a book by Selznick[50] is also directly relevant.

arguments between the "human relationists" and scientific-management advocates. Indeed, it seems that it is no longer adequate to perceive organization as an analog to the machine as Max Weber indicated: ". . . [bureaucracy is like] a modern judge who is a vending machine into which the pleadings are inserted together with the fee and which then disgorges the judgment together with its reasons mechanically derived from the code."[51] Nor is it reasonable to view the organization solely in terms of the socio-psychological characteristics of the persons involved at work, a viewpoint that has been so fashionable of late.[*] Rather, the approach that should be taken is that of these quoted writers: organizations are to be viewed as "open systems" defined by their primary task or mission and encountering boundary conditions that are rapidly changing their characteristics.[†] Given this rough definition, we must locate some effectiveness criteria and the institutional prerequisites that provide the conditions for the attainment of these criteria.

THE SPIRIT OF INQUIRY AS A MODEL FOR ORGANIZATION

Findings are science's short-range benefits, but the method of inquiry is its long-range value. I have said that the invention of organization was Man's first most important achievement; I now add that the development of inquiry will be his second. Both of these inventions change the species and are necessary for its survival. But both must become a part of the nature of Man himself, not just given house room in certain groups. Organization is by now a part of every man, but inquiry is not. The significant product of science and education will be the incorporation within the human animal of the capability and habit of inquiry.[54]

Whether our work is art or science or the daily work of society, it is only the form in which we explore our experience which is different; the need to explore remains the same. This is why, at bottom, the society of scientists is more important than their discoveries. What

[*] See Bennis[52] for elaboration of this point.
[†] Wilson lists six "areas of social activity; each of which contains a number of significant social institutions and social groups. These areas may be rather summarily labelled as: (i) Government, (ii) Consumers, (iii) Shareholders, (iv) Competitors, (v) Raw material and power suppliers, and (vi) Groups within the firm."[53] These represent some of the boundary conditions for the manager.

science has to teach us here is not its techniques but its spirit; the irresistible need to explore.[55]

It has been asserted throughout this chapter that organizations must be viewed as adaptive, problem-solving systems operating and embedded in complicated and rapidly changing environments. If this view is valid, then it is fair to postulate that the methodological rules by which the organization approaches its task and "exchanges with its environments" are the critical determinants of organizational effectiveness. These methodological rules or operating procedures bear a close resemblance to the rules of inquiry or scientific investigation. Therefore, the rules and norms of science may provide a valuable, possibly necessary, model for organizational behavior.

First, it should be stated what is meant and what is not meant by "science" in this context. I do not mean the findings of science, the vast array of data that scientists produce. Nor do I mean barren operationalism—what some people refer to as "scientism"—or the gadgetry utilized for routine laboratory work. Rather, what is meant may be called the scientific "temper" or "spirit." It is this "spirit of inquiry," which stems from the value position of science and which such authors as Dewey, Bronowski, Geiger, and Sanford have emphasized, that must be considered if our world is to survive. This position says essentially that the roles of scientist and citizen cannot be sharply separated. As Waddington put it:

> The true influence of science is an attitude of mind, a general method of thinking about and investigating problems. It can, and I think it will, spread gradually throughout the social consciousness without any very sharp break with the attitudes of the past. But the problems for which it is wanted face us already; and the sooner the scientific method of handling them becomes more generally understood and adopted, the better it will be.[56]

Now it is necessary to look a bit more closely at what is meant by this "scientific attitude." This complex includes many elements, only two of which are considered here. The first may be called the "hypothetical spirit," the feeling for tentativeness and caution, the respect for probable error. As Geiger says: ". . . the hypothetical spirit is the unique contribution scientific method can offer to human culture; it certainly is the only prophylactic against the authoritarian mystique so symptomatic of modern nerve failure."[57]

The second ingredient is experimentalism, the willingness to expose ideas to empirical testing, to procedures, to action. The hypothetical stance without experimentalism would soon develop into a rather arid scholasticism. Experimentalism without the corrective of the hypothetical imagination would bring about a radical, "dust-bowl" empiricism lacking significant insight and underlying structures capable of generalization. These two features, plus the corrective of criticism, are what is meant by the methodological rules of science; it is the *spirit of inquiry*, a love of truth relentlessly pursued, that ultimately creates the objectivity and intelligent action associated with science.

But the scientific attitude of which I speak can most easily flourish under specific conditions usually associated with the social organization of the scientific enterprise. A number of social scientists, inspired by the work of Parsons[58,59] and Merton,[60] have examined the society of scientific enterprise.[61,62,63,64] What they have said is important for the argument presented here. Only when the social conditions of science are realized, can the scientific attitude exist. As Sanford pointed out:

> Science flourishes under that type of democracy that accents freedom of opinion and dissent, and respect for the individual. It is against all forms of totalitarianism, of mechanization and regimentation. . . . In the historical development of the ends that are treasured in Western societies there is reason to believe that science has had a determining role. Bronowski again: Men have asked for freedom, justice, and respect precisely as science has spread among them.[65]

Or as Parsons states:

> Science is intimately integrated with the whole social structure and cultural tradition. They mutually support one another—only in certain types of society can science flourish and conversely without a continuous and healthy development and application of science such a society cannot function properly.[66]

What are the conditions that constitute the ethos of science? Barber identifies five that are appropriate to this discussion: rationality, universalism, individualism, communality, and disinterestedness.[67] A brief word about each of these is in order. The goal of science is understanding, understanding in as abstract and general a fashion as possible. "Universalism," as the term is used here, means that all men have morally equal claims to discover and to understand. Individualism, according to Barber, expresses itself in science as antiauthoritarianism; no authority but the authority of science need be accepted or trusted. Communality is close to the utopian Communist slogan: "From each according to his abilities, to each according to his needs." This simply means that all scientific peers have the right to share in existing knowledge; withholding knowledge and secrecy are cardinal sins. The last element, disinterestedness, is to be contrasted with the self-interest usually associated with organizational and economic life. Disinterestedness in science requires that role incumbents serve others and gain gratification from the pursuit of truth itself. These five conditions constitute the moral imperatives of the social organization of science. They are, of course, derived from an "ideal type" of system, an empirically imaginable possibility but a rare phenomenon. Nevertheless, insofar as they are imperatives, they do in fact determine significantly the behavior of scientific organization.

There are two points to be made in connection with this model of organization. The first was made earlier but may require reiteration: The spirit of inquiry can flourish only in an environment where there is a commitment toward the five institutional imperatives. The second point is that what is now called the "human relations school"* has been preoccupied primarily with the study of those factors which this chapter has identified as the institutional imperatives of the science of organization. In fact, only if we look at the human relationists' approach with this perspective do we obtain a valid view of their work. For example, a great deal of work in human relations has focused on "communication," [69] "participation,"[70] and "decision making." Overgeneralizing a bit, we can say that most of the studies have been (from a *moral* point of view) predicated on, and lean toward, the social organization of science as has been outlined here. Note, for instance, that many studies have shown that increased participation, better communication (keeping the worker "informed"), more "self-control," and decreased authoritarianism are desirable ends. Because of their emphasis on these factors, the researchers and theoreticians associated with human relations research have sometimes been perceived as "softheaded," unrealistic, too academic, and even utopian. In some cases, the social scientists themselves have invited these criticisms by being mainly interested in demonstrating that these participative beliefs would lead to heightened morale and, on occasion,

* See Bennis.[68]

to increased efficiency. So they have been accused by many writers of being advocates of "happiness" or a moo-cow psychology.*

These are invalid criticisms, mainly because the issue is being fought on the wrong grounds. One of the troubles is that the social scientists have not foreseen the full implications of their studies. Rather than debating the viability of socio-psychological variables in terms of the traditional effectiveness variables, which at this point is highly problematical, they should be saying that the only way in which organizations can develop a scientific attitude is by providing conditions where it can flourish. In short, the norms of science are both compatible and remarkably homogeneous with those of a liberal democracy. We argue, then, that the way in which organizations can master their dilemmas and solve their problems is by developing a spirit of inquiry. This can flourish only under the social conditions associated with the scientific enterprise (i.e., democratic ideals). Thus it is *necessary* to emphasize the "human side of enterprise," that is, institutional conditions of science, if organizations are expected to maintain mastery over their environment.†

Now, assuming that the social conditions of science have been met, let us return to the designated task of identifying those organizational criteria that are associated with the scientific attitude.

THE CRITERIA OF SCIENCE AND MENTAL HEALTH APPLIED TO ORGANIZATIONS

Perhaps no other area of human functioning has more frequently been selected as a criterion for mental health than the individual's reality orientation and his efforts at mastering the environment.[73]

I now propose that we gather the various kinds of behavior just mentioned, all of which have to do with effective interaction with the environment, under the general heading of competence.[74]

All aspects of the enterprise must be subordinated to . . . *its primary task*. It is not only industrial enterprises, however, which must remain loyal to their primary tasks. This is so of all human groups, for these are all compelled, in order to maintain themselves in existence, to

---

* See Baritz.[71]

† Shepard notes the irony that as research organizations expand their operations, they become more like the classical, ideal type of bureaucracy. See Shepard [72] for another approach to the social conditions of science.

undertake some form of appropriate action in relation to their environment. . . . An organism, whether individual or social, must do work in order to keep itself related to its external environment, that is, to meet reality.[75]

These quotations provide the framework for the following analysis. They express what has been the major concern throughout this chapter: that, when organizations are considered as "open systems," adaptive structures coping with various environments, the most significant characteristic for understanding effectiveness is competence, mastery, or (the term that has been used in this chapter) problem solving. It has been shown that competence can be gained only through certain adaptations of science: its attitude and social conditions. It is now possible to go a step further by underlining what the above quotations reveal, that the criteria of science bear a close kinship to the characteristics of what mental-health specialists and psychiatrists call "health."

There is an interesting historical parallel between the development of criteria for the evaluation of mental health and the evolution of standards for evaluating organizational health. The terms "mastery," "competence," and "adaptive, problem-solving abilities" are relatively new to both fields. In the area of organizational behavior, they are replacing the old terms "satisfaction" and "work competence." Similarly, an important change has taken place in the mental-health field, which has had some of the same problems in determining adequate criteria. Rather than viewing health exclusively in terms of some highly inferential intrapsychic reconstitutions, these specialists are stressing "adaptive mechanisms" and "conflict-free," relatively autonomous ego-functioning, independent of id energies. The studies of White,[76] Rapaport,[77] Erikson,[78] Hartmann,[79] and other so-called ego psychologists all point in this direction.

The main reason for the confluence of organizational behavior and mental health is basically quite simple. Both the norms of science and the methodology of psychotherapeutic work have the same goal and methodology: to perceive reality, both internal and external, and to examine unflinchingly the positions of these realities in order to act intelligently. It is the belief here that what a patient takes away and can employ *after* treatment is the methodology of science, the ability to look facts in the face and to use the hypothetical and experimental methods—the spirit of inquiry—in understanding experience.

Sanford has said in this connection:

> . . . most notably in Freud's psychoanalytic method of investigation and treatment. (This method is in my view, Freud's greatest, and it will be his most lasting contribution.) By the method I mean the whole contractual arrangement according to which both the therapist and patient become investigators, and both objects of careful observation and study; in which the therapist can ask the patient to face the truth because he, the therapist, is willing to try to face it in himself; in which investigation and treatment are inseparable aspects of the same humanistic enterprise.[80]

And in Freud's words: "Finally, we must not forget that the relationship between analyst and patient is based on a love of truth, that is, on the acknowledgement of reality, and that it precludes any kind of sham or deception."[81]

It is now possible to postulate the criteria for organizational health. These are based on a definition by Marie Jahoda, according to which a healthy personality " . . . actively masters his environment, shows a certain unit of personality, and is able to perceive the world and himself correctly."[82] Let us take each of these elements and extrapolate it into organizational criteria.

1 *"Actively masters his environment": adaptability* In terms of this chapter, this characteristic coincides with problem-solving ability, which in turn depends upon the organization's flexibility. Earlier it was pointed out that flexibility is the freedom to learn through experience, to change with changing internal and external circumstances. Another way of putting it, in terms of organizational functioning, is to say that it is "learning how to learn." This is equivalent to Bateson's notion of "deutero-learning," the progressive change in rate of simple learning.[83]

2 *"Certain unit of personality": the problem of identity* In order for an organization to develop adaptabilty, it needs to know who it is and what it is to do; that is, it has to have some clearly defined identity.* The problem of identity, which is central to much of the contemporary literature in the mental-health field, can in organizations be examined in at least two ways: (1) by determining to what extent the organizational goals are understood and accepted by the personnel and (2) by ascertaining to what extent the organization is perceived veridically by the personnel.

---

* See Selznick[84] for similar emphasis.

As to the problem of goals, Selznick pointed out:

> The aims of large organizations are often very broad. A certain vagueness must be accepted because it is difficult to foresee whether more specific goals will be realistic or wise. This situation presents the leader with one of his most difficult but indispensable tasks. *He must specify and recast the general aims of his organization so as to adapt them, without serious corruption, to the requirements of institutional survival.* This is what we mean by the definition of institutional mission and role.[85]

The same point is made by Simon, Smithburg, and Thompson: "No knowledge of administrative techniques, then, can relieve the administrator from the task of moral choice—choice as to organizational goals and methods and choice as to his treatment of the other human beings in his organization."[86]

In addition to the clear definition of mission, which it is the responsibility of the leader to communicate, there also has to be a working consensus on the organization of work. Wilfred Brown's work is extremely useful in this connection. He enumerates four concepts of organization: (1) the *manifest* organization, or the one which is seen on the "organization chart" and which is formally displayed; (2) the *assumed* organization, or the one that individuals perceive as the organization (were they asked to draw their phenomenological view of the way that things work); (3) the *extant* organization, or the situation as revealed through systematic investigation, say, by a student of organizations; and (4) the *requisite* organization, or the situation as it would be if it were "in accord with the real properties of the field in which it exists."

"The ideal situation," Brown goes on to say, "is that in which the manifest, the assumed, the extant, and the requisite are as closely as possible in line with each other."[87] Wherever these four organizational concepts are in contradiction, we find a case of what Erikson calls "identity diffusion."[88] Certainly this phenomenon is a familiar one to students and executives of organizations. Indeed, the great attention paid to the "informal group" and its discrepancy with the formal (the difference between the manifest and the assumed organizations or between the manifest and the extant) testifies to this.

Another useful analogy to the mental-health field shows up in this discussion. Many psychotherapeutic schools base their notions of health on the degree to which the individual brings into harmony the various "selves" that make up his personality. According to Fromm-Reichmann: ". . . the successfully treated mental patient, as he then knows himself, will be much the same person as he is known to others."[89]

Virtually the same criterion is used here for organizational health, i.e., the degree to which the organization maintains harmony—and knowledge—about and among the manifest, assumed, extant, and requisite situations. This point should be clarified. It is not necessary to organizational health that all four concepts of organization be identical. Rather, all four types should be recognized and allowance made for all the tensions attendant upon their imbalance. It is doubtful that there will always be total congruence in organizations. The important factor is recognition; the executive function is to strive toward congruence insofar as it is possible.

3 *"Is able to perceive the world and himself correctly": reality-testing* If the conditions requisite for an organization are to be met, the organization must develop adequate techniques for determining the "real properties" of the field in which it exists. The field contains two main boundaries, the internal organization and the boundaries relevant to the organization. March and Simon, in their cognitive view of organization, place great emphasis on adequate "search behavior." Ineffective search behavior—cycling and stereotypy—are regarded as "neurotic."[90]

However, it is preferable here to think about inadequate search behavior in terms of perception that is free from need-distortion.[91] Abraham Maslow places this in perspective: "Recently Money-Kyrle, an English psychoanalyst, has indicated that he believes it possible to call a neurotic person not only *relatively* inefficient, simply because he does not perceive the real world as accurately or as efficiently as does the healthy person. The neurotic is not only emotionally sick—he is cognitively *wrong!*[92] The requisite organization requires reality-testing, within the limits of rationality, for successful mastery over the relevant environments.*

In summary, then, I am saying that the basic features of organization rely on adequate methods for solving problems. These methods stem from the elements of what has been called the "scientific attitude." From these ingredients have been fashioned three criteria of

---

* See March and Simon[93] for a formal model of search behavior and an excellent discussion of organizational reality-testing.

organizational mechanisms, which fulfill the prerequisites of health. These criteria are in accord with what mental-health specialists call "health" in the individual.

Undeniably, some qualifications have to be made. The mensuration problem has not been faced, nor have the concrete details for organizational practice been fully developed. Nonetheless, it has been asserted that the processes of problem solving—of adaptability—stand out as the single most important determinant of organizational health and that this adaptability depends on a valid identity and valid reality-testing.*

SOME IMPLICATIONS OF THE SCIENCE MODEL FOR ORGANIZATIONAL BEHAVIOR

There is one human characteristic which today can find a mode of expression in nationalism and war, and which, it may seem would have to be completely denied in a scientific society. That is the tendency to find some dogma to which can be attached complete belief, forthright and unquestioning. That men do experience a need for certainty of such a kind can scarcely be doubted. . . . Is science, for all its logical consistency, in a position to satisfy this primary need of man?[94]

We are not yet emotionally an adaptive society, though we try systematically to develop forces that tend to make us one. We encourage the search for new inventions; we keep the mind stimulated, bright, and free to seek out fresh means of transport, communication, and energy; yet we remain, in part, appalled by the consequences of our ingenuity and, too frequently, try to find security through the shoring up of ancient and irrelevant conventions, the extension of purely physical safeguards, or the delivery of decisions we ourselves should make into the keeping of superior authority like the state. These solutions are not necessarily unnatural or wrong, but historically they have not been enough and I suspect they will never be enough to give us the serenity and competence we seek. . . . We may find at least part of our salvation in identifying ourselves with the adaptive process and thus share . . . some of the joy, exuberance, satisfaction and security . . . to meet the changing time.[95]

* Dr. M. B. Miles has suggested that an important omission in this approach is organization "memory" or storage of information. Organizations modeled along the lines suggested here require a "theory" based on an *accumulated* storage of information. This is implied, I believe, in the criterion of adaptability.

The use of the model of science as a form for the modern organization implies some profound reforms in current practice, reforms that may appear to some as too adventurous or utopian. This criticism is difficult to deny, particularly since not all the consequences can be clearly seen at this time. However, let us examine a few consequences that do stand out rather sharply.

1 *The problem of commitment and loyalty* Although the viewpoint does have its critics, such as William H. Whyte, Jr., most administrators desire to develop high commitment and loyalty to the organization. Can the scientific attitude, with its ascetic simplicity and acceptance of risk and uncertainty, substitute for loyalty to the organization and its purpose? Can science, as Waddington wonders, provide the belief in an illusion that organizational loyalty is thought to provide? The answer to this is a tentative "yes and no." Substituting the scientific attitude for loyalty would be difficult for those people to whom the commitment to truth, to the pursuit of knowledge, is both far too abstract and far too threatening. For some, the "escape from freedom" is a necessity, and the uncertain nature of the scientific attitude would be difficult to accept. However, it is likely that even these individuals would be influenced by the adoption of the science model by the organization. Loyalty to the organization per se would be transformed into loyalty and commitment directed to the spirit of inquiry. What effect would this have on commitment?

Gouldner, in another context, has supplied an important clue. He pointed to a difference between individuals in terms of two organizational roles, "locals" and "cosmopolitans."[96] The cosmopolitan derives his rewards from inward standards of excellence, internalized and reinforced through professional (usually scientific) identification. On the other hand, the local (what Marvick calls the "bureaucratic orientation"[97]) derives his rewards from manipulating power within the hierarchy. The locals are considered to be better organization men than the cosmopolitans. Loyalty within the scientific organizational conditions specified here would be directed not to particular ends or products or to work groups but to identification with the adaptive process of the organization.

2 *Recruitment and training for the spirit of inquiry* There are some indications that the problems of recruitment and training for the social organization of science are not as difficult as has been expected. For one thing, as Bruner has shown,[98] today's schoolchildren

are getting more and better science teaching. It is to be hoped that they will learn as much about the attitude of science as they will about its glamour and techniques. In addition, more and more research-trained individuals are entering organizations.* As McGregor points out: "Creative intellectual effort by a wide range of professional specialists will be as essential to tomorrow's manager as instruments and an elaborate air traffic control system are to today's jet pilot."[100] Individuals trained in scientific methodology can easily adapt to, in fact will probably demand, more and more freedom for intellectual inquiry. If McGregor's and Leavitt and Whisler's[101] prognostications are correct, as they presently seem to be, then there is practically no choice but to prepare a social milieu in which the adaptive, problem-solving processes can flourish.

As to training, only a brief word needs to be said. The training program of the National Training Laboratories[102] and the work of Blake,[103] Blansfied,[104] and Shepard[105] are based rather specifically on developing better diagnosticians of human behavior. It is apparent from such training studies that the organization of tomorrow, heavily influenced by the growth of science and technology and manned by an increasing number of professionals, will be based on inquiry.

3 *Intergroup competition* Blake and Mouton, guided partly by the work of the Sherifs,[106] have disclosed for examination one of organization's most troublesome problems, intergroup conflict and collaboration. These chronic conflicts probably dissipate more energy and money than any other single organizational disease. Intergroup conflict, with its "win-lose" orientation, its dysfunctional loyalty (to the group or product, not to the truth), its cognitive distortions of the outsider (the "enemy"), and its inability to reach what has been called "creative synthesis," effectively disrupts the commitment to truth. By means of a laboratory approach, Blake and Mouton have managed to break

> . . . the mental assumptions underlying win-lose conflict. Factually based mutual problem identification, fluidity in initial stages of solution, proposing rather than fixed position taking, free and frequent interchange between representatives and their constituent groups and focussing on communalities as well as differences as the basis for achieving agreement and so on, are but a few of the ways which have been experimentally demonstrated to increase the likelihood of

* See Harbison[99] on this point.

arriving at mutually acceptable solutions under conditions of collaboration between groups.[107]

What the authors do not explicitly say but only imply is that the structure of their experimental laboratory approach is based on the methods of inquiry that have been advocated in this chapter. Theirs is an action-research model, in which the subjects are the inquirers who learn to collect, use, and generalize from data in order to understand organizational conflict. Rational problem solving is the only means presently known by which organizations may be rid of persistent intergroup conflict.

Loyalty, recruitment and training, and intergroup hostility are by no means all the organizational consequences that this chapter suggests. The distribution of power, the problems of group cohesiveness,[*] the required organizational fluidity for arranging task groups on a rational basis, and the change in organizational roles and status all have to be considered. More time and energy than are now available are needed before these problems can be met squarely.

However, one thing is certain: whatever energy, competence, and time are required, it will be necessary to think generally along the lines outlined here. Truth is a cruel master, and the reforms that have been mentioned or implied may not be altogether pleasant to behold. The light of truth has a corrosive effect on vested interests, outmoded technologies, and rigid, stereotyped patterns of behavior. Moreover, if this scientific ethos is ever realized, the remnants of what are now known as "morale" and "efficiency" may be buried. For the spirit of inquiry implies a confrontation of truth that may not be "satisfying" and a deferral of gratification that may not, in the short run, be "efficient." However, this is the challenge that must be met if organizations are to cope more successfully within their increasingly complicated environments.

NOTES

1. "Muggeridge and Snow," *Encounter,* vol. 27, p. 90, February, 1962.
2. Snow, C. P., *The Two Cultures and the Scientific Revolution,* Mentor Books, New American Library of World Literature, Inc., New York, 1962.

[*] It is suspected that group cohesiveness will decrease as the scientific attitude infuses organizational functioning. With the depersonalization of science, the rapid turnover, and some expected individualism, cohesiveness may not be functional or even possible.

3. Bronowski, J., *Science and Human Values,* Harper & Row, Publishers, Incorporated, New York, 1959.

4. Sanford, N., "Social Science and Social Reform," Presidential address for SPSSI at the Annual Meeting of the American Psychological Association, Washington, Aug. 28, 1958.

5. Katzell, R. A., "Industrial Psychology," in P. R. Farnsworth (ed.), *Annual Review of Psychology,* Annual Reviews, Inc., Palo Alto, Calif., 1957, pp. 237–268.

6. Jahoda, M., *Current Concepts of Positive Mental Health,* Basic Books, Inc., Publishers, New York, 1958.

7. Pfiffner, J. M., and F. P. Sherwood, *Administrative Organization,* Prentice-Hall, Inc., Englewood Cliffs, N.J., 1960.

8. Jahoda, *op. cit.*

9. Wasserman, P., *Measurement and Evaluation of Organizational Performance,* McKinsey Foundation Annotated Bibliography, Graduate School of Business and Public Administration, Cornell University, Ithaca, N.Y., 1959.

10. Katzell, *op. cit.*

11. Aitken, H. G. J., *Taylorism at Watertown Arsenal: Scientific Management in Action, 1908–1915,* Harvard University Press, Cambridge, Mass., 1960.

12. Likert, R., "Measuring Organizational Performance," *Harvard Business Review,* vol. 36, pp. 41–50, March-April, 1958.

13. Argyris, C., "The Integration of the Individual and the Organization," Paper presented at the University of Wisconsin, Madison, Wis., May, 1961.

14. Argyris, C., *Personality and Organization,* Harper & Row, Publishers, Incorporated, New York, 1957.

15. Whyte, W. H., Jr., *The Organization Man,* Simon and Schuster, Inc., New York, 1956.

16. Haire, M., "What Price Value?" *Contemporary Psychology,* vol. 4, pp. 180–182, June, 1959.

17. Kahn, R., F. C. Mann, and S. Seashore, "Human Relations Research in Large Organizations. II," *Journal of Social Issues,* vol. 12, no. 2, p. 4, 1956.

18. Pfiffner and Sherwood, *op. cit.*

19. Likert, *op. cit.*

20. Kahn et al., *op. cit.*, introduction.

21. Parsons, T., "Suggestions for a Sociological Approach to the Theory of Organizations. I," *Administrative Science Quarterly,* vol. 1, pp. 63–85. 1956.

22. Bennis, W. G., "Leadership Theory and Administrative Behavior: The Problem of Authority," *Administrative Science Quarterly,* vol. 4, no. 3, pp. 259–301, December, 1959.

23. Selznick, P., "Foundations of the Theory of Organizations," *American Sociological Review,* vol. 13, pp. 25–35, 1948.

24. Selznick, *op. cit.*

25. Caplow, T., "The Criteria of Organizational Success," in K. Davis and W. G. Scott (eds.), *Readings in Human Relations,* McGraw-Hill Book Company, New York, 1959, p. 96.

26. Urwick, L. F., "The Purpose of a Business," in K. Davis and W. G. Scott (eds.), *Readings in Human Relations,* McGraw-Hill Book Company, New York, 1959, pp. 85–91.

27. Comrey, A. L., "A Research Plan for the Study of Organizational Effectiveness," in A. H. Rubenstein and C. J. Haberstroh (eds.), *Some Theories of Organization,* Dorsey-Irwin Press, Homewood, Ill., 1960, p. 362.

28. Bronowski, J., *The Common Sense of Science,* Modern Library, Inc., New York, no date.

29. Paul, B., "Social Science in Public Health," *American Journal of Public Health,* vol. 46, pp. 1390–1393, November, 1956.

30. Ridgway, V. F., "Dysfunctional Consequences of Performance Measurements," in A. H. Rubenstein and C. J. Haberstroh (eds.), *Some Theories of Organization,* Dorsey-Irwin Press, Homewood, Ill., 1960, pp. 371–377.

31. March, J., and H. Simon, *Organizations,* John Wiley & Sons, Inc., New York, 1958, chap. 7.

32. Argyris, C., *Organizational Development: An Inquiry into the Esso Approach,* Yale University Press, New Haven, Conn., July, 1960.

33. Shepard, H., "Three Management Programs and the Theories behind Them," in *An Action Research Program for Organization Improvement,* Foundation for Research on Human Behavior, Ann Arbor, Mich., 1960.

34. Gibb, J. R., and R. Lippitt (eds.), "Consulting with Groups and Organizations," *Journal of Social Issues,* vol. 15, no. 2, pp. 1–74, 1959.

35. Lippitt, R., J. Watson, and B. Westley, *The Dynamics of Planned Change,* Harcourt, Brace & World, Inc., New York, 1958.

36. Bennis, W. G., K. Benne, and R. Chin, *The Planning of Change,* Holt, Rinehart and Winston, Inc., New York, 1961.

37. Walker, C. R. (ed.), *Modern Technology and Civilization,* McGraw-Hill Book Company, New York, 1961.

38. Mann, F. C., and F. W. Neff, *Managing Major Change in Organizations,* Foundation for Research on Human Behavior, Ann Arbor, Mich., 1961.

39. Kahn et al., *op. cit.*

40. Leavitt, H. J., "Effects of Certain Communication Patterns on Group Performance," *Journal of Abnormal and Social Psychology,* vol. 46, pp. 38–50, 1951.

41. Smith, S., "Communication Pattern and the Adaptability of Task-oriented Groups: An Experimental Study," unpublished paper, Massachusetts Institute of Technology, Cambridge, Mass., 1950.

42. Leavitt, H. J., "Unhuman Organizations," Address presented at the Centennial Symposium on Executive Development, School of Industrial Management, Massachusetts Institute of Technology, Cambridge, Mass., Apr. 27, 1961.

43. Kubie, L. S., *Neurotic Distortions of the Creative Process,* Porter Lectures, Series 22, University of Kansas Press, Lawrence, Kans., 1958.

44. Brown, W., *Exploration in Management,* John Wiley & Sons, Inc., New York, 1960.

45. Bertalanffy, L. V., "The Theory of Open Systems in Physics and Biology," *Science,* vol. 111, pp. 23–29, 1950.

46. Emery, F. E., and E. L. Trist, "Socio-technical Systems," Paper presented at the 6th Annual International Meeting of the Institute of Management Sciences, Paris, September, 1959.

47. *Ibid.*

48. Wilson, A. T. M., "The Manager and His World," Paper presented at the Centennial Symposium on Executive Development, School of Industrial Management, Massachusetts Institute of Technology, Cambridge, Mass., Apr. 27, 1961.

49. Leavitt, "Unhuman Organizations."

50. Selznick, P., *Leadership in Administration,* Row, Peterson & Company, Evanston, Ill., 1957.

51. Bendix, R., *Max Weber: An Intellectual Portrait,* Doubleday & Company, Inc., Garden City, N.Y., 1960.

52. Bennis, *op. cit.*

53. Wilson, *op. cit.,* p. 3.

54. Thelen, H., *Education and the Human Quest,* Harper & Row, Publishers, Incorporated, New York, 1960.

55. Bronowski, *Science and Human Values.*

56. Waddington, C. H., *The Scientific Attitude,* Penguin Books, Inc., Baltimore, 1941.

57. Geiger, G., "Values and Social Science," *The Journal of Social Issues,* vol. 6, no. 4, pp. 8–16, 1950.

58. Parsons, T., *The Social System,* The Free Press of Glencoe, New York, 1951, chap. 8.

59. Parsons, T., "The Professions and Social Structure," in *Essays in Sociological Theory,* The Free Press of Glencoe, New York, 1949, chap. 8.

60. Merton, R., "The Sociology of Knowledge" and "Science and Democratic Social Structure," in *Social Theory and Social Structure,* The Free Press of Glencoe, New York, 1949, chaps. 8 and 12.

61. Barber, B., *Science and the Social Order,* The Free Press of Glencoe, New York, 1952.

62. Bush, G. P., and D. H. Hattery, *Teamwork in Research,* American University Press, Washington, D.C., 1953.

63. Marcson, S., *The Scientist in American Industry,* Industrial Relations Section, Princeton University, Princeton, N.J., 1960.

64. Rubenstein, A. H., and H. A. Shepard, *Annotated Bibliography on Human Relations in Research Laboratories,* School of Industrial Management, Massachusetts Institute of Technology, Cambridge, Mass., February, 1956.

65. Sanford, *op. cit.*

66. Barber, *op. cit.*

67. *Ibid.*

68. Bennis, *op. cit.*

69. Berkowitz, N., and W. Bennis, "Interaction in Formal Service-oriented Organizations," *Administrative Science Quarterly*, vol. 6, no. 1, pp. 25–50, June, 1961.

70. McGregor, D., *The Human Side of Enterprise*, McGraw-Hill Book Company, New York, 1960.

71. Baritz, L., *The Servants of Power*, Wesleyan University Press, Middletown, Conn., 1960.

72. Shepard, H., "Superiors and Subordinates in Research," *Journal of Business*, vol. 29, pp. 261–267, October, 1956.

73. Jahoda, *op. cit.*

74. White, R. W., "Motivation Reconsidered: The Concept of Competence," *Psychological Review*, vol. 66, no. 5, pp. 297–333, September, 1959.

75. E. L. Trist in Brown, *op. cit.*

76. White, *op. cit.*

77. Rapaport, D., "The Theory of Ego Autonomy: A Generalization," *Bulletin of the Menninger Clinic*, vol. 22, no. 2, pp. 13–35, January, 1958. (See also "The Structure of Psychoanalytic Theory," *Psychological Issues*, vol. 2, no. 2, monograph 6, 1960.)

78. Erikson, E., "Identity and the Life Cycle," *Psychological Issues*, vol. 1, no. 1, monograph 1, 1959.

79. Hartmann, H., *Ego Psychology and the Problem of Adaption*, International Universities Press, Inc., New York, 1958.

80. Sanford, *op. cit.*

81. Freud, S., "Analysis Terminable and Interminable," in E. Jones (ed.), *Collected Papers*, vol. 5, Basic Books, Inc., Publishers, New York, 1959.

82. Jahoda, *op. cit.*

83. Bateson, G., "Social Planning and the Concept of Deutero-learning," in T. M. Newcomb and E. L. Hartley (eds.), *Readings in Social Psychology*, 1st ed., Holt, Rinehart and Winston, Inc., New York, 1947, pp. 121–128.

84. Selznick, *Leadership in Administration*, chap. 3.

85. *Ibid.*

86. Simon, H. A., D. W. Smithburg, and V. A. Thompson, *Public Administration*, Alfred A. Knopf, Inc., New York, 1950.

87. Brown, *op. cit.*

88. Erikson, *op. cit.*

89. Fromm-Reichmann, F., *Principles of Intensive Psychotherapy*, The University of Chicago Press, Chicago, 1950.

90. March and Simon, *op. cit.*

91. Katzell, *op. cit.*

92. Jahoda, *op. cit.*

93. March and Simon, *op. cit.*, p. 50 and chap. 6.

94. Waddington, *op. cit.*

95. Morison, E., "A Case Study of Innovation," *Engineering Science Monthly*, vol. 13, pp. 5–11, April, 1950.

96. Gouldner, A., "Locals and Cosmopolitans: Towards an Analysis of Latent Social Roles. I," *Administrative Science Quarterly*, vol. 2, pp. 281–306, 1957.

97. Marvick, D., *Career Perspectives in a Bureaucratic Setting*, University of Michigan Government Study 27, University of Michigan Press, Ann Arbor, Mich., 1954.

98. Bruner, J., *The Process of Education*, Harvard University Press, Cambridge, Mass., 1961.

99. Harbison, F. H., "Management and Scientific Manpower," Paper presented at the Centennial Symposium on Executive Development, School of Industrial Management, Massachusetts Institute of Technology, Cambridge, Mass., Apr. 27, 1961.

100. McGregor, D., "New Concepts of Management," *Technology Review*, vol. 63, no. 4, pp. 25–27, February, 1961.

101. Leavitt, H. J., and T. L. Whisler, "Management in the 1980's," *Harvard Business Review*, vol. 36, pp. 41–48, November-December, 1958.

102. Bradford, L. P., J. R. Gibb, and K. D. Benne (eds.), *T-group Theory and Laboratory Method*, John Wiley & Sons, Inc., New York, 1964.

103. Blake, R. R., and J. S. Mouton, "Developing and Maintaining Corporate Health through Organic Management Training," unpublished paper, University of Texas, Austin, Tex., 1961.

104. Blansfield, M. G., and W. F. Robinson, "Variations in Training Laboratory Design: A Case Study in Sensitivity Training," *Personnel Administration*, vol. 24, no. 2, pp. 17–22, 49, March-April, 1961.

105. Shepard, "Three Management Programs and the Theories behind Them."

106. Sherif, M., and C. Sherif, *Groups in Harmony and Tension*, Harper & Row, Publishers, Incorporated, New York, 1953.

107. Blake, R. R., and J. S. Mouton, "Industrial Warfare to Collaboration: A Behavioral Science Approach," Korzybski Memorial Address, Apr. 20, 1961.

4

changing patterns of leadership[*]

The problem is to find a form of association which will defend and protect with the whole common force the person and good of each associate, and in which each, while uniting himself with all, may still obey himself alone, and remain as free as before. This is the fundamental problem[1]

How is it possible to create an organization in which the individuals may obtain optimum expression and, simultaneously, in which the organization itself may obtain optimum satisfaction of its demands?[2]

We have not learned enough about the utilization of talent, about the creation of an organizational climate conductive to human growth. The blunt fact is that we are a long way from realizing the potential represented by the human resources we now recruit into industry.[3]

Santayana once remarked that history has a curious way of repeating itself unless it is understood. The three quotations above seem to lend some support to this apothegm, for the first dates from 1762, while the latter two are taken from recent works on organizational

[*] First published in *Harvard Business Review* as "Revisionist Theory of Leadership," pp. 26–36, 146–150, January-February, 1961.

theory. All three are concerned with the same pivotal problem, quite possibly the essential problem of the Western tradition: the relationship of the individual and his fulfillment to the demands and constraints of some supra-individual entity.* History has presented us with this explosive legacy, transformed and ossified through many stages and forms, but ultimately reducible to the age-old puzzle of the uneasy balance between individual and organizational needs, between freedom and authority.

On the surface, the conflict seems inevitable. To make matters worse, it probably is deepened by the dominant emphasis in American ideology, which tends to understress principles of authority in favor of exalting the rights of the individual.† Perhaps the best recent demonstration of this riddle is reflected in the past presidential campaign. Both candidates seemed to be promising to create greater national purpose and a strong executive office and also to preserve the eternal verities of freedom and individuality.‡

Organizational and group theories are similarly honeycombed with this duality. For Chester I. Barnard, satisfying the requirements of efficiency (personnel relations) and effectiveness (productivity) is the prime task of the effective manager.[4] Harold J. Leavitt refers to "pyramids and people";[5] Argyris, to the essential conflict between the restricted nature of the formal organization and the individual "self-actualization"; and McGregor, to "theory X" and "theory Y" stressing either the organization's or the individual's goals.

How these seemingly incompatible demands can be fulfilled simultaneously presents today's managers with their most formidable

* For a concise, popularly written account from the history-of-ideas point of view, see J. Bronowski and Bruce Mazlish, *The Western Intellectual Tradition: From Leonardo to Hegel*, Harper & Row, Publishers, Incorporated, New York, 1960. Whereas earlier writings deal with the relationship of man to the state, the church, and the nation, our present-day concern appears to be mainly with man and organization. Witness the popularity of the recent polemic of William H. Whyte, Jr., *The Organization Man*, Simon and Schuster, Inc., New York, 1956.

† The best single book on the social and philosophical undertones of this issue is Kenneth D. Benne's *A Conception of Authority*, Bureau of Publications, Teachers College, Columbia University, New York, 1943. My debt to this book is shown throughout.

‡ This was written about the 1960 election. The conflict was as real in 1964, however, with one protagonist advocating "individualism" and the other calling for the "Great Society."

challenge. It is my contention that *effective leadership depends primarily on mediating between the individual and the organization in such a way that both can obtain maximum satisfaction.* But aside from the practical considerations, this conflict and its resolution provide a sharp analytical tool with which we can analyze the tortuous twists and turns, the zigzag fads, and the massive reversals-of-emphasis in leadership theory.

Before we consider some recent books on leadership in organization, we must review recent history and map out, rather arbitrarily, some landmarks which provide the building blocks of contemporary thought.* The two major pillars upon which current theory stands I shall refer to here as "scientific management" and the "human relations" approach.

SCIENTIFIC MANAGEMENT

The first approach, really scientific management *and* bureaucracy, describes a body of theory (prevalent from 1910 to 1935) which tended to view organizations as if they existed without people. Max Weber, the German sociologist, contributed the first fully developed theory of bureaucracy.[6] For Weber, bureaucracy was a descriptive term for characterizing what we now call "formal, large-scale organizations."

Two main influences on Weber probably contributed to his later theory: (1) He was deeply impressed by the growth of industrial organizations in his native country and by his military experience in the German army, and (2) he was concerned with human frailty and the general unreliability of human judgment and passion.

His answer was to develop an apparatus of abstract depersonalization, a system that would rationally dispense solutions without the friction of subjective coloring and human error.

Writing about the same time as Weber (1910) was an American engineer, Frederick W. Taylor, who more than any other individual advanced the professionalization of management.[7] Taylor, the "father of scientific management," attempted to rely on a "third force" that would mediate between man and the organization. Whereas Weber

---

* A more detailed explanation of these factors, and of a great many other points only touched on here, can be found in my article, "Leadership Theory and Administrative Behavior: The Problem of Authority," *Administrative Science Quarterly*, December, 1959.

emphasized the legal domination of "role" or position in a status hierarchy, Taylor stressed the impersonal rationality of measurement.

Loosely speaking, the classical organizational theory developed from these roots. But possibly even more important than those structures which took shape from the theories were the assumptions, both hidden and explicit, which the classical theorists made about "human nature." They created organizations which could be construed as pre-designated, omniscient machines, and any deviation from prediction was probably occasioned by the fact that man is regrettably unpredictable and unstable or by outright engineering inadequacies. Henry Ford, the prophet of this earlier age, put it neatly when he said: "All we ask of the men is that they do the work which is set before them." Man was viewed as a passive, inert instrument, performing the tasks assigned to him.

In classical theory, then, the conflict between the man and the organization was neatly settled in favor of the organization. The only road to efficiency and productivity was to surrender man's needs to the service of the bloodless machine.

HUMAN RELATIONS

The second group of theories (thriving from 1938 to 1950) represents what is appropriately called the "human relations" approach. Here people are regarded essentially as if they existed without organizations. It is often jokingly said that the Ford Motor Company has grown so much that if "old Henry" were alive today, there would be no place for him in the organization. What happened to create this change, this shift away from the mechanical resolution typified by Weber and Taylor and characterized by Henry Ford?

What precipitated the change was the formulation of the human relations model, crystallized in the early 1930s by Fritz Roethlisberger and W. J. Dickson in *Management and the Worker*.[8] Now, the dominant focus of organization was transformed from a rational model, free from the friction of man's emotions, to a model which appears less determined (or mechanistic) and hence more unfathomable. That is, the new look in organizational theory took cognizance of unanticipated consequences of organizations—workers' feelings, attitudes, beliefs, perceptions, ideas, sentiments (exactly those elements of passion Weber believed escaped calculation).

Management—partly through the seminal work of several social scientists—began to take seriously not only the formal organizational chart but also the informal and interpersonal contexts. The major assumption of the human relations model was that man could be motivated to work more productively on the basis of fulfilling certain social and psychological needs. This "new look" of organizations was no less "rational" than the earlier machine model, except that man's motivation was a trickier and more elusive concept than the concept of the machine.

The men primarily associated with this pioneering work are Elton Mayo, with his emphasis on the significance of the human group and *affiliation* as the strongest human need; Kurt Lewin, who stressed the promise of democratic and group decision making as well as the importance of *participation* in motivating people; J. L. Moreno, with his emphasis on *positive feelings* and liking as fundamentals in effective group action; and Carl Rogers, the founder of "nondirective therapy," who underscored the need for understanding, *empathy,* and self-realization. These men and their associates, spanning the range of the behavioral sciences, forged the conceptual framework of the human relations approach.

Let us now return to our original focus, the conflict between man and the organization. For the human relations model, there is no essential conflict; satisfying the workers' social and psychological needs is entirely congruent with the organization's goals of effectiveness and productivity. Thus there is no need for an authority to govern between these forces.

The leader is seen as a facilitator in this context, as an agent who helps smooth the pathway toward goal achievement. This model assumes that there is no essential conflict between individual satisfaction and organizational satisfaction, that the former (whether described as "morale," "job satisfaction," or whatever) will lead to greater efficiency, and that authority, insofar as it exists, attempts to facilitate forces which will increase personal satisfaction.

If the reader feels that in my description of the classical and human relations models of organization I have been guilty of exaggeration and of building straw men, he is right. I have not meant to imply that Weber et al. were proposing a "brave new world" where all man's impulses are controlled and dictated wholly by the organization. Nor do I really believe that the human relations proponents were postulating a world of "Huck Finns" actualizing themselves.

I have tried, however, to dramatize in fairly stark terms the key differences between the two models. And when the contrast is made between the broad outlines of the theories, it is clear that the earlier vision elevated the apparatus, the structure, and took man as a given, while the more recent focus on human relations has worked the other side of the street.

Undoubtedly, the building of knowledge goes on in this way. Otto Neurath, the mathematician, once compared the development of science to a man repairing a leaky boat. As he patches up one side while standing on the other, dry side, the latter starts leaking, so he shifts over to the new dry side, and so on and so forth. If such jerky rhythm and patchwork characterize most knowledge building, then in any reversal of emphasis, such as that evoked by the human relations movement, exaggeration of an inattention to some factors inevitably occurs. After any revolution in thought, the debris in terms of fads, unsubstantiated theories, and overstatements has to be put in perspective and incorporated into more formal theory.

THE REVISIONISTS

Accordingly, since 1950 a number of authors have attempted to reconcile and integrate classical and modern organizational theory. I shall refer to these theorists as the "revisionists." In general, they share a common concern for revising the native, unsubstantiated, and unrealistic aspects of the human relations approach without sacrificing its radical departure from traditional theory. These revisionists, only three of whom will be discussed here,* have modified their view for any number of reasons, but the chief ones are probably related to new research findings and some "reality" considerations.

As to research findings, the idea that productivity is strongly correlated with morale turns out to be more a wish than reality. As Rensis Likert put it: "On the basis of a study I did in 1937, I believed that morale and productivity were positively related; that the higher the morale, the higher the production. Substantial research findings since then have shown that this relationship is much too simple."[9]

The fact of the matter is that we are not at all clear today about the relationship of morale to productivity, nor, indeed, are we sure

* Other writers such as Philip Seiznick, Mason Haire, William F. Whyte, Rensis Likert, Herbert Shepard, Alvin W. Gouldner, Herbert A. Simon, Abraham Zaleznik, and many others deserve to be mentioned.

that there *is* any interdependence between them; Likert and his associates have found organizations with all the logical possibilities— high morale with low productivity, low productivity with low morale, etc.

Other research findings, as well, have challenged some of the basic assumptions of the human relations model, for example, whether attention to group process factors leads to greater efficiency of group operations, whether the leader who attempts to get close to the men is a more efficient leader, and whether the leader can or should avoid hostile and aggressive attitudes directed toward him by his men.

In general, then, the revisionists recognize clearly that organizational theory must take into account such factors as purpose and goal, status and power differentials, and hierarchy. And, finally, they have come to know that leadership ultimately has to act in ways other than, or in addition to, leading a group discussion.

In this connection, it is particularly illuminating to note that Douglas M. McGregor, an early advocate of human relations and a colleague of Kurt Lewin, began formulating his new theories (which I shall discuss later) after six years of line experience as a college president.

I think McGregor's final note to the alumni and faculty of the college deserves to be printed in full, for its honesty and for its attempt to spell out a significant change in attitude, a change which typifies the prevailing currents in recent organizational theory. Space considerations do not permit this, but the following excerpt captures the main point:

> I believed, for example, that a leader could operate successfully as a kind of adviser to his organization. I thought I could avoid being a "boss." Unconsciously, I suspect, I hoped to duck the unpleasant necessity of making difficult decisions, of taking the responsibility for one course of action, among many uncertain alternatives, of making mistakes and taking the consequences. I thought that maybe I could operate so that everyone would like me, that "good human relations" would eliminate all discord and disagreement.
>
> I couldn't have been more wrong. It took a couple of years, but I finally began to realize that a leader cannot avoid the exercise of authority any more than he can avoid responsibility for what happens to his organization.[10]

The utopian wish to escape conflict, to avoid tough decisions, to create the "happy family," and to stress group and interpersonal factors tinctured the writings of the early human relations students. Yet this was an indispensable antidote, a required emphasis, given the impersonal models of the classical era.

Now the revisionists are concerned with external, economic factors, with productivity, formal status, and so on, but not to the exclusion of the human elements that the traditional theorists neglected. At this point, let us consider the works of some of these revisionists.

PESSIMISTIC RESOLUTION

Robert N. McMurry has presented a cogent case for a Weberian model of organization led at the top by strong and mature personalities. What is needed, he concludes, is "benevolent autocracy."[11] His reasoning is rather interesting. While he believes that "bottom-up" or consultative management (a species of the human relations model) is preferable ideologically, it is not practical, nor is it congruent with what he knows about personality functioning. (He holds a Ph.D. in psychology, and he has had considerable experience as an industrial consultant in this area.)

Managers are hard-driving entrepreneurs, and many of them are stubbornly destructive people. Only about 10 per cent of them *really* believe in the human relations approach. Furthermore, the bureaucratic personality does not want responsibility and independence; it prefers regimentation, routinization, and structure. "It just isn't possible in business," McMurry claims, "to delegate much autonomy below the top echelons of management."[12]

This melancholy view of the "bureaucratic personality" (whatever that truly is) goes on to show that, even if preferred, a human relations viewpoint, which McMurry equates with a radical version of group dynamics, is not really practical.

Benevolent autocracy, on the other hand, gets its results because it rigidly structures and controls the relation of the supervisors to their subordinates. Its major virtue is that it works and makes the best out of the worst. It works because a strong autocrat, who can evoke binding loyalty, respect, and distant worship, dictates, commands, and controls the organization by occupying the only room at the top. "The typical bureaucrat," McMurry says, "is incapable of conceiving or building sound leadership principles on his own initiative."[13]

Let us assume, for the moment, that McMurry's position is valid.

What we see in this approach is a virtuous and popularized psycho-analytic justification for rigid autocracy on the presumptive basis that this is the way people are. McMurry's strong autocrat, whom he does not discuss in any detail (nor does he account for his recruitment or his development), sounds like a nostalgic and romantic image of the old-time entrepreneur: strong, wise, smart, aggressive, the good father, a man utterly independent.

While McMurry's ideas seem to have a close kinship to the classical model of organization, with the resolution of the conflict clearly favoring the organization, he does not hold with the legal and/or scientific rationales of Weber or of Taylor. Rather, he creates the "great man" (the benevolent autocrat).*

When we examine McMurry's thesis more closely, we see that it resolves the conflict between man and the organization by postulating certain human needs which appear to be compatible with a tightly controlled hierarchy: man wants to be dependent, man is incapable of taking responsibility, man needs a strong leader, and so forth. And, most importantly, McMurry appears to assume these needs are fixed and immutable.

Here is where the rub comes. If McMurry's diagnosis of the situation is correct (and I strongly question it, for I have never seen a "typical bureaucrat"), is there no possibility for change, no possibility for producing more mature and able personnel, no possibilty for creating organizational conditions where individuals can take responsibility? McMurry's answers are not very clear.

And if the human relations model has tried to feature man as it would have liked him to be (denying reality), then McMurry appears to be taking man as he is, i.e., denying the possibility of change. Even Freud, known for his tragic view of man and his recognition of the difficulty of human change, once said: "Certainly men are like this, but have you asked yourselves whether they need be so, whether their inmost nature necessitates it?"

UTOPIAN RESOLUTION

Chris Argyris's *Personality and Organization* provides a neat counterfoil to McMurry. For, while they both start with the nature and

---

* For a renewed plea for the great man, see Eugene Jennings, *The Anatomy of Leadership*, Harper & Row, Publishers, Incorporated, New York, 1960.

importance of the human condition within organized settings, they end up with totally opposite diagnoses and conclusions.

Argyris, more than any other recent author, comes directly to grips with the man-organization problem. He feels that the individual's needs and formal organization's demands are basically incompatible. The outcome of this frustration can be inferred and observed through a variety of defense mechanisms and other pathological behaviors on the part of the individual which ultimately lead to the attenuation of the organization's goals and his own mental health.

Let us take a closer look. Argyris postulates a "total personality" signified by a number of dimensions: passivity to activity, dependence to independence, behavioral inflexibility to flexibility, subordinate to superordinate positions, and the like. His model assumes that these dimensions reside on a continuum and that the healthy personality develops along the continuum toward "self-actualization."

In contrast, formal organization is characterized by conditions which stultify this "growth": task specialization, chain of command, unity of direction, span of control, and other repressive and restrictive devices. The picture we get from Argyris, then, is that of an organizational behemoth slowly but surely grinding down the individual's need for growth and actualization.

The contrast between Argyris and McMurry now becomes focused:

For McMurry, most personnel are children (according to Argyris's and his own criteria), and that is the *only way they can and want to be.*

Argyris argues, on the other hand, that that is the way they are, to be sure, but that the organization forces them into this mold and that they can be vastly different.

Argyris does not pretend to solve this dilemma but suggests three possibilities which would enhance work in the industrial organization and thus lead to greater human potentiality: (1) job enlargement, (2) employee-centered leadership, and (3) reality leadership.

These suggestions are not fully developed, nor is their meaning clear. Mason Haire comments, for example, that reality leadership is ". . . flexible leadership tailored to the situation, not too directive, not too non-directive, not too employee-centered, but firm when it should be firm, and like the song in *South Pacific*, broad where it should be broad."[14]

What these proposals lack in clarity, they make up in promise. Through improved "diagnostic skill" on the part of the manager (meaning greater competence in interpersonal relations) and through the use of a staff specialist who will help management and the organization to attain these skills, a fusion process will occur which will help to bring about the optimal actualization of both the organization and the individual.

There are two main difficulties that I have with Argyris's thesis. The first has to do with his notion of "self-actualization," and the second with what he means by "optimal":

1 "Self-actualization" is a term used rather loosely by some psychologists to explain that an individual will "realize his full potential." It is a fuzzy term, drenched in value connotations both of what people are like and of what they can become. I have as much difficulty seeing concretely the self-actualized man as I do seeing the typical bureaucrat.

In order for an abstraction to be meaningful, there must be empirical and experiential validity for it. And when I ask for examples of the self-actualized person, the proponents suggest people like Einstein, Goethe, Spinoza, William James, Schweitzer, Beethoven, and Thoreau.*

The criteria used are not at all obvious, for when they are explored, it is clear that individuals like Lucky Luciano and Adolf Hitler deserve equal consideration as candidates. It is also clear that, for the most part, those public figures who are termed "self-actualizers" rarely fall into the category called "managerial leaders" (or, for that matter, rarely are they alive now!) but fall rather within the area of the arts and sciences.

The heart of the matter is that the assumptions about human behavior made by Argyris and McMurry lead them to construct totally different organizational models. For McMurry, humans are slothful and need leading; for Argyris, humans, if left free, will move naturally toward growth. As for my own belief, I, like Machiavelli, hold that man is both good and evil and that certain conditions in the organization will accentuate the expression of one or the other. Man's goodness and/or badness, this ambivalence, is part of the human condition and, as such, has to be considered in any theory of organization.

* See particularly Abraham Maslow, *Motivation and Personality*, Harper & Row, Publishers, Incorporated, New York, 1954.

2 Related to this point is the idea of "optimizing." This term refers to Argyris's notion that effective leadership can successfully fuse the organization's and the individual's needs in such a way that both will arrive at some peak point.

If this is so, then what becomes of the inevitable conflict between the two? If Argyris is correct, his solution is very similar to the human relations one: greater need-satisfaction on the part of the workers yields higher productivity for the organization. Yet this solution tries to avoid, unsuccessfully, the calculus of values so essential to the problem. For it is clear that simultaneous optimization is not feasible, that there are accommodation and relinquishment of some objectives on both sides, and that the best possible solution will be one wherein neither employer nor employee is at his peak value but where sufficient personnel satisfaction is reached at a viable rate of organizational efficiency.

THE TRAGIC VIEW

Another system of thought, in many ways similar to Argyris's, is now developing; it attempts to deal with the inherent tension between individual needs and organizational demands. It has taken shape in McGregor's recent book, *The Human Side of Enterprise*.

Unlike the quest for optimization, this view seeks no more than a satisfactory resolution. Unlike actualization, it settles for a "commitment toward maturity." Instead of a unidirectional tendency toward growth, it recognizes the basic ambivalence and conflicts within the personality. At its most hopeful, this view asserts that from this basic conflict, new and creative resolutions *may* emerge, but not necessarily. In that sense, this view is tragic.

Taking Peter Drucher's phrase "management by objective," McGregor has recast four principles that outline a new approach to organizational leadership.

1 The starting point is the clear recognition that "if there is a single assumption which pervades conventional organizational theory it is that authority is the central, indispensable means of managerial control."[15] McGregor shows the limitations of various forms of organizational authority based on role or status compared with authority based on task or goal demands, i.e., objectives. Under this concept, management by objective comes about through "target setting," a joint

effort where superior and subordinate attempt to develop the ground rules for work and productivity.*

2   There is the principle of "interdependence," or collaboration between superior and subordinate. This is essential if the two parties are to agree on some mutually satisfactory target.

3   Another principle has to do with the "belief evidenced in practice that subordinates are capable of learning how to exercise effective self-control."[16] Self-control, because it is not governed by external forces, is apparently one of McGregor's indications of maturity.

4   This position asserts the need for "integration," i.e., the bringing together and working through of the differences between individual and organizational needs. This idea was missing in the earlier conclusion of proponents of the human relations approach. According to McGregor: "The central principle which derives from Theory Y is that of integration: the creation of conditions such that members of the organization can achieve their own goals *best* by directing their efforts toward the success of the enterprise."[17]

Self-control, collaboration, and integration—these are the main ingredients of the McGregor approach. Although this approach does not claim theoretical completeness, a number of questions must be raised.

Take the concept of self-control. As I understand it, self-control comes about through the internalization of standards, not through external incentives, and through satisfying tasks, not on the basis of reward-punishment schedules.

But do all or most jobs in industry induce this "instinct of workmanship"? Can we expect assembly-line workers, maintenance personnel, or other workers performing relatively repetitive tasks to be motivated from within? Or is self-control more likely and possible in those jobs where there is a high degree of responsibility and autonomy?

McGregor bases a good deal of his theory on collaboration between subordinate and superior. Like Argyris, he recommends training in human relations to facilitate a process whereby both parties can develop skills and engage in this collaborative activity.

But we have to ask: Can individuals working in organized settings manage to deal and work collaboratively with their superiors?

* For further elaboration, see Douglas M. McGregor, "An Uneasy Look at Performance Appraisal," *Harvard Business Review*, p. 89, May-June, 1957.

Can superiors and subordinates manage to perceive each other as human beings with all their limitations and strengths, as helpers, coordinators, and also as persons with *realistic power?* These questions have to be deferred for empirical investigation, but, right now, we can see no simple solution.

Along these lines, Samuel Goldwyn was reputed to have said to his staff one day: "I want you all to tell me what's wrong with our operation even if it means losing your job!" And this is the point. Authenticity in a relationship which depends on "leveling" and honesty is a prime requisite for collaboration. Authenticity and authority seem almost antithetical to each other. Can they be combined? McGregor feels they can, over a period of time, as long as there is a "commitment to maturity."

But the main strength of McGregor's position is that he, more than other recent students of organizational behavior, has attempted to stress the sticky problem of integration of task requirements with the individual's growth. Role incumbency, personal factors, coercion, external rewards and punishments, and "selling and persuasion" are replaced by objective stress on organizational purpose and attainment. It is the "tragic view" because it comes to grips fully with the calculus of values and because it recognizes the trading, negotiations, and accommodations necessary to realize a true integration.

These brief summaries of the revisionist authors do not do full justice to their ideas; they are far more complex and provisional than I have indicated here. They also provide hope for future research and theory in organizations, work which can illuminate even more clearly the thorny issues which they raise and leave exposed to scientific scrutiny. They are to be praised, moreover, for realizing that leadership is the fulcrum on which the demands of the individual and the demands of the organization are balanced. The classical human relations models minimized this conflict by assuming a similarity between these requirements. At other times, theorists simply dismissed the concept of authority as irrelevant or as nonexistent.

We have a great deal more to learn about leadership. And where the revisionists seem to require particular help is in their theory of the nature of change. Change which facilitates the motivation and skills of managers and their employees and which allows them to develop more authentic human relationships, more true collaboration, and a more reality-centered leadership all within the highly structured organization must always be sought. We must all join the prophet J. H. Leckie, who said: "And whoever would think truly of authority must think reverently of freedom."

NOTES

1. Rousseau, J., *The Social Contract,* tr. by Charles Frankel, Hafner Publishing Company, Inc., New York, 1949, p. I.i.
2. Argyris, C. "The Individual and Organization: Some Problems of Mutual Adjustment," *Administrative Science Quarterly,* p. 24, June, 1957.
3. McGregor, D., *The Human Side of Enterprise,* McGraw-Hill Book Company, New York, 1960, p. vi.
4. Barnard, C. I., *The Functions of the Executive,* Harvard University Press, Cambridge, Mass., 1950.
5. Leavitt, H. J., *Managerial Psychology,* The University of Chicago Press, Chicago, 1958, pp. 257–262.
6. Bendix, R., *Max Weber: An Intellectual Portrait,* Doubleday & Company, Inc., Garden City, N. Y., 1960.
7. Taylor, F. W., *Scientific Management,* Harper & Row, Publishers, Incorporated, New York, 1948.
8. Roethlisberger, F. J., and W. J. Dickson, *Management and the Worker,* Harvard University Press, Cambridge, Mass., 1939.
9. Likert R., "Developing Patterns in Management," *Strengthening Management for the New Technology,* American Management Association, New York, 1955, p. 13.
10. McGregor, D., "On Leadership," *Antioch Notes,* pp. 2–3, May, 1954.
11. McMurry, R. N., "The Case for Benevolent Autocracy," *Harvard Business Review,* p. 82, January-February, 1950.
12. *Ibid.,* p. 12.
13. *Ibid.,* p. 90.
14. Haire, M., "What Price Value?" *Contemporary Psychology,* p. 181, June, 1959.
15. McGregor, *The Human Side of Enterprise,* p. 18.
16. McGregor, D., *Notes on Organizational Theory,* Massachusetts Institute of Technology, Cambridge, Mass., 1957, p. 11. (mimeographed.)
17. McGregor, *The Human Side of Enterprise,* p. 49.

part two

planning and controlling organizational change

What we have all witnessed and participated in in the past two or three decades has been called the "rise of the rational spirit," the belief that science can help better the human condition. The following five chapters describe one indication of this trend, the attempts by behavioral scientists to apply their knowledge (primarily sociological and psychological) toward the improvement of human organizations.

Three assumptions underlie what is to follow: (1) that the proportion of contemporary change that either is planned for, or arises from, deliberate innovation is much higher than in former times; (2) that man's wisdom and mundane behavior are short of perfection insofar as they regulate the fate and selective adaptation of human organization; and (3) that considering the complexity and uncertainty of managing these social systems, behavioral scientists can assist in helping their functioning and effectiveness.[*]

The following five chapters will deal with the entire range of strategic, methodological, and conceptual issues brought about by this new development in the application of the behavioral sciences.

[*] I have been aided in this formulation by Wilbert E. Moore's *Social Change*, Prentice-Hall, Inc., Englewood Cliffs, N.J., 1964. Most of the material contained in Chaps. 5 to 7 and in Chap. 9 was included in a keynote address to the International Operational Research Association, Cambridge, England, September 14, 1964.

5

*applying behavioral sciences
to planned organizational change*

THE NOTATION OF PLANNED CHANGE

Planned change is a method which employs social technology to solve
the problems of society. The method encompasses the application of
systematic and appropriate knowledge to human affairs for the purpose of creating intelligent action and choices. Planned change aims
to relate to the basic disciplines of the behavioral sciences as engineering does to the physical sciences or as medicine does to the biological disciplines.* Thus, planned change can be viewed as a crucial
link between theory and practice, between knowledge and action. It
plays this role by converting variables from the basic disciplines into
strategic instrumentation and programs. In historical perspective, the
development of planned change can be viewed as the result of two

---

* It falls far short of this aim as of today, partly because of the relatively
less mature state of the behavioral sciences and even more because of the
lack of tradition in the application of the behavioral sciences.

forces: complex problems of modern (organizational) society requir-
ing expert help and the growth and viability of the empirical
behavioral sciences. "Behavioral sciences" is a term coined in the
period following World War II by the more empirically minded of
the profession in order to "safeguard" the social disciplines from the
nonquantitative humanists and the depersonalized abstractions of the
econometricists. Typically, the field is thought to contain six disciplines:
psychology, sociology, anthropology, political science, history, and
economics. Planned change, as the term is used here, relies most
heavily on the sociological and psychological disciplines.*

The process of planned change involves a *change-agent*, who is
typically a behavioral scientist brought in to help a *client-system*,
which refers to the target of change.† The change-agent, in *collaboration* with the client-system, attempts to apply *valid knowledge* to the
client's problems. These four elements in combination—change-agent,
client-system, valid knowledge, and a deliberate and collaborative relationship—circumscribe the class of activities referred to as "planned
change." The terms are imprecise and somewhat ambiguous, but it
is hoped that their meaning will be clarified through a discussion
of concrete illustration.

These four elements also help distinguish planned change from
other forms of change. Planned change differs from "technocracy" in
that it attempts to implement research results and relies more heavily
on the relationship between change-agent and client-system. Planned
change differs from most "coercive" change programs in that the
change-agent has no formal power over the client-system. Planned
change differs from spontaneous and secondary innovations in that
it is a conscious and deliberate induction process.

Table 3 presents a typology where eight species of change may
be identified. Along the horizontal axis are shown two variables,
dichotomized for convenience: mutual goal setting and deliberateness
of change. Along the vertical axis, power distribution between the

---

* For a recent inventory of scientific findings of the behavioral sciences,
see Berelson and Steiner;[1] for the best single reference on the philosophical
foundations of the behavioral sciences, see Kaplan.[2]

† These terms, "change-agent" and "client-system," are awkward, but sub-
stitutes which would satisfy aesthetic criteria do not come to mind. And
these terms are coming into wider usage. See Lippitt et al.[3] for a fuller
account of these terms. See also Bennis et al.[4]

TABLE 3 Typology of change processes

	Collaborative		Noncollaborative	
	Mutual goal setting		*Goals set by only one or neither side*	
Power ratio	Deliberate on the part of one or both sides of the relationship	Nondeliberate on the part of both sides	Deliberate on the part of one side of the relationship	Nondeliberate on the part of both sides
.5:.5	Planned	Interactional	Technocratic	Natural
1:0	Indoctrinational	Socialization	Coercive	Emulative

change-agent and client-system is shown: .5:.5 indicates a fairly equal distribution of power, and 1:0 indicates a tilted or unequal power distribution. (In other words, in a .5:.5 power ratio, each party has the capability of influencing the other; in a 1:0 ratio, only one party is susceptible to influence.) "Valid knowledge" is omitted from the paradigm since it is, for the present, subsumed under "mutual goal setting." In a later section (page 92) we shall return to the question of valid knowledge and its relevance to planned change.

Planned change entails mutual goal setting, an equal power ratio (eventually), and deliberateness on the part of both sides.

Indoctrination involves mutual goal setting and is deliberate, but it involves an imbalanced power ratio. Many schools, prisons, and mental hospitals or other "total institutions"[5] fall into this category.

Coercive change is characterized by nonmutual goal setting, an imbalanced power ratio, and only one-sided deliberateness. Coercive change, as we are using the term, may be exemplified by the thought-control and "brainwashing" practices of the Chinese.[6,*]

---

* The distinctions between indoctrinational and coercive changes are complex. When all is said and done, hospital administrators and prisoner-of-war commandants may employ similar processes and techniques. There are probably more similarities than would be expected between forms of "acceptable" social influences, such as psychotherapy or teaching, and "unacceptable" forms, such as brainwashing. This paradigm, like all others, creates an ideal and abstract model to which empirical occurrences do not neatly conform. See my typology of change process.[7]

Technocratic change may be distinguished from planned change by the nature of the goal setting. The use of technocratic means to bring about change relies solely on collecting and interpreting data. Technocratic change, then, follows primarily an "engineering" model: the client defines his difficulties as deriving from inadequate knowledge and assumes that this lack of knowledge is accidental or a matter of neglect—not something that is functional to the system itself. The technocrat colludes in this assumption and merely makes and reports his findings.*

Interactional change is characterized by mutual goal setting, a fairly equal power distribution, but no deliberateness on either side of the relationship. (*Unconsciously* either may be committed to changing the other in some direction.) Such changes can be observed among good friends and married couples and in various other nondeliberate transactions among people. Change does occur in such relationships, possibly with beneficial effects, but there is a lack of self-consciousness about it and thus a lack of any definite change-agent–client-system relationship.

Socialization change has a direct kinship with hierarchical controls. Parent-child relationships would be the most obvious example, although the counselor-camper and teacher-pupil relationships would also be instances.

Emulative change takes place for the most part in formal organizations where there is a clear-cut superior-subordinate relationship. Change is brought about through identification with, and emulation of, the "power figures" by the subordinates.

Natural change refers to that class of changes brought about with no apparent deliberateness and no goal setting on the part of those involved in it. Primarily it is a residual category encompassing all accidents, "quirks of fate," unanticipated consequences, spontaneous innovations, etc.

This typology is crude: in nature we can rarely observe these change processes exemplified so neatly. In addition, the distinctions made in it are somewhat arbitrary and certainly not all-inclusive. In order to give the notion of planned change more meaning and subtance, it might be useful to compare it with some characteristics of operations research.

---

* See Gouldner[3] for a full discussion of the technocrat as a change-agent.

PLANNED CHANGE COMPARED WITH
OPERATIONS RESEARCH*

My knowledge of OR stems from three sources: lay articles on OR that one might see in popular periodicals such as *Scientific American* or in Shuchman[9]; more recently, and in preparation for this paper, the basic introductory books recommended by OR professionals; and most of all, the OR "pros" who occasionally sit at the dining table at MIT across from me and talk mysteriously and cheerfully about their work in such a way that I hesitate to ask even the most elementary questions, such as: What do you *really* do? And I ruefully sense a kinship, the mutual incapacity to explain to each other the basic nature of our work. But as I read over some of the literature recently, I was encouraged by certain similarities between OR and what I mean by planned change. It may be useful to discuss these now.

SOME SIMILARITIES BETWEEN
OR AND PLANNED CHANGE

Both are relatively recent *developments*. Both were products of World War II. As I understand it, OR was "founded" just before World War II, developed its status during the war, and flourished thereafter. Planned change, as was true of almost all applied behavioral research, was begun in earnest following World War II and was facilitated and promoted by practitioners who learned during the war that science could be practical.† Later on, I will have more to say about the relationship between science and action, but I should stress at this point that while there have been in the past fruitful liaisons between the behavioral sciences and action in rural sociology, in applied economics, and in clinical psychology—to mention only a few—the quality and quantity of these linkages have taken a significant upturn since World War II. From a pastime, the application of knowledge became a profession.

* This section was written especially for the OR personnel attending the conference for which this paper was written. I have decided to retain it as I think it puts the idea of planned change in better focus.

† Kurt Lewin, one of the leaders of this group, was fond of saying: "There is nothing so practical as a good theory."

Both OR and planned change are problem-centered, as contrasted to the basic disciplines, which emphasize *concept* or *method*. This is a matter of emphasis only, for OR and applied research, in general, have often provided significant inputs to the concepts and methods of their parent basic disciplines. This is not a one-way street.*

Both OR and planned change emphasize improvement and optimization of performance. To that extent, they are *normative* in their approach to problems; that is, they attempt to maximize goals under certain conditions.

Both OR and planned change rely heavily on *empirical science* as their main means of influence. Ellis Johnson points out that the ". . . majority of practitioners of operations research were trained in the basic sciences rather than in engineering or administration."[11] Similarly, practitioners of planned change were mostly trained in psychology, sociology, or anthropology. To both, the old maxim, "Knowledge is power," seems appropriate as a model of action.

Both OR and planned change rely on a relationship with clients based on *confidence* and *valid communication*.

Both OR and planned change emphasize a *systems* approach to problems, meaning essentially an awareness of the interdependencies within the internal parts of the system as well as boundary maintenance with its environment.

Finally, both OR and planned change appear to be most effective when working with *systems which are complex, rapidly changing, and probably science-based*. It will be useful to quote Johnson again on this point:

> In those large and complex organizations for whom once-reliable constants have now become "galloping variables" because of the impact of increasing complexity, trial and error must give way to planning, and acceptance of marginal improvement must give way to an organized search for opportunities to make major shifts in the means of achieving organizational objectives. Today, so many industrial and other organizations are so huge, and major operations are so expensive, that a single major "wrong" decision may be fatal; trial and error becomes "trial and catastrophe."[12]

These characteristics, then—newness, problem orientation, normative approach, basis in science, collaborative relationship with

---

* See Gouldner[10] for a brilliant exposition on the contributions of applied research to "pure" theory.

clients, systems approach, and effectiveness in rapidly changing environments—show some of the points of common interest and approach of OR and planned change. Let us turn now to some of the differences.

SOME DIFFERENCES BETWEEN OR AND PLANNED CHANGE

Perhaps the most crucial difference between OR and planned change has to do with the *identification of strategic variables,* that is, with those factors which appear to make a difference in the performance of the system under study. The marked difference in the selection of variables must undoubtedly stem from a unique "frame of reference" which leads to divergent problem-definitions. Ackoff and Rivett, for example, classify OR problems in the following way:[13]

Inventory	Routing
Allocation	Replacement
Queuing	Competition
Sequencing	Search

A similar inventory of problems in the planned-change field would probably include the following:

Identification of appropriate mission and values	Utilization of human resources
Human collaboration and conflict	Communication between hierarchical ranks
Control and leadership	Rapid growth
Coping with, and resistance to, change	Management and career development

The divergence of problem-definition leads to the selection of different variables. OR practitioners tend to select economic or engineering variables—most certainly variables which are quantitative and measurable and which appear to be linked directly to the profit and efficiency of the system. Not so of the planned-change practitioners. While there are vigorous attempts to measure rigorously and to conduct evaluation studies, the variables selected tend to be less amenable to statistical treatment and mathematical formulation. Upon even a superficial perusal of some of the literature on planned change and OR, the difference is evident: a significantly lower ratio of tables and mathematical formulas in the former.

An interesting example of the difference in variable identification and selection can be seen if we compare an example of OR with an example of planned change. Ackoff and Rivett, in their introductory chapter, report a case where OR was called on to help a major commercial airline decide how often it should run a class for stewardesses and how large the class should be. This led to a study of the following factors: cost of running the school, forecasts for future requirements, forecasting procedures, expenses and salaries of all personnel, maximum possible average number of flying hours per stewardess that could be obtained, factors in stewardesses' job satisfaction, number of reserve stewardesses required at each air base, number of bases and where they should be located, how flights should be assigned, etc., etc. As Ackoff and Rivett conclude:

> What originally appeared to be a simple and isolated problem turned out to be interconnected with almost all other operating problems of the airline. With extension of the problem the solutions to the parts could be interrelated to assure best overall performance. This avoided a "local" improvement which might result in overall loss of efficiency.[14]

Compare the airline's case with a report of C. Sofer, a sociologist who employs techniques of planned change in his role as a social consultant to a variety of organizations. A small firm called upon him to help in the selection of a senior manager.* This "presenting symptom" led to a series of disclosures and causal mechanisms which Sofer uncovered during a series of talks and meetings with the top management group. The case itself unraveled a complicated cat's cradle of factors including family relationships (among the top management group), fantasies and mistrust among members of the management group, management and career development, selection procedures, etc. Sofer helped the firm overcome these problems through counseling, through devising new organizational structures, through a training program, and through developing improved selection devices. The case was completed in about three years with follow-up consultations from time to time.

When we compare the two cases, what differences appear? First and foremost, as we said before, the problems identified as crucial for the success of the enterprise. In the case of OR, the problems identified appear to be more concrete, more measurable, and more

* This example is taken from Sofer's *Organization from Within.*[15] We shall return to this book later on when we take up the strategy and theory of planned organizational change.

obviously related (at least in the short run) to the success of the enterprise, i.e., profits and losses. Sofer identified problems and variables which were less measurable, more subjective in that they were *felt* as problems by the participants, and less obviously linked to the firm's success.

But beyond this, there appear to be some equally marked differences in the two approaches to organizational change. In the example given by Sofer, he concerns himself directly with his relationship to the client, studies this very carefully, and attempts to "use" this relationship both as a diagnostic instrument and as a training device. Even apparently "trivial" decisions, such as whether or not to have lunch with his clients, come under scrutiny:

> My staying to lunch was consistent with what is now a not uncommon Institute [Tavistock] pattern of associating to a certain degree with "clients" outside the professional situation as strictly defined. Not to do so would seem unnatural to them and highly discrepant from the ordinary conventions of business relationships to which they are accustomed. There is also the more positive reason that through such association clients are more likely to remain reality-oriented in their perceptions of the social consultant and to regard him simply as another human being who brings a particular type of expertise to bear on their problems.[16]

So a second major difference between OR and planned organizational change has to do with the *perceived importance* of the *relationship with the client*. The development and maintenance of this relationship are crucial elements in all planned-change programs. And *not solely*, or even most importantly, for "good human relations." Instead, the quality and the nature of the relationship are used as indicators for the measure of progress and as valid sources of data and diagnosis. This is not to say that OR practitioners do not concern themselves with matters of this kind. Undoubtedly they do, and probably the most successful of them operate with great sensitivity toward their clients. But if one looks at what they *say* about their work, there is no question that practitioners of planned change are clearly more *self-conscious* and concerned with the human interactions between client and change-agent.°

° It may be that the extent to which science and instrumentation can be used in effecting change is directly and inversely proportional to the use of personal elements of the relationship. We shall return to this speculation later on.

A third major difference can now be identified. In the airline case, the OR practitioner devoted the majority of his time to *research*, to problem solving. In the case Sofer presents, while there was some research effort and data gathering, perhaps slightly more time was spent on *implementation through programs* of one kind or another: counseling, training programs, selection procedures, management development schemes, etc.

A fourth major difference has to do with the degree to which OR and planned-change practitioners take seriously the idea of a *system* in their approaches. Though I said earlier that both were systems-oriented, it seems that this is less stringently upheld in most cases of planned change. Sofer dealt almost exclusively with the top management group, and though the actions taken may have "percolated" down to lower echelons, there is a wide zone of uncertainty regarding the effects of this program on other parts of the system. In a case cited by Argyris[17] which will be discussed later on, we shall see how a particular change program in only one part of the system may create negative disturbances and unanticipated consequences in other parts of the system.*

Two other differences should be mentioned before going on. First, the idea of an interdisciplinary team, so central to OR, does not seem to be a part of most planned-change programs. Usually, only one or two men work on a program. It is true that these change-agents are themselves "generalists" and are capable of bridging disciplines. Yet it is a lack, compared with OR. Many times, for example, an economist or an engineer would add significantly to the change-agent's skills—particularly as they relate to the measurement of effectiveness and performance variables.†

One thing that emerges from a study of these two approaches to organizational change is a realization of the complexity of modern organization. Look through the kaleidoscope one way, and a configur-

---

* See Bavelas and Strauss[18] for a classic case where positive change in one part of a system created such perturbations in adjacent parts of the system that the entire program was scrapped.

† Another factor may be that there is a greater homogeneity of theory among OR practitioners. I do, however, mistrust this observation, no matter how valid it is. My mistrust is based on a fundamental law of social perception; i.e. the "others" always seem more alike to the "outsider" ("Well, they all look alike to me.").

ation of the economic and technological factors appears; tilt it, and nothing appears except the pattern of external environment surrounding the firm. Tilt it again, and what emerges is a pattern of the internal human relations problems confronting the organization. The practitioners of planned organizational change more often than not tend to focus on these last-named human factors and their effects upon the performance of the system.*

A FOCUS OF CONVENIENCE FOR PLANNED ORGANIZATIONAL CHANGE

So far, I have discussed planned change in its broadest context without carefully distinguishing it from applied or developmental research in general. Let us turn to that task now and develop what George Kelley refers to as a "focus of convenience" for planned organizational change. Earlier I defined planned change as a deliberate and collaborative process involving a change-agent and a client-system which are brought together to solve a problem or, more generally, to plan and attain an improved state of functioning in the client-system by utilizing and applying valid knowledge.† This is still a vague and general definition, and I will have to make two aspects of it clearer, particularly the notion of a "collaborative relationship" and that of "valid knowledge."

I have implied in the last section that the outcome of a planned-change effort depends to some extent on the relationship between the client and the change-agent. So let us turn, first, to that. Criteria for evaluating the nature and quality of this relationship can be based on the following questions: (1) How well is the relationship under-

---

* This is not the place to elaborate on some of the issues involved in the identification of variables *internal* to the system or *external* to the system. This has been one of the pivotal issues dividing economists from social psychologists and other so-called human relationists. It is not unlike the debate Arthur Koestler wrestles with in his distinction between the yogi and the commissar, between those who turn *inward* for insight, for therapy, and for Nirvana and those who turn *outward* to the external environment for the location of variables of promise. This distinction seems to have lost a good deal of its impact recently, almost primarily because of the work of Tavistock groups, particularly Emery and Trist,[19] as well as Wilson,[20] who have brought the *environment* and boundary maintenance back into the mainstream of organizational theory and research.

† For a fuller treatment of some of these ideas, see Bennis.[21]

stood and veridically construed by both parties? (2) To what extent do both parties determine the course and fate of the planned-change program? (3) To what extent is the relationship open to examination and reconstruction by one or both parties? In other words, a deliberate and collaborative relationship can be optimized in a planned-change induction only when the following exist:

1   A joint effort that involves mutual determination of goals
2   A "spirit of inquiry"—a relationship that is governed by data, publicly shared
3   A relationship growing out of the mutual interaction of the client and the change-agent
4   A voluntary relationship between the change-agent and the client, with either free to terminate the relationship after joint consultation
5   A relationship where each party has equal opportunities to influence the other

Now, what is meant by "valid knowledge"? Generally speaking, the criteria for valid knowledge are based on the requirements for a viable applied behavioral science research, that is, an applied behavioral science that

1   Takes into consideration the behavior of persons operating within their specific institutional environments
2   Is capable of accounting for the interrelated levels (person, group, role, and larger organization) within the context of the social change
3   Includes variables that the policy maker and practitioner can understand, manipulate, and evaluate
4   Allows, in specific situations, selection of variables most appropriate to a specific planned change in terms of its own values, ethics, and moralities
5   Accepts the premise that groups and organizations as units are as amenable to empirical and analytical treatment as the individual
6   Takes into account external social processes of change as well as the interpersonal aspects of the collaborative process
7   Includes propositions susceptible to empirical test, focusing on the dynamics of change

The definition and criteria for planned change presented here must be construed as an arbitrary goal and not as an existing reality. To my knowledge, there is no program which fulfills these requirements fully. This realization raises the final consideration in this focus of convenience: the arbitrary selection of those change-agents working on organizational dynamics. This particular class of change-agents was selected not only because of my greater familiarity with their work but for two other factors as well. First, they seem to fulfill the criteria outlined to a greater extent than other change-agents.* Second, equally important in the choice of emphasis is the belief that changes in the sphere of organizations—primarily *industrial*—in patterns of work and relationships, in structure, in technology, and in administration promise to be some of the most significant changes in our society.†

NOTES

1. Berelson, B., and G. A. Steiner, *Human Behavior*, Harcourt, Brace & World, Inc., New York, 1964.

* There are others, from an assortment of fields, who undoubtedly deserve discussion here but who have to be omitted primarily for space reasons. I am referring to the work of rural sociologists such as Loomis, Sower, and Moe (see Rogers[22] for a recent summary of this work); to community and hospital and psychiatric change-agents such as Caplan, Lindemann, S. Levine, L. Howe, B. Paul, D. Klein, the Cummingses, and the Rapoports; to applied anthropologists working on directed culture change such as Holmberg, Goodenough, Kimball, and Barnett; and to those change-oriented economists Hagen, Hoselitz, Rosenstein-Rodan, and Eckaus. Each of these branches implies a research and theoretical tradition which falls beyond the scope of this chapter but which will be touched on briefly in the next section.

† I do not exclude socialist societies from this statement. As Parsons pointed out, the one common feature between so-called capitalist systems and socialist systems is the presence of bureaucracy. In the United States, it is my guess that industrial bureaucracies are the most radical, innovative, and adventurous in adapting new ways of organizing—far ahead, it seems to me, of the government, universities, and labor unions, who appear rigid and stodgy in the face of rapid change. Industrial bureaucracies, at least in the United States, are acting with a verve and imagination regarding rapid change which, I wager, not only will be copied but will be a model for future organizational change programs in other institutions. For an elaboration of this point, see Slater and Bennis.[23]

2. Kaplan, A., *The Conduct of Inquiry*, Chandler, San Francisco, Calif., 1964.

3. Lippitt, R., J. Watson, and B. Westley, *The Dynamics of Planned Change*, Harcourt, Brace & World, Inc., New York, 1958.

4. Bennis, W. G., K. D. Benne, and R. Chin (eds.), *The Planning of Change*, Holt, Rinehart and Winston, Inc., New York, 1961.

5. Goffman, E., *Asylums: Essays on Social Situations of Mental Patients and Other Inmates*, Anchor Books, Doubleday & Company, Inc., Garden City, N.Y., 1961.

6. Schein, E. H., I. Schneier, and C. H. Barker, *Coercive Persuasion: A Sociopsychological Analysis of the "Brainwashing" of American Civilian Prisoners by the Chinese Communists*, W. W. Norton & Company, Inc., New York, 1961.

7. Bennis et al., *op. cit.*, p. 154.

8. Gouldner, A. W., "Engineering and Clinical Approaches to Consulting," in *ibid.*, pp. 643–653.

9. Schuchman, A., *Scientific Decision Making in Business*, Holt, Rinehart and Winston, Inc., New York, 1963.

10. Gouldner, A. W., "Theoretical Requirements of the Applied Social Sciences," in Bennis et al., *op. cit.*, pp. 83–95.

11. Johnson, E. A., "Introduction," in McCloskey and Trefethen (eds.), *Operation Research for Management*, The Johns Hopkins Press, Baltimore, 1954, p. xii.

12. *Ibid.*, p. xix.

13. Ackoff, R. L., and P. Rivett, *A Manager's Guide to Operations Research*, John Wiley & Sons, Inc., New York, 1963, p. 34.

14. *Ibid.*, p. 17.

15. Sofer, C., *The Organization from Within*, Tavistock, London, 1961.

16. *Ibid.*, p. 8.

17. Argyris, C., *Interpersonal Competence and Organizational Effectiveness*, Dorsey Press, Homewood, Ill., 1962.

18. Bavelas, A., and G. Strauss, "Group Dynamics and Intergroup Relations," in Bennis et al., *op. cit.*, pp. 587–591.

19. Emery, F. E., and E. L. Trist, *The Causal Texture of Organizational Environments*, Tavistock Institute, London, 1963. (Mimeographed.)

20. Wilson, A. T. M., "The Manager and His World," paper presented at the Centennial Symposium on Executive Development, Alfred P. Sloan School of Management, Massachusetts Institute of Technology, Cambridge, Mass., April 27, 1961.

21. Bennis, W. G., "A New Role for the Behavioral Sciences: Effecting Organizational Change," *Administrative Science Quarterly*, vol. 8, pp. 125–165, 1963.

22. Rogers, E. M., *Diffusion of Innovations*, The Free Press of Glencoe, New York, 1962.

23. Slater, P. E., and W. G. Bennis, "Democracy Is Inevitable," *Harvard Business Review*, vol. 42, pp. 51–59, 1964.

6

planned organizational change in perspective

It is important at this juncture to recognize some aspects—theoretical, social, and historical—of planned organizational change which may not be obvious to the general reader and which should be illuminated before going on.

RELATIONSHIP BETWEEN SYSTEMS OF KNOWLEDGE AND ACTION

It is probably true that the United States has a more practical attitude toward knowledge than any other country.[1] Harrison Salisbury was impressed with the disdain European intellectuals seem to show for practical matters. Even in Russia, he reported, where one would least expect it, there is little interest in the "merely useful."[2] He was struck during his recent travels by the almost total absence of liaison between research and practical application. He saw only one great

95

agricultural experimental station on the American model. In that case, professors were working in the fields. They told Salisbury: "People call us Americans."

There may not be many American professors working in the fields, but they can be found almost everywhere else: in factories,[3] in the government,[4] in underdeveloped countries,[5] in backward areas of the United States,[6] in mental hospitals,[7] in jobs concerned with international matters,[8] in educational systems,[9] and in practically all the institutional crevices that Ph.D. candidates can worm their way into. They are advising, counseling, researching, recruiting, developing, consulting, training, and working for the widest variety of clients imaginable. This is not to say that the deep ambivalence which Americans have toward the intellectual has disappeared—witness the nomination of Goldwater—but it does indicate that the academic intellectual has become *engaged* with spheres of action in greater numbers, with more diligence, and with higher aspirations than at any other time in history.*

The behavioral sciences have been directly implicated in this trend. Recent additions to the vocabulary of the behavioral scientist which can be said to reflect this trend are the following: "clinical sociology," "policy sciences," "action research," "action anthropology," "change-agents," "social catalysts," "human and social engineers," "sociotherapy," "milieu therapy," "knowledge centers," and others. Also, within the past three years, the three primary professional associations of psychology, sociology, and anthropology have been devoting more and more annual meeting time to the problems of application and utilization. The University of Michigan's Institute of Social Research has recently added a third major division under Floyd Mann's direction: a Center for Research on the Utilization of Scientific Knowledge. There has also been a growing literature on planned social change through the uses of the behavioral sciences.[11] Finally, a more subtle trend can be detected: a growing concern with normative planning, with new forms of social architecture, with "realistic" and "vivid" utopias, and with more radical assumptions about social values.[12]

These signs and activities all point in the same direction: toward an emerging *action* role for the behavioral scientist. The *manipulative standpoint,* as Lasswell calls it, is becoming distinguished from the

---

* To the point where other intellectuals have questioned this hyperactivity on behalf of the "establishment." See Baritz[10] for one such statement.

contemplative standpoint and is increasingly ascendant insofar as knowledge utilization is concerned.*

SOME REASONS FOR EMERGENCE OF AN ACTION ROLE

It may be useful to speculate about the reasons for this shift of emphasis, this tendency toward a more direct role of action intervention and manipulation on the part of the behavioral scientist. Most important, but trickiest to identify, are those causative factors bound up in the warp and woof of "our times and age," what is called the *Zeitgeist*. There has been a shift in the intellectual climate of opinion, perhaps aroused by the threat of atomic destruction and reinforced by the exigencies of our time. "The world community of scientists," according to C. P. Snow, "has a final responsibility upon it—a greater responsibility than is pressing on any other body of men. . . . I cannot prove it, but I believe that, simply because scientists cannot escape their own knowledge, they won't be able to avoid showing themselves disposed to good."[15] And from my own vantage point, more and more behavioral scientists are committed to action programs and research projects of significance, pertaining to war and peace, problems of Negro-white relations, problems of economic development, etc. So there seems to be a growing disenchantment with the moral neutrality of the scientists and a willingness to risk scientific method on urgent social problems.

Related to a shift in *Zeitgeist*, and possibly caused by it, may be a general tendency to regard the applied social sciences with less condescension. To be sure, "pure" research still implies that applied research is somehow "impure," but while still not as honorific as pure research, applied or action research does not carry the same opprobrium it once did.

A third reason for this shift of emphasis, perhaps the most crucial, is simply that we know more. Since World War II, when the results

* It is beyond the scope of this chapter to discuss some of the *value* implications of the manipulative standpoint. Certainly, science suffers when it becomes the servant of any higher authority. And though it is alive with problems, unless we can discover ways to utilize science to influence policy formulations without losing its soul, science cannot realize its full potential. For excellent discussions of the "value" issues, see Kaplan,[13] whose point of view I follow, and Benne and Swanson.[14]

of applied research could not be brushed aside, and following postwar developments when the impetus for application accelerated, we have obtained large bodies of research and diverse reports on the application of research. Writing in 1951, Merton and Lerner commented on the lack of codified and systematic experience in application.[16] Today, we are in a better position to assess the results and potentialities of applied social sciences precisely because there are more complete reports and analyses available to us.*

Finally, we must mention a fourth factor which has played a key role in the action orientation of the behavioral scientist and which will be of special concern to us throughout this chapter. It has to do with the fate and viability of human organization, particularly as it has been discussed and conceptualized as "bureaucracy." In the past three decades, Weber's vision of organization has been increasingly challenged, not only by practitioners who are facing, firsthand, some problems that current practices and policies of organization cannot cope with, but by the behavioral scientists as well. In the previous section, I presented an inventory of organizational problems as perceived by the managers. A catalog of problems and shortcomings of bureaucracy, as perceived by the behavioral scientists, was presented in Chapter 1. (See footnotes 18 to 27 for examples of these criticisms.) The general meaning of this should be clear: managers and practitioners, on the one hand, and organizational theorists and researchers, on the other, are dissatisfied with the current practices of organizational behavior and are searching for new forms and patterns of organizing work. However wrong their diagnoses may be (and there is no firm evidence for their prognostications), a good deal of activity and many change programs are being generated by this impetus to revise and supplement the idea of bureaucracy in the face of these perceived theoretical and practical exigencies.

* While this chapter was being written, for example, the Foundation for Research on Human Behavior sponsored a conference on organizational change and the behavioral sciences. Over a period of five days, about a dozen behavioral scientists and an equal number of industrial practitioners concerned with organizational improvement reported on change programs utilizing the behavioral sciences. These papers are currently being edited for publication by Zand and Buchanan.[17]

THE CONTEMPORARY STATE OF THEORIES OF
SOCIAL CHANGE

If there is one truth most social theorists agree on and on which they can arrive at a quick consensus, it is the lack of a viable theory of social change.

Wilbert E. Moore, an intrepid sociologist, says: "The mention of 'theory of social change' will make most social scientists appear defensive, furtive, guilt-ridden, or frightened."[28]

K. D. Naegele, in the introductory essay on social change in the monumental *Theories of Society*, volume II, says: "At the gate of the study of social change stands a host of half-truths."[29]

Finally, Martindale reports an admission made by ". . . leading sociologists that its theory of social change *is the weakest branch of sociological theory.*" (Emphasis his.) He goes on to say: "This confession by some of the most highly placed persons in American sociology has usually been accompanied by the assurance that sociology's lack of an adequate theory of change is either of no great importance or merely a temporary state of affairs. One cannot wonder whether this confession and smug reassurance proceed from breathtaking *naiveté* or from an unctuous philistinism."[30]

Sherlock Holmes was reviewing the case. "Then, of course," he reflected, "there is the curious incident of the dog barking in the night."

"But," said Watson, "there was no dog barking in the night."

"Precisely, my dear Watson," said Holmes. "That is what I find so curious."

What Holmes might find so curious about the present state of theories of social change, and what I find so curious, is that they are silent on matters of *directing* and *implementing* change. What I object to—and I include the "newer" theories of neo-conflict,[31] neo-functionalism,[32] and neo-evolutionary theories[33]—is that they tend to identify and explain the dynamic interactions of a system without providing a clue pertaining to the identification of strategic leverages for alteration. They are theories suitable only for *observers* of social change, not theories for *participants* in, or practitioners of, social change. They are theories of *change* and not theories of *changing*.

PREREQUISITES FOR A THEORY OF CHANGING

According to Robert Chin, a theory of changing must do the following: *

1   It must provide levers or handles for influencing the direction, tempo, and quality of change and improvement, i.e., variables that are accessible to control. Variables which "explain" and are casual may be the *least alterable;* hence, a science of "causes" may not be adequate for a theory of changing. For example, we do know that urbanization causes population explosion, but the applied demographer can do little to reduce the birthrate by manipulating the degree of urbanization. Demographers can, however, control contraceptive materials and information. So, most of all, a theory of changing must include manipulable variables.

2   It must take into account the roles of a change-agent and a client-system, each with its own system of values, perceptions, and rights of self-determination; e.g., in the preceding example, it may be that the use of contraceptives in a Catholic country will render this independent variable virtually useless because it conflicts with the client-system's values. In addition to manipulability, then, the variable must not violate the client-system's values.

3   It must take into account the cost of usage. Prohibitive costs may again rule out a highly controllable and value-resonant variable.

4   It must provide a reliable basis of diagnosing the strength and weakness of the conditions facing the client-system.

5   It must account for phases of intervention so that the change-agent can develop estimates for termination of his relationship with the client-system, "self-takeoff" points, etc.

6   It must be able to be communicated with a minimum of distortion to the client-system without destroying its effectiveness.

7   It must be able to assess its own appropriateness for different client-systems.

Such a theory does not now exist, and this probably explains why the change-agents, whom we shall discuss in the next main section (pages 113–119), appear to write like "theoretical orphans." More

* I am deeply indebted to my colleague Robert Chin for many of the ideas presented here. See his articles.[34] See also Gouldner.[35]

important, it also explains why so many change programs based on theories of social change have been inadequate. Let us turn now to some of the most commonly used models of knowledge utilization and assess their effectiveness.

TRADITIONAL CHANGE PROGRAMS BASED ON SOCIAL KNOWLEDGE

The term "traditional" is used here because it describes the thinking of most scholars concerned with adapting knowledge to social-change programs. I would also wager that these so-called traditional ideas are accepted as conventional wisdom and "common sense" in our society. I shall describe eight of the most commonly used programs and then question the assumptions on which they are based.

EIGHT TYPES OF CHANGE PROGRAMS*

It is possible to identify eight types of change programs if we examine their strategic rationales: exposition and propagation, elite corps, human relations training, staff, scholarly consultations, circulation of ideas of the elite, developmental research, and action research.

Exposition and propagation may be the most popular type of change program. It rests almost entirely on the assumption that knowledge is power, that ideas change the world, and that the men who possess "truth" will utimately lead the world. Myrdal presents the case for this method: "My thesis is that, while, there was little participation on the part of social scientists in the actual technical preparation of legislation and still less in administering induced social changes, *their influence was due in the main to their exposition and propagation of certain general thoughts and theories.*"[37] (Emphasis added.)

The *elite-corps* program is based on the idea of "getting the *right man* in the job." Perhaps the best-known contemporary version of this program is the one advocated by C. P. Snow: Get scientists in government.[38] And in a recent issue of *Encounter*, R. H. S. Crossman writes in a manner supporting Snow.[39] The elite-corps idea grows from the justified realization that ideas by themselves (exposition and propagation) do not constitute action and that a strategic *role* (such as that

---

* For a fuller exposition of these ideas, see Bennis.[36]

of a civil servant or a member of Parliament) is a necessity for ideas to be implemented.

A version of the elite-corps idea can be observed in a good deal of the writings in the human relations training field. It is similar to the elite-corps idea in that it depends upon the knowledge and skills of men in power positions; its difference lies in the type of knowledge it requires of the elite. The program of *human relations training* hopes to inculcate key executives with the necessary insight, wisdom, and diagnostic sensitivity. In other words, human relations training attempts to translate concepts from the behavioral sciences so that they take on personal referents for the executives.*

The idea of *staff* is to provide a source of intelligence within the client-system such that the appropriate intelligence is available when needed. As Myrdal says, the strategy of the staff idea ". . . is to observe and to analyze actual situations and short and long term developments and, on this basis, to plan rationally the immediate policy reactions to events of a government, an interest organization, or a business firm."[42] Examples of staff are the work of social anthropologists advising military governors after World War II, staff work in large organizations, etc.†

By *scholarly consultations*, Zetterberg[44] means a procedure whereby science can be made useful to clients. It includes exploratory inquiry, scholarly understanding, scholarly confrontation, discovery of solutions, and, finally, scientific advice to the client. It is an unusual approach when compared with the others. For rather than taking a research orientation toward the client's problems, the adviser considers the problem in terms of available sociological theory and literature and deduces solutions from combinations of propositions already known.

Circulation of ideas to the elite is a strategy based on a very early idea in American history. The American Revolution, according to historians, was partly triggered by the Council for Correspondence, a remarkable chain letter linking the recipient rebels to a program of action. The idea is simple: "If you want to change things, then get

---

* In addition to human relations training, some advise forms of psychotherapy and psychoanalysis for the translation of theory into practice. See Levinson et al.[40] and Holt.[41]

† For a survey of the role of staff in administration, see Barnett.[43]

your ideas to the people in power, or people who influence someone who can influence someone in power."*

The idea of a *developmental research,* as a counterpart to the developmental research of the research and development labs, was advanced recently by Mason Haire:

> The one thing which, more than any other, seems to keep the social sciences from being socially useful is the lack of developmental research. By "developmental research" I mean a kind of work midway between the rarefied aloofness of laboratory tests of theoretical propositions and the somewhat pebble-picking particularity of applied research. It is the research that asks the question, "If this proposition is true in principle, how does it find expression in the operational context of action?" . . . Developmental research would be directed exactly toward the problem of helping people to see, given new theoretical insights, *how* something could be done substantially differently or better.[46]

Like Zetterberg's scholarly-confrontation method, developmental research has to do with seeing whether an idea can be brought to an engineering stage. Unlike the former method, developmental research is directed toward a particular problem, not necessarily a client, and is concerned more with implementation and program. (Incidentally, I would wager that *no* developmental research is being done today in the behavioral sciences.)

Action Research (or applied research) is the last program we shall discuss that aims to apply the behavioral sciences to improve systems performance. The term was coined by Kurt Lewin, and the best statement of its methods and aims can be found in an article by three of his followers.[47] "It is a field," according to them, "which developed to satisfy the needs of the socio-political-individual who recognizes that, in science, he can find the most reliable guide to effective action, and the needs of the scientist who wants his labors to be of maximal social utility as well as of theoretical significance."

In all ways but one, action research is identical to the traditional functions of applied research; that is, it is research undertaken to solve a problem for a client. What distinguishes action research is the nature

* A recent example of this strategy is *The Liberal Papers,* a series of papers inspired by a group of intellectuals who communicated their ideas to a receptive congressional audience.[45]

of the roles of the researchers and subjects in the research endeavor. In the typical applied-research project, the roles are differentiated and static. In action research, the roles may change and reverse. For example, it is not uncommon in action-research programs for the subjects to become researchers and for the researchers to engage in action steps in place of the subjects who they are studying.

CRITIQUE OF THE EIGHT CHANGE PROGRAMS

Although the the eight change programs differ in terms of their objectives, their values, and their means of influence, and although each has its own programmatic implications, they are similar in wanting to use knowledge to gain some socially desirable end. Each seems successful or promising, if current usage is any criterion, and each has its avid supporters and detractors. Intrinsic to the eight programs, I believe, is a bias or flaw which can be questioned and which probably weakens its full impact. Four biases are particularly visible.

Rationalistic Bias: No Implementation or Programs

Present to a greater or lesser degree in all the schemes is the belief that knowledge equals power. Obviously there is some truth in this. But why should the dissimenation of knowledge by itself lead to influence, particularly if the knowledge affects deeply held motives, beliefs, and attitudes, particularly those reinforced by group norms and power blocs? I do not want to minimize the importance of facts and knowledge—certainly, they do play a role in social change; yet in most of the strategies discussed, there is an almost total reliance on rationality. Knowledge *about* something does *not* lead automatically to intelligent action, no matter how "right" the idea. Intelligent action requires *commitment* and *programs* as well as truth.

Technocratic Bias: No Spirit of Collaboration

Related to the rationalistic bias is the assumption that if a program is presented, the client can carry it out with dispatch. We see this most clearly in the strategies related to applied research: scholarly consultation and developmental and applied research. Zetterberg, for example, says: "The client is presented with a translation of the theoretical solutions into the client's language and with references to his specific situation. In short he is told what to do."[48]

But this technocratic approach to planned change rarely works without some form of collaboration between the change-agent and the client. And the degree to which collaboration is required is probably related to the type of change anticipated: the more it involves socio-psychological factors—as opposed to technical—the more collaboration is required. Elliott Jaques is worth quoting in this regard:

> In practice the problem usually boils down to the relationship between the "expert" and the administrator or the executive responsible. We already know how difficult this relationship becomes even in the domain of the physical sciences and engineer; how much farmers, for example, often resent the intrusion of the government agriculture expert with his new and supposedly superior methods. *How much more difficult does the problem of establishing a satisfactory relationship become, however, where not crops but the changing of human behavior itself becomes the target of scientific endeavor?*[49] (Emphasis added.)

F. L. W. Richardson, the action anthropologist, puts it more strongly: "One conclusion, however, is certain; namely, a social scientist's success in an action role, similar to that of a practicing psychiatrist, often depends more on interpersonal than on rational skills."[50]

Why are collaboration and interpersonal skills so necessary in facilitating social change? Because any significant change in human organization involves a rearrangement of patterns of power, association, status, skills, and values. Some individuals and groups may benefit; others may lose. Some may view an anticipated change as "threatening" and reject it, and others may view it as "enhancing" and embrace it.* In any case, change typically involves risk and fear. The trust and support of the change-agent during the period of greatest stress may help to "ready" the client for the change.

Another crucial reason lies at the foundation of this need for collaboration. It has to do with important value differences between change-agents and clients. For the most part, clients are practitioners, managers, men of action. Change-agents tend to be academicians, scholars, researchers, men of contemplation. Inevitably, there are bound to be value conflicts between these two orientations; inevitably there are bound to be ambivalences, false starts, worries, and concerns about the other party to the relationship. Without an opportunity for these fears and worries to be discussed and "worked through," without

---

* For discussions of "resistance to change," see Mann & Neff.[51]

an opportunity for each party to "test" the competence and confidence of the other, it is doubtful whether the change program can realize its full intent.*

Individualistic Bias: No Organization Strategy

The trouble with those strategies associated with C. P. Snow and G. Myrdal as well as human relations training programs is their assumption that if men in power possess the right ideas they will act in accordance with those ideas. Undoubtedly there is some truth in this, as there is in the rationalistic strategy. But it denies completely the organizational *forces* and *roles* surrounding the individual; in short, this strategy tends to place altogether too much reliance on the individual.

There is a great deal of evidence which questions this assumption. For example, there is simply no guarantee that a wise individual who attains power will act wisely. The noted political scientist Hans Morgenthau (in his review of a book written by an intellectual economic historian who took a highly placed job with the U.S. State Department) writes:

> How could such a mind produce such trash? The answer lies in the corruption of power and the defenselessness of the intellectual in the face of it. The intellectual as a social type is singularly deprived of the enjoyment of power and eminently qualified to understand its importance and what it means not to have it. Thus campuses and literary circles abound with empire builders, petty politicians, and sordid intriguers—all seekers after power, the substance of which eludes them.

* Perhaps the most glaring example in recent history of the failure to develop (or even consider!) the required form of collaboration between client and change-agent can be seen in the early work of F. W. Taylor and his colleagues in "scientific management." To this day, in some government bureaus, stopwatches—the hated emblem of the "time-and-motion boys"—are not allowed to be used by a government industrial engineer. The trouble with Taylor was that he was not *scientific* enough; that is, he did not consider the relationship between the engineer and the client as falling within the domain of scientific management. Another corollary to this can be seen within the Freudian psychoanalytic movement. In the early days, Freud considered it adequate to examine the unconscious of his patients and to tell them what he learned. In some cases, he even analyzed dreams by mail. It turned out that this was not the way to help patients, at least not permanently. Later on, the analysis of relationship and resistance became the hallmark of successful treatment.

When an intellectual finds himself in the seat of power he is tempted to equate the power of his intellect with the power of his office. As he could mould the printed word to suit his ideas so he now expects the real world to respond to his actions.[52]

Perhaps *role corrupts:* both the role of powerlessness and the role of power. For example, Unilever Ltd., if I understand their management development program, aims at early selection of talent, an elite corps of bright young men. But mindful of the fact that bureaucratic norms may corrupt or mistrain this cadre, Unilever attempts to accelerate their progress through the bureaucratic structure and rush them to the top.[53]

The point of all this is that there is no guarantee that placing certain types of people in management—or training them or psychoanalyzing them or making scientists of them—leads to more effective action. Psychoanalytic institutes, according to Clara Thompson, are stricken with the same human predicaments as any other organization;[54] scientists act like administrators—or even more so—when they gain power,* and graduates of human relations training programs tend to act like nonalumni shortly after their return to their organizational base.†

The staff idea, proposed by Myrdal, is limited by the unresolved tensions in the staff-line dilemma noted by students of organizational behavior. This solution ignores, as well, something touched on earlier: the conflicts derived from the role of the intellectual working in bureaucratic structures. Merton catalogs some of these conflicts in his treatment of the problem.[57] He also suggests that the high turnover of expert personnel in public bureaucracies not only is a matter of *client* dissatisfaction but also is the "product of the cumulative frustrations experienced by the intellectual who has been previously conditioned to a sense of personal autonomy and cannot abide the visible constraints imposed by a formal organization."[58]

For all these reasons—organization norms, influence of role pressures, naïveté with respect to power, fade-out effects, value collisions—the idea of getting the right man in the job, the elite

---

* See Jungk[55] for an example of how scientists, such as Oppenheimer, acted more like administrators, forsaking personal and scientific moral imperatives for imperatives of the organization, against their colleagues' expectations.

† This "fade-out" effect has been frequently commented upon and studied. See Fleishman and Argyris.[56]

strategy, has serious drawbacks, primarily because it focuses on the individual and not on the organization.

Insight Bias: No Manipulability

Many of these strategies, but particularly those associated with human relations training programs, reflect a bias held by most clinical psychologists: insight leads to more effective functioning. This is a more sophisticated solution than the purely rationalistic mode, for insight, though usually ill-defined, implies an emotional as well as an intellectual grasp of an issue. My major quarrel is not with the formulation that insight leads to change, though this is presently being challenged by some.[59] What is more serious in the insight approach is the lack of provision of strategic variables, i.e., those accessible to control. How does personal insight get translated into effective programs of change? It is not obvious that insight leads directly to sophistication in rearranging social systems or in making strategic organizational interventions. If anything, planned change depends on the policy maker's controlling the relevant variables. Insight provides these as far as personal manipulation goes, but the question still remains: How can that lead directly to the external manipulation of social factors?

NOTES

1. Lazarsfeld, P. F., in collaboration with S. S. Spivack, *Observations on Organized Social Research in the United States: A Report to the International Social Science Council,* Columbia University Press, New York, 1961. (Mimeographed.)

2. Salisbury, H. E., *To Moscow and Beyond,* Harper & Row, Publishers, Incorporated, New York, 1960, p. 136.

3. Argyris, C., *Interpersonal Competence and Organizational Effectiveness,* Dorsey Press, Homewood, Ill., 1962; Blake, R. R., and J. S. Mouton, *The Managerial Grid,* Gulf Publishing Company, Houston, 1964; Burns, T., and G. M. Stalker, *The Management of Innovation,* Quadrangle, Chicago, 1962; Jaques, E., *The Changing Culture of a Factory,* Tavistock, London, 1951; Lawrence, P., *The Changing of Organizational Behavior Patterns,* Harvard University Press, Cambridge, Mass., 1958; Rice, A. K. *The Enterprise and Its Environment,* Tavistock, London, 1963; Spencer, P., and C. Sofer, "Organizational Change and Its Management," *The Journal of Management Studies,* vol. 1, pp. 26–47, 1964; Walker, C. R., *Modern Technology and Civilization,* McGraw-Hill Book Company, New York, 1962; "Major Issues in Modern Society," in R. J. Smith (ed.), *Human Organization,* 1962, p. 21.

4. Barnett, H. G., *Anthropology in Administration*, Row, Peterson & Company, Evanston, Ill., 1956; Hilsman, R., *Strategic Intelligence and National Decisions*, The Free Press of Glencoe, New York, 1956.

5. Foster, G. M., *Traditional Cultures and the Impact of Technological Change*, Harper & Row, Publishers, Incorporated, New York, 1962; Goodenough, W. H., *Cooperation in Change*, Russell Sage Foundation, New York, 1963; Hagen, E., *On the Theory of Social Change*, Dorsey Press, Homewood, Ill., 1962; McClelland, D. C., *The Achieving Society*, D. Van Nostrand Company, Inc., Princeton, N.J., 1961; Spicer, E. H. (ed.), *Human Problems in Technological Change*, Russell Sage Foundation, New York, 1952; Tax, S., "The Uses of Anthropology," in S. Tax (ed.), *Horizons of Anthropology*, Aldine Publishing Co., London, 1964; Almond, G. A., and S. S. Coleman (eds.), *The Politics of the Developing Areas*, Princeton University Press., Princeton, N.J., 1960.

6. Kimball, S. T., and M. Pearsall, *The Tallageda Story*, University of Alabama Press, University, Ala., 1954.

7. Stanton, A. H., and M. S. Schwartz, *The Mental Hospital*, Basic Books, Inc., Publishers, New York, 1954; Caudill, W., *The Psychiatric Hospital as a Small Society*, Harvard University Press, Cambridge, Mass., 1958.

8. Klineberg, O., *The Human Dimension in International Relations*, Holt, Rinehart and Winston, Inc., New York, 1964.

9. Miles, M. B. (ed.), *Innovation in Education*, Bureau of Publications, Teachers College, Columbia University, New York, 1964.

10. Baritz, L., *Servants of Power*, Wesleyan University Press, Middletown, Conn., 1960.

11. Bennis, W. G., A New Role for the Behavioral Sciences: Effecting Organizational Change," *Administrative Science Quarterly*, vol. 8, pp. 125–165, 1963; Freeman, H. E., "The Strategy of Social Policy Research," *The Social Welfare Forum*, pp. 143–160, 1963; Zetterberg, H., *Social Theory and Social Practice*, Bedminster Press, New York, 1962; Gibb, J.R., and R. Lippitt (eds.), "Consulting with Groups and Organizations," *The Journal of Social Issues*, vol. 15, 1959; Leeds, R., and T. Smith (eds.), *Using Social Science Knowledge in Business and Industry*, Richard D. Irwin, Inc., Homewood, Ill., 1963; Likert, R., and S. P. Hayes, Jr. (eds.), *Some Applications of Behavioral Research*, UNESCO, Paris, 1957; Glock et al., *Case Studies in Bringing Behavioral Science into Use*, Institute of Communication Research, Stanford, Calif., 1960.

12. Friedmann, J., *Issues in Planning Theory*, Massachusetts Institute of Technology, Cambridge, Mass., 1963 (mimeographed); Mead, M., "Toward More Vivid Utopias," *Science*, vol. 126, pp. 957–961, 1957; Mumford, L., *The Transformation of Man*, Harper & Row, Publishers, Incorporated, New York, 1956; Myrdal, G., *Value in Social Theory*, Harper & Row, Publishers, Incorporated, New York, 1958; Perlmutter, H. V., "On Social Architecture," Yale University, New Haven, Conn., 1961.

13. Kaplan, A., *The Conduct of Inquiry*, Chandler, San Francisco, Calif., 1964, chap. 10 (see especially sec. 45).

14. Benne, K. D., and G. Swanson (eds.), "Values and Social Science," *The Journal of Social Issues*, vol. 6, 1950.

15. Snow, C. P., "The Moral Un-neutrality of Science," in P. C. Obler and H. A. Estrin (eds.), *The New Scientist*, Anchor Books, Doubleday & Company, Inc., Garden City, N.Y., 1962.

16. Merton and Lerner, *op. cit.*, p. 56.

17. Zand, D., and P. Buchanan (eds.), *Organization Development: Theory and Practice*, in press.

18. Argyris, C., *Personality and Organization*, Harper & Row, Publishers, Incorporated, New York, 1957; Argyris, C., *Integrating the Individual and the Organization*, John Wiley & Sons, Inc., New York, 1964.

19. Argyris, *Interpersonal Competence and Organizational Effectiveness;* Whyte, W. H., Jr., *The Organization Man*, Simon and Schuster, Inc., New York, 1956.

20. Likert, R., *New Patterns of Management*, McGraw-Hill Book Company, New York, 1961; McGregor, D., *The Human Side of Enterprise*, McGraw-Hill Book Company, New York, 1960.

21. Gouldner, A. W., "Organizational Analysis," in R. K. Merton, L. Broom, and L. S. Cottrell, Jr. (eds.), *Sociology Today: Problems and Prospects*, Basic Books, Inc., Publishers, New York, 1959, pp. 404–412; Roethlisberger, F. J., and W. J. Dickson, *Management and the Worker*, Harvard University Press, Cambridge, Mass., 1941.

22. Shepard, H. A., "Three Management Programs and the Theories behind Them," in *An Action Research Program for Organization Improvement*, Foundation for Research on Human Behavior, Ann Arbor, Mich., 1960; Shepard, H. A., "Changing Interpersonal and Intergroup Relationships in Organizations," in J. March (ed.), *Handbook of Organization*, Rand McNally & Company, Chicago, in press; Slater, P. E., and W. G. Bennis, "Democracy Is Inevitable," *Harvard Business Review*, vol. 42, pp. 51–59, 1964.

23. Evan, W., "Due Process of Law in Military and Industrial Organizations," *Administrative Science Quarterly*, pp. 187–207, 1962.

24. Emery, F. E., and E. L. Trist, *The Causal Texture of Organizational Environments*, Tavistock Institute, London, 1963. (Mimeographed.)

25. Blake, R. R., H. A. Shepard, and J. S. Mouton, *Intergroup Conflict*, Foundation for Research on Human Behavior, Ann Arbor, Mich., 1964.

26. Argyris, *Integrating the Individual and the Organization;* Blake, R. R., and Mouton, J. S., *The Managerial Grid*, Gulf Publishing Company, Houston, 1964; Likert, *op. cit.*

27. Leavitt, H. J., "Unhuman Organizations," in H. J. Leavitt and L. Pondy (eds.), *Readings in Managerial Psychology*, The University of Chicago Press, Chicago, 1964, pp. 542–556; Leavitt, H. J., and T. L. Whisler, "Management in the 1980's," *Harvard Business Review*, pp. 41–48, 1958.

28. Moore, W. E., "A Reconsideration of Theories of Social Change," *American Sociology Review*, vol. 25, pp. 810–818, 1960.

29. Naegele, K. D., "Introduction," in T. Parsons, E. Shils, K. D. Naegele, and J. R. Pitts (eds.), *Theories of Society*, vol. II, The Free Press of Glencoe, New York, 1961, p. 1207.

30. Martindale, D., "Introduction," in G. K. Zollschan and W. Hirsch (eds.), *Explorations in Social Change*, Houghton Mifflin Company, Boston, 1964, p. xii.

31. Coser, L., *The Functions of Social Conflict,* The Free Press of Glencoe, New York, 1956; Dahrendorf, R., "Toward a Theory of Social Conflict," in W. G. Bennis, K. D. Benne, and R. Chin (eds.), *The Planning of Change,* Holt, Rinehart and Winston, Inc., New York, 1961, pp. 445–451.

32. Boskoff, A., "Functional Analysis as a Source of a Theoretical Repertory and Research Tasks in the Study of Social Change," in Zollschan and Hirsch, *op. cit.,* pp. 213–243.

33. Parsons, T., "Evolutionary Universals in Society," *American Sociology Review,* vol. 29, pp. 339–357, 1964.

34. Chin, R., "Models and Ideas about Changing," Paper Given at Symposium on Acceptance of New Ideas, University of Nebraska, November, 1963; Chin, R., "The Utility of System Models and Development Models for Practitioners," in Bennis *et al., op. cit.,* pp. 201–214.

35. Gouldner, *op. cit.*

36. Bennis, *op. cit.*

37. Myrdal, *op. cit.,* p. 26.

38. Snow, C. P., *Science and Government,* Harvard University Press, Cambridge, Mass., 1961.

39. Crossman, R. H. S., "Scientists in Whitehall," *Encounter,* vol. 23, pp. 3–10, 1964.

40. Levinson, H., C. R. Price, K. J. Munden, H. J. Mandl, and C. M. Solley, *Men, Management, and Mental Health,* Harvard University Press, Cambridge, Mass., 1962.

41. Holt, H., "The Psychoanalytic Psychiatrist as a Management Consultant," in G. Fisk (ed.), *The Frontiers of Management Psychology,* Harper & Row, Publishers, Incorporated, New York, 1964, pp. 68–84.

42. Myrdal, *op. cit.,* p. 29.

43. Barnett, *op. cit.*

44. Zetterberg, *op. cit.*

45. Roosevelt, J. (ed.), *The Liberal Papers,* Anchor Books, Doubleday & Company, Inc., Garden City, N.Y., 1962.

46. Haire, M., *Why Have the Social Sciences Contributed So Little to Industrial Relations?* University of California, 1962. (Mimeographed.)

47. Chein, I., S. Cook, and J. Harding, "The Field of Action Research," *The American Psychologist,* vol. 3, pp. 43–50, 1948.

48. Zetterberg, *op. cit.,* p. 136.

49. Jaques, E., "Social Therapy: Technocracy or Collaboration?" in Bennis et al., *op. cit.,* pp. 162–168.

50. Richardson, F. L. W., "Foreword," in Smith, *op. cit.,* p. 61.

51. Mann, F. C., and F. W. Neff, *Managing Major Change in Organizations,* Foundation for Research on Human Behavior, Ann Arbor, Mich., 1961; Zander, A., "Resistance to Change: Its Analysis and Prevention," in Bennis et al., *op. cit.,* pp. 543–548.

52. Morgenthau, H., "The Sweet Smell of Success," *N.Y. Review of Books,* vol. 2, p. 6, 1964.

53. Wilson, A. T. M., *op. cit.*

54. Thompson, C., "A Study of the Emotional Climates of Psychoanalytic Institutes," *Psychiatry*, vol. 21, pp. 42–52, 1958.

55. Jungk, R., *Brighter than a Thousand Suns*, Grove Press, Inc., New York, 1958.

56. Argyris, C., *Interpersonal Competence and Organizational Effectiveness;* Fleishman, E. A., "Leadership Climate, Human Relations Training, and Supervisory Behavior," *Personnel Psychology*, pp. 205–222, 1953.

57. Merton, R. K., *Social Theory and Social Structure*, The Free Press of Glencoe, New York, 1949.

58. *Ibid.*, p. 174.

59. Hobbs, N., "Sources of Gain in Psychotherapy," *The American Psychologist*, vol. 17, pp. 741–747, 1962.

7

change-agents,
change programs, and strategies

The foregoing chapter outlined some of the biases that inhere in traditional models of social change. They will serve as terms of comparison and evaluation in what follows. Now with these preliminary considerations and background factors out of the way, let us turn directly to the main business at hand.

THE CHANGE-AGENTS

In the October 7, 1963, edition of the *New York Times,* a large classified ad was printed announcing a search for "change-agents." It read:

> WHAT'S A CHANGE AGENT?
> A result oriented individual able to accurately and
> quickly resolve complex tangible and intangible
> problems. Energy and ambition necessary for
> success. . . .

Whatever doubts I had had up to this point about Madison Avenue's gifts for simplification and polish were lost. For I realized then and do now that any description of a change-agent I would advance would have to include more factors than "energy and ambition," though these two are probably required.

The change-agents I have in mind are *professionals*, men who, for the most part, have been trained and who hold doctorates in the behavioral sciences. Many of them hold university posts, and others work as full-time consultants, but they owe their professional allegiance to one of the behavioral science disciplines.

While change-agents are not a very homogeneous group, it may be useful to sketch out in broad terms some of their similarities:

1 *Their assumptions* They take for granted the *centrality of work* in our culture, to men and women at work in highly organized, instrumental settings like industries, hospitals, and universities. They are concerned with *organizational effectiveness*, however intangibly defined or measured. So they are concerned with improvement, development, and enhancement. While their prescriptions vary, their diagnosis of organizational health pivots on *interpersonal* or *group relationships* and the implications of these on changes in technology, structure, and tasks. Although they are aware of these three nonpersonal factors and occasionally focus on them, their main preoccupation is with people and the processes of human interaction.* Along these lines, it is important to point out that they are not interested in changing (or transferring) *personnel* but in the relationships, attitudes, perceptions, and values of the existing personnel.

2 *Their roles* They play a variety of roles as change-agents: researchers, trainers, consultants, counselors, teachers, and, in some cases, line managers. Some specialize in one, but for the most part they shift and switch from one to another.

Frequently, the change-agents are not actual members of the client-system; in other cases, they are. There are some who say that significant change depends on the impetus generated by an external agent.[2] They argue that only a skilled outsider-consultant can provide the perspective, detachment, and energy so necessary to effect a true

* Contrast this with another approach, of an engineering type, proposed by Chapple and Sayles,[1] where task, structure, and technology are utilized as independent variables.

alteration of existing patterns. Advocates of the internal model take the opposite stand. They argue that the insider possesses the intimate knowledge of the client-system (and the power to legitimize) that the external change-agent lacks. In addition, the internal change-agent does not generate the suspicion and mistrust that the outsider often does. His acceptance and credibility are guaranteed, it is argued, by his organizational status.*

Change-agents tend to be self-conscious about their roles and their role changes vis-à-vis their clients. They go into instructive detail describing their interventions.

3 *Their interventions* Change-agents intervene at different structural points in the organizations (person, group, intergroup, etc.) and at different times. Blake and Mouton[3] list nine major kinds of interventions which facilitate organizational development:

1 Discrepancy: calls attention to a contradiction in action or attitudes
2 Theory: research findings or conceptual understanding which helps the client-system gain perspective
3 Procedural: a critique of existing methods of solving problems
4 Relationships: focuses attention on tensions growing out of group and interpersonal relationships
5 Experimentation: setting up comparisons and testing of several actions *before* a decision is made
6 Dilemma: identifies significant choice points or exigencies in problem solving and attempts to understand assumptions and search for alternatives, if necessary
7 Perspective: an attempt to provide situational and historical understanding of problems through a detached study
8 Organization structure: identifies source of problem as bound in the structure and organizational arrangements
9 Cultural: focuses on an examination of traditions

4 *Their normative goals* These are stated with varying clarity and specificity, but there is unmistakable evidence that their goals

---

* Thus, General Electric in its change program uses internal change-agents (to gain credibility and to eliminate the typical fear that behavioral scientists are "headshrinkers," "brainwashers," etc.). However, these internal men are not placed within their own company departments.

imply a particular vision of man and organization and a particular set of values which lay the base for this version.

To a large extent, these normative goals are aroused by dissatisfactions with the effectiveness of bureaucratic organizations, set forth on page 6. These objections were probably most cogently articulated and given the greatest force by the writings of McGregor, Likert, and Argyris.[4] These three books are often cited as evidence, and they are used by change-agents as the foundation for various change programs.

Though each change-agent has in mind a set of unique goals, based on his own theoretical position and competencies as well as on the needs of the client-system, roughly speaking there are some general aims which most change-agents would agree to. Argyris provides a graphic model which can serve us as an example. In Fig. 2, he shows (at the far left) the purported value system which dominates modern organizations; i.e., bureaucratic values. These values, basically impersonal and task-oriented and denying humanistic and democratic values, lead to poor, shallow, and mistrustful relationships between members of the organization. Argyris calls these "nonauthentic" relationships and says that they tend to be "phony," unhelpful, and basically incomplete; that is, they do not permit the natural and free expression of feelings which often must accompany task efforts. These nonauthentic relationships lead to a state which Argyris calls "decreased interpersonal competence," a result of the shallow and threatening state of the relationships. Finally, without effective interpersonal competence among the managerial class, the organization is a breeding ground for mistrust, intergroup conflict, rigidity, etc., which in turn leads to a decrease in whatever criteria the organization is using to measure its effectiveness.

This is the paradigm: bureaucratic values tend to stress the rational, task aspects of the work and to ignore the basic human factors which relate to the task and which, if ignored, tend to reduce task competence. Managers brought up under this system of values are badly cast to play the intricate human roles now required of them. Their ineptitude and anxieties lead to systems of discord and defense which interfere with the problem-solving capacity of the organization.

Generally speaking, the normative goals of change-agents derive

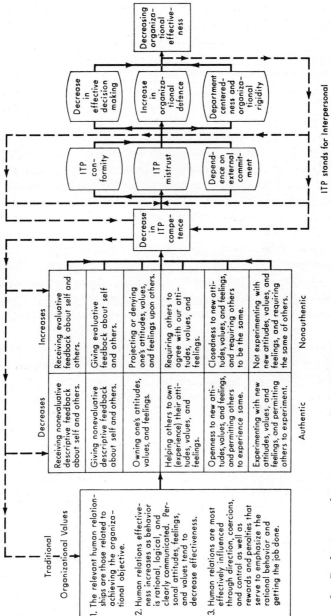

FIG. 2.   Predominant value system in modern organization[4]

117

in one way or another (explicitly or not) from this paradigm. Most commonly strived for are the following:

1 Improvement in interpersonal competence of managers.
2 A change in values so that human factors and feelings come to be considered legitimate.
3 Development of increased understanding between and within working groups in order to reduce tensions.
4 Development of more effective "team management," i.e., the capacity for functional groups to work competently.
5 Development of better methods of "conflict resultion"; rather than the usual bureaucratic methods of conflict resolution, which include suppression, denial, and the use of naked and unprincipled power, more rational and open methods of conflict resolution are sought after.
6 Development of organic systems. This normative goal, as outlined by Shepard and Blake,[6] is a strong reaction against the idea of organizations as mechanisms, which, they claim, has given rise to false conceptions (such as static equilibria, frictional concepts like "resistance to change," etc.) and, worse, to false notions of social engineering and change, e.g., pushing social buttons, thinking of the organization as a machine, etc. Organic systems, as Shepard and Blake conceive them,* differ from mechanical systems in the following ways:

Mechanical systems	*Organic systems*
Individual skills	Relationships between and within groups
Authority-obedience relationships	Mutual confidence and trust
Delegated and divided responsibility rigidly adhered to	Interdependencies and shared responsibility
Strict division of labor and hierarchical supervision	Multigroup membership and responsibility
Centralized decision making	Wide sharing of control and responsibility
Conflict resolution through suppression, arbitration, or warfare	Conflict resolution through bargaining or problem solving

* Burns and Stalker also develop the idea of organic and mechanical systems.[7] They state, however, in contradiction to Shepard that both may be appropriate under differing environmental and organizational conditions.

Change-agents conceptualize and discuss their normative goals in different ways; occasionally they work toward the same goal under different labels and for different goals under similar labels. But allowing for some exceptions, they would probably accept at face value the goals enumerated above. Where the differences among them come into sharper focus is in their choice of instruments or programs for implementing these normative goals.

PROGRAMS FOR IMPLEMENTING PLANNED ORGANIZATIONAL CHANGE

The discussion here will focus on three broad types of change programs that seem to be most widely used; training, consulting and research. Most frequently they are used in some combination depending on the needs of the client-system and the particular skills of the change-agent. For our purposes, we shall consider each of them separately.

Training

"Training" is an inadequate and possibly misleading word to use in this context as its dictionary meaning denotes "drill," "exercise," and the general notion of imparting skills through habit and rote learning. As the term is used here, it has a widely different meaning. It is used here to describe a particular variety of training which has been called "laboratory" training or education or "sensitivity" or "group dynamics" training and in most quarters "T-group training."[*] The idea of laboratory training originated at Bethel, Maine, in 1947 under the guidance of Bradford, Benne, and Lippitt, all of whom were influenced by Kurt Lewin. This group shared a common concern for the application of the behavioral sciences to practice and policy. The T group emerged as one of the most important components of laboratory training and has evolved over the past eighteen years into one of the main instruments for organizational change. Bradford, as director of the National Training Laboratories, has played a central role in the development of laboratory training; its growth was facili-

---

[*] For a popular account of laboratory training as it is used to implement organizational improvement, see Argyris.[8] For other writings on the same subject, see Schein and Bennis,[9] Blake and Mouton,[10] and Argyris.[11] For a theoretical background of laboratory training, see Bradford et al.[12]

tated through the active participation of a number of university-based behavioral scientists and practitioners.* Its main objective at first was *personal change,* or self-insight. Since the late 1950s or so, the emphasis has shifted away from personal growth to *organizational development.*†

As evidence of this shift, more and more laboratory training is conducted for specific organizations, using groups which follow organizational patterns rather than so-called "stranger" labs, where people come together from a variety of organizations and professions.

This is not the place to go deeply into the subject of laboratory training, but it might be useful to say a word or two more about it. It unfolds in an unstructured group setting where the participants examine their interpersonal relationships. The training process relies primarily and almost exclusively on the behavior experienced by the participants; i.e., the *group itself* becomes the focus of inquiry. Conditions are promoted whereby group members by examining data generated by themselves, attempt to understand the dynamics of group behavior, e.g., decision processes, leadership and influence processes, norms, roles, communication distortions, and effects of authority on a number of behavioral patterns, personality and coping mechanisms, etc. In short, the participants learn to analyze and become more sensitive to the processes of human interaction and acquire concepts to order and control these phenomena.

T groups are used in organizations today in the following ways:

Stranger labs   Executives from organizations attend labs as "delegates" representing their organizations. The parent organization hopes to improve the organization this way by "seeding" a sufficient number of managers.

Cousin labs   Organizations set up labs for individuals with similar organizational ranks but from different functional groups, e.g., all first-line supervisors or all general foremen.

---

* Tavistock Institute has played a similar role in England. Recently a group of European behavioral scientists set up their own counterpart to the National Training Laboratories in the United States.

† I date this more precisely as 1958 because at about this time the employee relations department of the Esso Company, under the leadership of Blake and Shepard, inaugurated a series of laboratory training programs in their refineries throughout the country. Other companies followed suit, but the original Esso programs laid the groundwork for future developments.[13]

Diagonal slices T groups are composed of members from the same company but of different ranks and from different departments. No man is in the same group with anyone from his own work group.

Family or functional groups These groups are identical to the intact group as indicated by the formal organization; e.g., a particular supervisor would be with his work group.

Decisions about type of composition of T group training are based on a variety of factors, e.g., the stage of organizational development of the client-system, particular exigencies facing the client-system, and the competencies of the change-agent. The extent to which laboratory training affects the organizational value system and structure is related to the T-group strategy utilized: the more it approaches the family group, the more the total organizational system is affected.

Consulting

For every type and style of training, there is an equivalent type of consulting. The type we shall be concerned with here is practiced by a number of change-agents and is perhaps best exemplified by the work of the Tavistock Institute.*

The change-agent qua consultant operates very much like the practicing physician or psychoanalyst: "In undertaking my work," writes Sofer, "I entered the same moral order as my respondents, helping them to maintain what was positive in their situation and to alter what was negative."[16] So the consultant starts from the chief "presenting symptom" of the client, articulates it in such a way that the causal and underlying mechanisms of the problem are understood, and then takes remedial action.

He employs an extensive repertory of instrumentation which he uses as flexibly as possible. Using himself, most of all, he aims to detect and get close to the important "data," to exploit every encounter he can in order to help the client-system see "reality." He uses situations, as they develop spontaneously, to work through the tensions and resistances associated with them. Most of all, he uses *himself*

---

* The work of Jaques, Sofer, and Rice in particular.[14] Sofer has been the most articulate in the sense of adumbrating the principles and assumptions behind this style of social consultancy, so I have used his book *The Organization from Within* most profitably for this paper. Beckhard,[15] in the United States, has also developed a procedure and a unique style with respect to the role of the management consultant.

as a *role model*. More important than the expertise and methodological help they contribute—and it is substantial—is the ". . . *manner* in which my colleagues and I defined and reconceptualized the problems."[17] To the extent that this role model is emulated by the management group, change can occur.

Heavy emphasis is placed on the strategy of role model because the main instrument is the change-agent himself: his skills, insight, and expertise. Sofer reveals this when he suggests that psychotherapy or some form of clinical experience in a mental hospital is necessary preparation for the change-agent.

Argyris provides an interesting example of change-agent qua consultant. He writes about two possible reactions clients have when their attempts to "seduce" him to give the "solutions" fail. One is the expression by the executives of sorrow and dismay. Another reaction is their insistence that, since he is the "expert" consultant, he *should* provide some answers. Argyris writes:

> Moreover, if their expectation of the researcher is that he should give some answers, because in the feedback situation he is the leader, what does this expectation imply concerning what they probably do to their subordinates? Perhaps this indicates that when they (as leaders) make a diagnosis, they feel they must make a prognosis. But if the above analysis is valid, what positive value is a unilateral prognosis? At best it gives their subordinates something tó shoot at (just as they are behaving toward the researcher.) But as they just experienced, if the leader (in this case, the researcher) is skilled enough to answer all their objections, he succeeds in making the diagnosis *his* and not theirs. Perhaps, this also occurs when they succeed in answering all the questions of their subordinates when they, as superiors, are "selling" a new policy of practice.[18]

So Argyris, as consultant, confronts the group with their behavior toward him as an analog of their behavior vis-à-vis their own subordinates. He continually searches for experiential referents in the existential ("here-and-now") encounters with his client-system which can be used heuristically for the fuller understanding of the client.

If the description of the role of the consultant makes it sound more ambiguous and vague than the training process, this probably reflects reality, for in the consultant approach, the processes of change and the change-agent's interventions are less systematic and less programmed than in either the training or the applied-research programs. Let us turn to the latter now.

Applied Research: The Utilization of Data as Feedback Intervention

Almost all planned-change programs utilize research results in one way or another. The particular form of applied or action research I am referring to now is the one in which research results are used systematically as an *intervention*. This type of program was developed primarily by the researchers at the University of Michigan's Institute for Social Research, most particularly by Floyd Mann and his associates.[19] Here is the way it works: Survey data are collected and then reported back to the particular departments (subjects) in "feedback" meetings where the subjects become clients and have a chance to review the findings, test them against their own experiences, and even ask the researchers to test some of their hypotheses. Rather than the traditional uses of research, of a technocratic variety, where the findings are submitted "in triplicate" and probably ignored, this method strives for active participation of the subjects.

In other words, most methods of research application collect information and report it. There the relationship ends. In the survey-feedback approach, the collecting and reporting of results is only the *beginning* of the relationship. On the basis of the research results—and partly because of them—the involvement and participation in the planning, collection, analysis, and interpretation of more data are activated. Objective information, knowledge of results, is the first step in planned change. But more than intellectual commitment is usually required. The survey-feedback approach is utilized in order to gain this extra commitment via active participation in the research process.

Richard Beckhard, too, utilizes data as the first step in his work as change-agent, both as a way of diagnosing the initial state of the client-system and as a way of using the data themselves as a springboard for discussions with the executive staff. His procedure is very similar to that of Mann and his associates, except that the data are collected through informal, nonstructured interviews which he then codes by themes about the managerial activities of the client. He then convenes a meeting with the particular subsystem on which the data were collected at an off-site location and uses the research headings as the basis for discussion. The following are examples of these themes:

1   Communications between president and line (or staff)
2   Line-staff communications
3   Location of decision making
4   Role clarification or confusion
5   Communications procedures[20]

I should reiterate that most planned-change inductions involve all three processes: training, consulting, and researching. In most cases, the change-agent himself tries to utilize all their functions. Some change-agents report, however, that they work in collaboration with others and that they divide their functions. For example, Argyris used L. Bradford as a trainer and Roger Harrison as a researcher.[21] Sofer employed his colleagues at Tavistock to augment the services he could perform. It is also true that some change-agents possess distinctive competencies which tend to direct their activities in certain channels.

What should be clear from the foregoing discussion are these three points: (1) Change-agents play a variety of roles; (2) clients play a variety of roles: subject, initiator and planner, client, and participant-researcher; and (3) the final shape of the change-agent's role is not as yet clear, and it is hazardous to describe exactly what they do on the basis of their reports.*

STRATEGIC MODELS EMPLOYED BY CHANGE-AGENTS

In order to gain a deeper understanding of how these change programs are used in practice, it might be useful to sample some of the strategies employed by change-agents. This turns out to be somewhat more difficult than one might think because quite often change-agents

---

* There are other matters with respect to these three functions which space and time limitations make it impossible to more than mention. For example, in *choosing* one particular intervention over another, one would have to consider the following factors: cost, time, degree of collaboration between change-agent and client-system required, ease of measurement of effects, state of target system, whether an internal or an external change-agent is required, the degree to which the program is "instrumented" (for example, Blake's change program is so precisely programmed and "laid out" that first-level line managers within the client-system can conduct their own program based on Blake's ideas without his presence), and the relationship between the type of change sought and the change indication process.

fail to report their strategies or to make them explicit—even to themselves. However, two quite different strategic models are available to us, one developed by R. R. Blake in his "managerial grid" scheme and one through some work I was associated with at an oil refinery.*

Blake has developed a change program based on his analytic framework of managerial styles.[22] On the basis of this twofold analytic framework, it is possible to locate five types of managerial strategies. One dimension is "concern for people"; the other is "concern for production." As Blake points out, the term "concern for" represents the degree of concern for, not the *actual* production of, people's activities. Figure 3 shows the grid and the eight managerial styles. Blake and his colleagues attempt to change the organization in the 9,9 direction.

In their strategic model employed to induce changes in the direction of "team management" (9,9), Blake and his colleagues specify six phases, which represent their most thorough and systematic work so far. Their strategy is based on experience with fifteen different factories, ranging in size from 500 to 5,000 employees.

Phase 1 takes place away from the plant location; factory members are exposed to behavioral science theory (managerial grid, etc.), take part in structural experiments, and participate in face-to-face feedback experiments and sessions of the T-group variety. All members of the managerial organization participate in the laboratory for a one- or two-week session. Groups are composed on a "diagonal-slice" basis. It is believed that this diagonal-slice deployment is the most strategic at first. It allows organizational and interdepartmental issues to be aired more easily than they can be when the usual organizational constraints are present.

Phase 2 is also conducted off site and focuses on *team training*. Training groups are composed of a particular boss and his immediate subordinates, starting with the top team and reaching lower levels later on. Thus, the unit of grouping is the actual "family" group, and actual conditions become the focus of analysis. This phase is based

* It might interest the reader to know that in this case, the strategy—if it can be called that—was strictly a *post hoc recapitulation* of what was done. In fact, it was not developed by the change-agents, themselves, but by Chris Argyris, who was asked to evaluate the program several years after its termination.

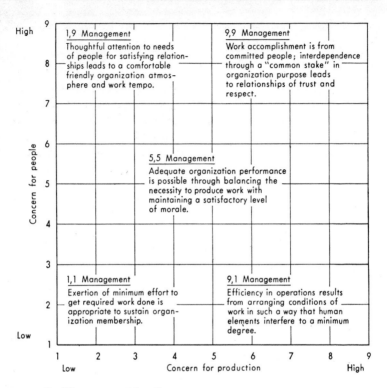

FIG. 3   The managerial grid

on the principle that if organizational change is to take place, it must be supported by the actual organizational groupings and must be exemplified and reinforced by top management.

Phase 3 is designed to achieve better *integration between functional groups* and between various organizational divisions, such as staff and line, technical and practical, sales and production, and so on. The normative goal of this horizontal linking is to create an organizational "culture" which can link relationships and articulate between departments in a more effective way than the bureaucratic model. In this phase, pairs of functional groups work together in order to solve the problems that exist between them. First they work as groups apart from each other, testing their image and stereotypes of their own group vis-à-vis the other and identifying obstacles to better integration. Then they get together and attempt to develop better methods of joint problem solving. This activity takes place, unlike that of the two previous phases, in the plant location.

Phase 4 gives real meaning to the concept of *planned change,* for it provides the mechanism for ensuring that the changes sought after are planned. In this phase, groups of from ten to twelve managers get together to *set goals for the total organization.* This composition is used at this stage in order to set targets that reflect the variety of forces present in the organization. After the issues, plans, and goal implementations are discussed by the various groups, they are summarized and used as the basis for an intensive organizational change effort.

Blake and his colleagues estimate that the time required for the first four phases, appreciation sessions, team training, horizontal linking, and setting of organizational goals may be two years or longer. Implementing them may require an additional two years or so.

In phase 5, the change-agent attempts to *help the organization realize the goals* established in phase 4. He deals with the organization much as a psychoanalyst would deal with a patient; in fact, the program during this phase resembles the consulting approach discussed earlier.

Phase 6, the final one, is directed toward *stabilizing the changes* brought about during the prior phases. Blake estimates that this period lasts for a year. The role of the change-agent is more passive during this period, and he is called upon for help less and less frequently. Rather than living with the client-system, he is available upon request. The main effort during this phase is to ensure the maintenance of the present state of functioning.

Figure 4 presents another strategy: a recapitulation by Argyris of a change program used by the New York headquarters team of a large oil company to improve the functioning of one of its smaller refineries in New England.[23] For some years, because of certain market changes, the refinery's profits had been declining, and there had been talk of closing it down.

The first change brought about was the recognition by headquarters that a new manager was needed who had the necessary technical skills and administrative experience, *plus* the assurance, for the future operation of the refinery. (See page 128.) This man was sent to two T-group training sessions in order to gain some awareness of the human problem existing in the refinery. Following this, the

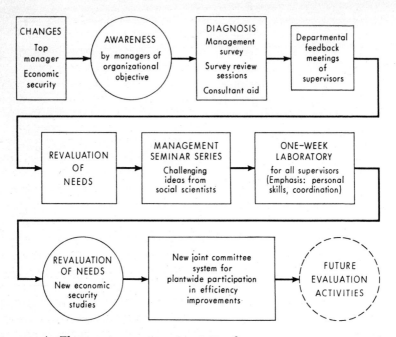

FIG. 4   Elements in one-year program in refinery

New York headquarters organizational development staff came on the scene and conducted a diagnosis through a survey and interviews of the total managerial staff (seventy) and a sample of the hourly employees (40 out of 350). About that time I was asked to consult with and help the New York headquarters staff and the refinery manager. Then, departmental feedback meetings with the supervisors were held and a reevaluation of needs was taken in coordination with the consulting group and top management (which at this point consisted of only the new refinery manager).

It was then decided that a laboratory program of T groups might be effective but possibly premature, and so a series of weekly seminars was held with the top management group (about twenty executives) focusing on new development in human relations. Speakers ranged over a wide variety of subjects, going from the Scanlon Plan to individual psychology. Following this, a one-week laboratory training program was held for all supervisors in diagonal-slice groupings, and then another reevaluation of needs was undertaken.

At this point some structural innovations were suggested and implemented. These included a top management committee consisting of all functional managers and a variety of project groupings working on a number of efficiency programs. During the very last phase of the program (not shown in the figure), the Scanlon Plan was adapted and installed at the refinery (incidentally, this was the first time the Scanlon program was undertaken in a "process" industry and the first time that a union agreed to the Scanlon Plan without a bonus automatically guaranteed).

It is difficult to know how typical or unusual these two planned-change strategies are; insufficient experience and reports dilute any generalizations that I would hazard. If they *are* typical, however, certain features of the strategies can be identified: (1) the length of time—Blake estimates five years, and the refinery program up to the point of the Scanlon Plan took two years; (2) the variety of programs utilized—research, consulting, training, teaching, and planning; (3) the necessity of cooperation with top management and the parent organization; (4) approaching the organization as a system, rather than as a collection of individuals; (5) phasing the program so that it evolves from individual to group to intergroup to overall organization; (6) the intellectual *and* emotional content of the program.

NOTES

1. Chapple, E. D., and L. R. Sayles, *The Measurement of Management,* The Macmillan Company, New York, 1961; Sayles, L., "The Change Process in Organization," in R. J. Smith (ed.), *Human Organization,* 1962, pp. 62–67.
2. Lippitt, R., J. Watson, and B. Westley, *The Dynamics of Planned Change,* Harcourt, Brace & World, Inc., New York, 1958; Seashore, C., and E. Van Egmond, "The Consultant-Trainer Role," in W. G. Bennis, K. D. Benne, and R. Chin (eds.), *The Planning of Change,* Holt, Rinehart and Winston, Inc., New York, 1961, pp. 660–666.
3. Blake, R. R., and J. S. Mouton, "A 9,9 Approach to Organization Development," in D. Zand and P. Buchanan (eds.), *Organization Development: Theory and Practice,* in press.
4. Argyris, C., *Interpersonal Competence and Organizational Effectiveness,* Dorsey Press, Homewood, Ill., 1962; Likert, R., *New Patterns of Management,* McGraw-Hill Book Company, New York, 1961; McGregor, D., *The Human Side of Enterprise,* McGraw-Hill Book Company, New York, 1960.
5. Argyris, *op. cit.,* p. 43.

6. Shepard, H. A., and R. R. Blake, "Changing Behavior through Cognitive Change," in Smith, *op. cit.*, pp. 88–96.

7. Burns, T., and G. M. Stalker, *The Management of Innovation*, Quadrangle, Chicago, 1962.

8. Argyris, C., "T-groups for Organizational Effectiveness," *Harvard Business Review*, vol. 42, pp. 60–74, 1964.

9. Schein, E. H., and W. G. Bennis, *Personal and Organizational Change through Group Methods*, John Wiley & Sons, Inc., New York, 1965.

10. Blake and Mouton, *op. cit.*

11. Argyris, *Interpersonal Competence and Organizational Effectiveness.*

12. Bradford, L. P., J. R. Gibb, and K. D. Benne, *T-group Theory and Laboratory Method*, John Wiley & Sons, Inc., New York, 1964.

13. *An Action Research Program for Organizational Improvement*, Foundation for Research on Human Behavior, Ann Arbor, Mich., 1960.

14. Jaques, E., *The Changing Culture of a Factory*, Tavistock, London, 1951; Rice, A. K., *The Enterprise and Its Environment*, Tavistock, London, 1963. Sofer, C., *The Organization from Within*, Tavistock, London, 1961.

15. Beckhard, R., "An Organization Improvement Program in a Decentralized Organized Organization," in Zand and Buchanan, *op. cit.*; Gibb, J. R., and R. Lippitt (eds.) "Helping a Group with Planned Change," *The Journal of Social Issues*, vol. 15, pp. 13–19, 1959.

16. Sofer, *op. cit.*

17. *Ibid.*

18. Argyris, *Interpersonal Competence and Organizational Effectiveness*, p. 104.

19. Mann, F., "Studying and Creating Change: A means to Understanding Social Organization," *Research in Industrial Relations*, Industrial Relations Research Association Publication 17, 1957; Mann, F., and H. Baumgartel, *The Survey Feedback Experiment: An Evaluation of a Program for the Utilization of Survey Findings*, Foundation for Research on Human Behavior, Ann Arbor, Mich., 1964; Mann, F., and R. Likert, "The Need for Research on the Communication of Research Results," *Human Organization*, vol. 11, pp. 15–19, 1952.

20. Beckhard, *op. cit.*

21. Argyris, *Interpersonal Competence and Organizational Effectiveness.*

22. Blake, R. R., J. S. Mouton, L. B. Barnes, and L. E. Greiner, "A Managerial Grid Approach to Organization Development: The Theory and Some Research Findings," *Harvard Business Review*, vol. 42, 1964.

23. Argyris, C., *Organization Development*, Yale University Press, New Haven, Conn., 1960.

8

*principles and strategies of directing organizational change via laboratory training**

INTRODUCTION

Two main uses or, put another way, two main target systems or client-systems for the Lab Training can be identified. One is the *individual:* his growth, interpersonal competence, and "self-actualization." The other target system is a *social system,* usually a formal organization or some subsystem or part of it.

In this chapter we shall focus on the *organization* as a change target for Lab Training. We choose this target system primarily because it is with social systems (and their subsystems) that the *strat-*

* This is a revision of a chapter in a book written in collaboration with Schein.[1] Although Lab (or T-group) Training is used as the pivotal type of change induction in this essay, please bear in mind that the principles and strategies apply equally to all classes of change programs involving the value and normative systems of the client population. This chapter appears by permission of the coauthor and the publisher.

tegic problems of Lab Training become manifest and where it is so crucial to understand the "fit" between Lab Training values and organizational goals. Where the individual is concerned, the problem of learning or change is ostensibly simpler; he can reject or accept, learn or not, without undue perturbation. When it comes to using Lab Training to change organizational systems, however, the strategic problems become impressive and complex, with seemingly untold unanticipated consequences and risks. So we propose here to examine some of the issues and dilemmas surrounding the use of Lab Training in effecting organizational change with the hope that increased understanding will lead to more effective utilization.

An Issue: Yogis and Commissars

Before going on to outline this chapter, let us take a short detour and discuss a general issue which lies behind the recent impetus to use Lab Training in improving social systems. We stated at the beginning of this chapter that the individual and the social system represent the twin change objectives. In fact, these goals reflect an interesting and ubiquitous tension—rarely stated as such, but always present—concerning the general direction of any change program. Over the years, since the beginning of Lab Training, the conflict has taken a variety of forms, but its capacity to arouse staff debates or arguments over training design or staff strategies has been monumental.

It is hard to state exactly what *the* issue is, but it is very reminiscent of Koestler's distinction between the yogi and the commissar, between those who turn *inward* for insight and Nirvana and those who turn *outward* for social salvation. It is the difference between those who believe in the manipulation of external forces—such as legal, technological, economic, and political factors—for the "good life" and those who look to the personality, to self-actualization, or to the individual for ultimate social improvement.

In the past eighteen years or so of Lab Training's existence, almost all training designs and strategies have—tacitly or explicitly—reflected this conflict. The debate takes different forms: sometimes it appears in the guise of "theoretical preferences," such as Lewin versus Freud or self-actualization versus organizational improvement; sometimes the argument oscillates between "utopianism" and "existential despair." However one finds that, most often, it is argued in terms of: "Who is the client?"—the organization or the individual.

For the most part, the dialogue which the debate has generated has been useful insofar as it has lifted up for analysis certain crucial issues such as (1) the problem of transfer of learning from the lab culture to other cultures and the durability of training effects on the individual *after* the lab, (2) the relationship between self-enhancement and organizational improvement—if any, and (3) the ethical-normative-value issues of transporting lab values into the fabric of the organization. We are a long way from resolving any of these issues, but one fortunate outcome of the debate is the increase in research and the improvement in conceptualization that it has forced.*

The shift in orientation from regarding solely the individual as the ultimate client to regarding the organization, or some other social unit, as the ultimate client is a fairly recent development. Before the late 1950s Lab Training was pretty much confined to a "cultural island" where strangers gathered, underwent an intensive experience, and left in two weeks abruptly—again, as strangers. It was difficult enough to evaluate the effects of the lab on the individual delegate; it was practically impossible to trace the effects on the organization. What data there were implied that the individual could not even maintain his own *self*-changes within the organization, much less modify the organization.

The predicament is real: How do you gain the advantages of a cultural island (particularly "unfreezing") and still transfer competencies and values internalized at the lab? Put another way, we can ask: Can you ensure lasting change of the individual without also changing the social fabric (norms, policies, values) of the organization?

The predicament has been solved over the past several years, as the preceding chapters have indicated, by bringing Lab Training to

---

* The reader is invited to read the excellent summary of research reported by Stock in Bradford et al.[2] See also, in the same book, the chapter by Benne for an excellent history of Lab Training associated with the National Training Laboratories.

the organization rather than the other way around. In other words, instead of sending individuals of a particular organization to a "stranger" lab, the organization has set up, in one form or another, its own Lab Training program.

But introducing Lab Training into the climate of a formal organization (such as a hospital, factory, university, or ship) brings about a set of strategic questions and raises certain issues of social change. In this chapter we would like to discuss and clarify these questions and issues.

OUTLINE OF CHAPTER

I. Background of, and perspectives on, the use of Lab Training for changing social systems
- ◆ A *Why this recent impetus toward the use of Lab Training for organizational improvement?*
- ◆ B *What are the conceptual goals of Lab Training with respect to organizational change?*
- ◆ C *What strategic models for inducing change are used?*

II. Considerations for the successful adoption of Lab Training by social systems
- ◆ A *State of the target system or subsystem*
  - • 1 *Are the learning goals of Lab Training appropriate?*
  - • 2 *Is the culutral state of the target system "ready" for Lab Training?*
  - • 3 *Are the key people in the target system involved in, or informed of, the Lab Training program?*
  - • 4 *Are members of the target system adequately prepared for, and oriented to, Lab Training?*
  - • 5 *Is voluntarism (regarding participation) ensured?*
- ◆ B *Role and competence of the change-agent*
  - • 1 *The change-agent's role*
  - • 2 *Competence required of the change-agent*
- ◆ C *Strategies of implementation*
  - • 1 *Who is the client?*
  - • 2 *What is the point of entry?*
  - • 3 *Which systems are involved?*
  - • 4 *To what extent can the change-agent involve the target system in planning and executing Lab Training?*

I. **Background of, and perspectives on, the use of Lab Training for changing social systems**

     ♦ *A Why this recent impetus toward the use of Lab Training for organizational improvement?*

Obviously, there are many causes to consider in the emergence of any social phenomenon. Similarly, in order to understand the use of Lab Training as an organizational instrument, many social forces must be mentioned. Labor supply, the professionalization of management, automation, the growing complexity of the enterprise, the large-scale and sprawling quality of organizations in conjunction with the need for better communication and decentralization, the improved education of the worker and the changing population characteristics of our work force, the network of boundaries and transactions which clogs up the turbulent environment of the organization, and a host of other factors must be included in even a superficial survey.* For us, the crucial factor is the inadequacy of present-day organizations to cope with the complexity of rapid change and problems of human collaboration. Adaptation and collaboration are two of the main problems confronting contemporary society, and our organizations will fail or succeed depending upon their mastery of these two tasks.

This is only a part of the explanation, however. The inadequacies of bureaucracy have been examined in detail by many organizational theorists for a number of years. These theorists have produced countless thoughtful suggestions and ideas about a new vision of social architecture which would be more in keeping with what is known about human motivation. *The point is that Lab Training provides the instrument whereby the normative goals and improvements set forth by theorists and practitioners of organizations can be achieved.*

Let us take some examples to clarify our meaning. Take the prob-

---

* See Bennis⁴ for a more detailed discussion.

lem of *intergroup conflict*. There is an urgent need to understand the network of interdependencies which stem from the myriad of specialties and complexity of technologies. Managers of large-scale operations frequently mention intergroup conflict and collaboration as one of their main problems. From a theoretical viewpoint, Likert[5] arrives at the same conclusion and suggests the importance of a "linking pin," a mechanism for integrating groups that are work-related. *But how is the mechanism developed?*

Or take the problem of *authority and leadership* in organizations. McGregor,[6] in particular, has focused in his writings on the archaic workings of authority systems in bureaucratic structures. What is now needed, asserts McGregor, are systems of collaboration, of colleagueship between superiors and subordinates, not the blind use of controls and coercions. What we now need is increased autonomy, not dependencies and counterdependencies. *But how are systems created and people "changed" so that bosses trust their subordinates enough to give them more autonomy, and how can subordinates learn to trust so that they can rely on self-control and collaboration?*

Lewin,[7] Allport,[8] and others have, for some time, produced evidence and arguments which show that as individuals participate directly in the decisions that are relevant to their work and life, they develop a higher state of morale and implement the decisions more effectively. *But how do organizations develop better and more responsive mechanisms for participative management?*

One final example: Argyris[9] and others have insisted that *interpersonal competence* is necessary to a manager. He must be able to size up a situation, be aware of human factors impinging on a situation, and develop a diagnostic sensitivity as well as behavioral flexibility in dealing with human problems. *But how do managers and other practitioners develop this interpersonal competence?*

The point of these examples is this. Ever since the historic studies of Mayo and Roethlisberger at Western Electric, there have been many profitable revisions and suggestions developed to improve the operations of the human organization. We have mentioned some of these in the examples above: better systems of collaboration, of adaptation, of authority; greater interpersonal competence; etc. There is no shortage of criticism or prescription. The problem is that there has been no organizational mechanism capable of implementing these suggestions. Lab Training appeared on the scene at the time when formal organizations were most pressed for revision, for change. *Lab Training provided an instrument whereby these normative goals and revisions could be translated into practice.*

> ♦ **B What are the conceptual goals of Lab Training with respect to organizational change?**

We have just been discussing the growth of Lab Training in terms of the needs and problems of the managers and practitioners, as they saw them. Now we want to shift our emphasis to the *change-agents* who have collaborated with these target systems. What do they have in mind as change goals?

Before answering this question, it might be useful to say a few words about the idea of a "change-agent." It is a rather new term and is used in many different ways.* (See Chapter 7, pages 113–119 for a detailed discussion of change-agents. For a general description of the change-agent's normative goals see p. 116.) We are using the term "change-agent" to refer to a person or group, practitioners or social scientists, who are using the theory which underlies Lab Training in order to improve the functioning and effectiveness of organizations. What do they have in mind as change goals?

The basic paradigm is: bureaucratic values tend to stress the rational, task aspects of the work and to ignore the basic human factors which relate to the task. Managers brought up in this system of values are badly cast to play the intricate human roles now required

---

* I stress their uniformities here, though there is a wide divergence of orientation, outlook, training, and experience. Some change-agents grew out of the tradition of Lewin and academic psychology, others were disciples of psychoanalytic practice; still others came from applied disciplines such as rural sociology or social work or education. Whatever their differences, they seem to receive their impetus as much from the urge to improve society as from simple curiosity about its working. They seem to be as intimately involved in affecting change as they are in studying it. They have developed a self-consciousness about the strategies of social change as well as about its goals. They are driven by a radical rather than conservative ethic, which means simply that their attitude toward social change springs from locating the ills of society in its institutions, where something can be done about them, rather than in human nature, where very little can be done about them. In short, the change-agents are not only *interpreting* the world in different ways; some intend to *change* it.

of them. Their ineptitude and anxieties lead to systems of discord and defense which interfere with the problem-solving capacity of the organization. The aims of change-agents, then, are (1) to effect a change in values so that *human factors and feelings come to be considered as legitimate* and (2) to assist in *developing skills among managers in order to increase interpersonal competence.*

There are variations to this paradigm, to be sure; for example, "changed attitudes toward our own role, role of others, and organizational relationships," or increased adaptibility of the organization to external stress, etc. But basically, the variations show up more sharply in the *strategic models* employed to induce the change than they do in the conceptual goals. Let us turn to that now.

♦ C   What strategic models for inducing change are used?

This question has to do with the problem of *how:* How are change agents selected? How do they achieve their goals? How do they gain their influence and power? In order to get a foothold on these issues, let us pose two central questions: (1) Are the change-agents internal or external to the target system; i.e., are they regular employees of the target system or not? (2) What is the basis of the change-agent's power or ability to exert influence on the target system?

1. Change-agents: internal or external? Whether or not the change agents are actual members of the target system or not is a crucial question to practitioners and students of organizational change. There are some who say that a significant change cannot occur without the impetus generated by the external agent.[11,12] They argue that only a skilled outsider-consultant can provide the perspective, detachment, and energy so necessary to effect a true alteration of existing patterns. There are advocates of the internal model, though, who take the opposite stand. They argue that the insider possesses the intimate knowledge of the target system that the external change-agent lacks. In addition, the internal change-agent does not generate the suspicion and mistrust that the outsider often does. His acceptance and credibility are guaranteed, it is argued, by his organizational status.

2. What is the source of the change-agent's power? Generally speaking, he derives his power and influence from a combination of two sources: *expert* power and *legitimate* power. As these terms sug-

gest, the change-agent is seen as possessing certain skills and competencies (expert power), or he is seen as occupying a certain office or holding status in an organization which legitimizes his influence (legitimate power.)*

Now we are in a better position to return to our main question concerning the various strategic models of change. In our experience, the most common model used is the *external* change-agent employing *expert* power. We call this the "Consultant" model because outside change-agents are employed as consultants to the organization (usually, but not always, to the personnel division), and they attempt to help the target system build adequate Lab Training programs. In some cases, the consultants actually conduct Lab Training; in other cases, they coordinate Lab Training activities along with other consulting functions.

Perhaps an example of the consultant model would help clarify its nature. The work of Shepard and other consultants at the Space Technology Laboratories may be one of the best models of this approach. In this case, Shepard acts as consultant to the director of industrial relations. In the course of their work together it was decided that "career development" (preparing managers for the future) was one of the most important problems facing the organization. Following this, Shepard worked most intensively with the manager in charge of career development. A sequence of activities followed, all worked out with Shepard collaborating with this man and the director of industrial relations, finally leading to team training.†

At the other extreme from the consultant model is the line model, a strategy by which the change-agent is internal to the target system and possesses legitimate power. A company president or any line leader who utilizes Lab Training would be an example of this. Alfred J. Marrow, president of the Harwood Manufacturing Company, repre-

---

* We have ignored some of the more personal and intangible elements which enter into questions of strategy, such as the change-agent's personality, charisma, etc. These personal factors are rarely written about explicitly and only infrequently are recognized as such. For these reasons, we do not feel at all confident in stressing anything but their *presence*. See Chap. 9 for a fuller discussion of the change-agent's power.

† See Argyris[13] for a step-by-step analysis of the consultant model. It is the most clearly written account of this model.

sents this approach to Lab Training. Marrow works directly with the external consultants—being a psychologist as well as an entrepreneur—conducts his own T groups, participates in labs, and generally takes an active role in conducting and coordinating Lab Training in his own organization. The president of Non-Linear Systems, Andrew Kaye, and the president of Minnesota Mining, Hugh Harrison, are both, to some extent, examples of the line model.*

A more popular model than the line model, but less so than the consultant model, is the staff model, as exemplified by Shepard while he was at Esso and, more recently, by Buchanan at Esso International. In this model, change-agents are drawn directly from the headquarters staff of the organization; for example, Shepard and his colleagues (some of whom were outside consultants) went to the Baton Rouge refinery in 1959 and 1960 to conduct two-week residential labs for the entire managerial staff of the refinery. The staff model, then, is similar to the consultant model in that it emphasizes expert power, but it is similar to the line model in that its change-agents are drawn from inside the target system.

A purer case of the internal change-agent model was developed by the General Electric Company and is now used by that company in their Business Effectiveness Program. In this case, change-agents (called "catalysts") are trained by headquarters staff and outside consultants to go to a target system (a General Electric location) and "live in" as internal change-agents for as long as it takes to effect a change along the lines specified by the program. Some catalysts have been on location for as long as two years; others terminate after several months. What should be stressed here, for our analysis, is that the change-agents are *paid* and are considered regular employees of the target system itself.

Let us summarize now. Models implementing Lab Training for improving organizations can be viewed along two dimensions, internal versus external and legitimate power versus expert power. If the choice of change strategy is *internal*, then legitimate or expert power can be utilized. The General Electric catalyst program is an example

---

* The extent to which these men actually conduct Lab Training varies. What is most characteristic of the line model is that the top line management—rather than staff—takes the leadership in instituting and sustaining Lab Training.

of the internal-expert model; the work of Alfred J. Marrow at Harwood is an example of the internal-line model. If the choice of the change strategy is *external*, then only one power alternative is open, that of expert, for legitimate power, by definition, must be drawn from sources internal to the target system. There are many examples of the external-expert model. We have already mentioned the work of Argyris, Blake, Shepard, McGregor, and others. It is probably the most widely used of the approaches we have singled out.

The classification we have developed for the uses of change strategies is crude, to be sure, and it ignores some of the more ingenious variations, but we would wager that over 90 per cent of the change efforts utilizing Lab Training can be grouped in it. At the same time, however, new models are now being developed which may make this classification obsolete.

It seems increasingly clear to us that *combinations* and appropriate *sequencing* of these approaches may prove to be most useful. There are more and more signs, for example, that internal and external change-agents, *in concert,* are more effective than either internal or external change-agents working alone. Moreover, a combination of legitimate and expert power cannot help but be more effective, other things being equal, than either working independently of the other. The evidence is far from conclusive at this point, but from certain trends we now see developing, new models for implementing organizational change will be used which rely on external *and* internal change-agents in combination and using legitimate *and* expert power. What this implies is a *team effort* involving a diverse set of skills, status, and roles in order to induce the organizational change. We believe this will prove to be the most useful strategy in the future.

II. Considerations for the successful adoption of Lab Training by social systems

In this section we shall examine the conditions that facilitate the adoption of Lab Training by target systems. We shall consider first the state of the target system or subsystem and, second, the role and competence of the change-agent. Then we shall discuss the interaction between the change-agent and the target system in the strategy of implementation.

♦ A *State of the target system or subsystem**

In considering the state of the target system, a number of questions must be asked:

1 Are the learning goals of Lab Training appropriate?
2 Is the cultural state of the target system "ready" for Lab Training?
3 Are the key people in the target system involved in, or informed of, the Lab Training program?
4 Are members of the target system adequately prepared for, and oriented to, Lab Training?
5 Is voluntarism (regarding participation) ensured?

•1 *Are the learning goals of Lab Training appropriate?*

To what extent do the goals relate to the effectiveness of the target system? We can think of many target systems where the answer to these questions may be negative because of market, technological, and competitive conditions. Serious attention must be given, particularly in the early stages, to the appropriateness of Lab Training change goals for the particular target system. A great deal of effort, at first, must be directed to diagnosing the target system's needs in relation to the anticipated outcomes of Lab Training. Are the outcomes relevant to the effectiveness of the target system? Is Lab Training timely, economical, congruent with the anticipated target-system trends, etc.? Later on, after discussing the cases where Lab Training failed, this question of appropriateness will again be raised.

•2 *Is the cultural state of the target system "ready" for Lab Training?*

Let us be as clear as we can about what we mean by "cultural readiness." Each target system transmits and maintains a system of values which permeates the organizational climate and which is used as a basis for action and commitments. This does not mean that values are always adhered to, but it usually means that those who exemplify the values are rewarded and that those who violate them are

---

* The boundaries of the target system which Lab Training affects may be a part (or subsystem) of the larger target system. For example, a target system like ALCAN has been directing the bulk of its Lab Training change program at one of its three main divisions. And in the Esso change program, the refinery, a subsystem, became the chief target system. We shall come back to this point later in our discussion of the strategy of implementation.

punished. Lab Training also has a set of values which we specified as authenticity, choice, collaboration, and the expression of feelings among others. There is always bound to be *some* conflict between these values of Lab Training and the values of the target system, but situations should be avoided where the two sets of value systems clash extraordinarily.

The degree and range of value conflicts provide some of the best clues for diagnosing the cultural state of the target system. That is, if the discrepancy between Lab Training values and the target system's values can be realistically assessed, a fairly good idea about the target system's readiness can be obtained. Let us sample some of the most important dimensions of the cultural state.

The *legitimacy of interpersonal relationships,* in terms of both their effects on the work and the degree to which members of the target system view them as susceptible to change, is an important aspect of the target system's culture. In many target systems, interpersonal phenomena are not considered appropriate to discuss, germane to the task, or legitimate as a focus of inquiry. As Henry Ford once said about his own philosophy of management: "You just set the work before the men and have them do it." While this view is becoming slowly outdated by modern techniques of management, there are still many situations where interpersonal influence is regarded as invalid, not legitimate, or an invasion of privacy.

Another cultural variable which must be taken into account is the *control and authority system presently employed by the target system.* If it is too rigid and authoritarian, it may be too much at variance with the values of Lab Training for easy adoption.

The presence and intensity of conflict within the target system represent still another cultural factor which must be considered. It is difficult to generalize about conflict in terms of its relationship to the adoption of Lab Training. The impression we gain, however, is that it is best not to introduce Lab Training under conditions of intense conflict. In this case, the organization is under stress and may be *too* "plastic"; Lab Training may be only a temporary dodge or a tool in a power play by one of the protagonists, or it may be used later on as a convenient scapegoat. This is not to say that Lab Training may not be strategic to employ during periods of conflict but only that the type, causes, and intensity of conflict must be examined in relationship to the Lab Training program.

The internal boundary system of the target system must be carefully examined in order to avoid situations where Lab Training values are internalized in one subpart of the system, only to be rejected by, and cause disruptions in, an adjacent system.* In other words, the interdependence of the parts within the target system must be carefully scrutinized so that unanticipated changes in some parts of the system do not "backfire" and create negative repercussions in another part of the target system.

The last item to consider in assessing the cultural readiness of the target system is the most difficult to render in objective terms, and yet it is possibly the single most important factor in estimating the probability of success. *It has to do with the change-agent's relationship with the target system,* in particular the quality and potentiality of the relationship.

If the change-agent believes that it is possible to establish a relationship with the target system based on a healthy, realistic understanding of his role and with realistic expectations regarding the change, then a change program may be indicated. But if the relationship is based on fantasy, unrealistic hopes, fear, worship, or intimidation, then the change-agent and/or the target system must seriously reexamine the basis for their joint work.†

We are suggesting that one of the best ways of diagnosing cultural readiness has to do with the way the target system reacts to, and establishes a relationship with, the change-agent. The quality and

---

* Bavelas and Strauss[14] report an interesting example of this. A subunit of girls on an assembly line developed an ingenious and new method which increased their job satisfaction and improved their performance significantly. The only trouble was that it had repercussions on interdependent parts of the organization. The program eventually had to be scuttled. Though we know of no such case, it will be interesting to identify sources of strain that Lab Training might create with the target system's *external* boundary system: suppliers, customers, government, employee sources, etc. It is doubtful that it would generate the same degree of strain as internal interdependencies, but it still bears examination.

† Let us be clear about this. We mean that if the change-agent cannot *foresee* a healthy relationship in the future, he might well reconsider the Lab Training program. We do not think it is possible for the relationship to be totally trusting and realistic during the beginning phases of work. In any case, the main point we want to stress is the diagnostic validity of the relationship; the problems that inhere in that are probably symptomatic of the problems to be encountered.

vicissitudes of this encounter—insofar as it is a replica of the intended change program—provide an important clue regarding the fate of the Lab Training change program.

What we mean by "readiness," then, is the degree of value conflict between Lab Training values and the target system's values in terms of (1) the legitimacy of interpersonal phenomena; (2) the range, depth, and intensity of conflicts and modes of conflict resolution; (3) concepts of control and authority; (4) interdependence of parts of the target system; and (5) the relationship between change-agent and target system. Though they are difficult to measure precisely, they must be given thorough attention, and an assessment must be made before Lab Training can be introduced.

Assuming that the cultural readiness of the target system has been carefully assessed and found to be appropriate, then we must ask:

> • 3   *Are the key people in the target system involved in, or informed of, the Lab Training program?*

It can be disastrous if the people most affected by Lab Training are not involved in, informed of, or even advised of, the Lab Training program. To guarantee this commitment, a great deal of energy and time must be devoted to assessing the extent to which the Lab Training is supported by the key people and the attitudes individuals generally hold regarding Lab Training.

> • 4   *Are members of the target system adequately prepared for, and oriented to, Lab Training?*

The usual forms of *preparation* and *orientation* do not seem too effective for Lab Training, primarily because the written (or spoken) word rarely conveys the sense of the experience. Lab Training, if anything, is experience-based, and words, without an experiential referent, often tend to confuse and, in some cases, cause more apprehension than necessary.

Some introductory *experiences* often prepare and orient future participants adequately. We have tried a "miniature" lab (waggishly called by one of the participants an "instant" lab) to simulate as accurately as we could the lab environment. In this case, an entire lab was compressed into one full day of training. In other situations we have executed a specific training exercise with some prospective delegates in order to give them a feel for the learning environment of

Lab Training. In any case, we are advocating some experience-based orientation in order to provide a reasonable facsimile of lab life.

In our consideration of the state of the target system, we must consider one last factor:

• 5   *Is voluntarism (regarding participation) ensured?*

We feel this is an important, perhaps crucial, factor for the successful adoption of Lab Training by target systems. We think it is crucial not only for the obvious ethical reasons but also for realistic learning considerations. In order for a participant to profit the most from Lab Training, he must not feel coerced or pushed into experiencing it.* Involuntary attendence is particlarly hard to avoid in those cases where the entire organization undergoes Lab Training and where there is a tacit rejection of those who refuse to attend. Still it is important for target systems to provide as much choice and voluntarism regarding Lab Training as possible. And this is done by (1) providing the individuals with as much orientation as possible so that choice is meaningful (simply to ask a person whether he wants to attend Lab Training when he has no understanding of it is ridiculous!) and (2) keeping organizational pressure to attend at a minimum.

In this section, on the state of the target system, we have presented a series of factors to be taken into account in order to increase the probability of the successful adoption of Lab Training. In order to summarize this section as well as to make explicit the sequence of choices, we have constructed a five-step model shown in Table 4.

♦ B   Role and competence of the change-agent

We mentioned earlier that the idea of "change-agentry," as we are using the term here, is very new. And because of its novelty, its fundamental outline is still emerging. Thus the role of the change-agent is protean, changing, difficult to grasp, and practically impossible to generalize about. However, it may be useful to make some tentative remarks about it in this section.

---

* This often creates the dilemma of the people most in need of the Lab Training experience resisting it and those who least need it volunteering for it. However unsatisfactory the resolution of this dilemma is, nothing would be gained, and a lot possibly lost, if people were captive to the experience.

TABLE 4   Five-step model for diagnosing state of target system

1 Are Lab Training change goals appropriate to target system?	If *not, stop* and reconsider appropriateness of Lab Training.

If *yes,* then:

2 Is the "cultural state" of target system prepared for Lab Training?	If *not, stop* and examine areas where more preparation is needed or where value conflicts should be reduced.

      Degree and type of value conflict?
      Legitimacy of interpersonal phenomena?
      Degree, range, intensity, and resolution of conflict?
      Concepts of control and authority used?
      Interdependence of target system?
      Relationship of trust and confidence between change-agent and target system?

If *yes,* then:

3 Are key people involved and committed?	If *not, stop* and examine ways to develop more commitment to program.

If *yes,* then:

4 Are members of the target system adequately prepared for, and oriented, to Lab Training?	If *not, stop* and examine ways to develop more commitment to program.

If *yes,* then:

5 Is voluntarism (regarding participation) ensured?	If *not, stop* and examine attitudes toward Lab Training, or *why* people do or do not want to go to labs. After diagnosis, attempt to indicate the place of Lab Training in career development accurately.

• 1   The change-agent's role

There are a number of things we would like to call attention to about the role of the change-agent and then go on to discuss each of them in more detail. The change-agent's role must be construed as being professional, marginal, ambiguous, insecure, and risky.

First, the role of the change-agent is *professional;* that is, he counts heavily on a body of certified knowledge in order to realize his aims, under guidance of certain ethical principles, and with the client's interest—not his own—in mind. This last point should be emphasized; the change-agent must defer his own personal gratification in his dealings with the target system, his client. Particularly in dealing with something as important as a large and complex organization —where the change-agent's actions may affect thousands of individuals—he must continually check his own needs, motives, and wishes against the reality of the client's needs.*

Second, the role of the change-agent is *marginal;* that is, he does not have formal membership in the target system or a band of colleagues working close by. Typically he works alone, and his marginality can work to his advantage and to his discomfort. On the positive side, the marginality can enhance his detachment and perception; it can also create insecurity and an absence of mechanisms (like colleagues) for reality-testing. In any case, both the target system and the change-agent have to come to terms with the idea of marginality.†

Third, the role of the change-agent is *ambiguous.* Essentially this means that the basic concept of the change-agent is not widely understood and evokes a wide range of meaning. If one responds to the question "What do you do?" with the answer "I am a psychologist," it does not evoke the same bewilderment as the response "I am a change-agent." (In fact, the responder might be well advised not to answer in that vein.) The ambiguity of the role betrays its lack of legitimacy as well as credibility. It also involves certain risks like drawing suspicion and hostility *because* of its ambiguity. On the other

---

* The change-agent must be made painfully aware of some of the unconscious gratifications of his role too, so that these can be brought under control. We have in mind fantasies of high-powered manipulation or of satisfying an uncontrollable urge for power and omnipotence.

† In a recent case we heard about, a change-agent reported to work for his first day on the job, and the plant manager requested him to do some work which seemed to be inappropriate for a change-agent; that is, it was work which one of the managers should have been doing. The change-agent refused to carry out functions which properly belonged to management. In this case the manager could not come to terms with the marginal role of the change-agent.

side, it can also be helpful in providing the necessary latitude and breadth which more precisely defined roles do not allow.

Fourth, the role of the change-agent is *insecure*. This stems from a variety of causes: the precarious employment basis of the change-agent (the fact that he may be the most expendable person under certain conditions); inadequate knowledge and the lack of guidelines for many of his actions; the profound resistances which develop when one attempts to change an organization—all these factors tend to make the role insecure.

Fifth, and related to the insecure elements in the change-agent's role, is the *risky* quality inherent in it, the risk not only to the target system but also to the agent's professional status. As we shall see in the next section, the complexity of organizational change and some of its unanticipated consequences can lead to totally undesirable outcomes.

In sum, we view the change-agent's role as professional, marginal, ambiguous, insecure, and risky. Let us continue this discussion by identifying some of the competencies required for achieving success in the role.

• 2   Competence required of the change-agent

This must encompass a wide range of knowledge, including conceptual-diagnostic knowledge cutting across the entire sector of the behavioral sciences, theories and methods of organizational change, knowledge of sources of help, and orientation to the ethical and evaluative functions of the change-agent's role.

In addition to this intellectual grasp, the change-agent must also possess operational and relational skills. He must be able to listen, observe, identify, and report; he must have the ability to form relationships and inspire trust; and he must have a high degree of behavioral flexibility.

The change-agent must also be able to "use himself," to be in constant communication with himself, and to recognize and come to terms with (as much as is humanly possible) his own motivations. Particularly in the diagnostic stages of the work, the change-agent must observe how the target system deals with him. Quite often, as we mentioned earlier, the interaction between the change-agent and the target system is crucial for understanding and reaching a conclusion with respect to the state and readiness of the target system. In short, the change-agent should be sensitive and mature.

Finally, the change-agent should act congruently ("authentically"), that is, in accordance with the values he is attempting to superimpose upon the target system's value system. It will not do for the change-agent to impose democratic or humanistic values in an authoritarian or inhuman manner. If the change-agent is concerned with creating more authenticity and collaboration, he must behave in ways that are in accord with these values. We say this not only for the obvious ethical reasons but for deeper reasons as well. The fact of the matter is that so much of the change-agent's influence grows out of his relationship with the target system and the extent to which he is emulated as a role model that any significant discrepancies between his actions and his stated values cannot help but create resistance.

These are the requirements for the effective achievement of the change-agent's role, and they sound almost saintly. We would not expect to find many such supermen among us, but we would expect this job description to be used as something to aim for.

♦ C   Strategies of implementation

We have examined the state of the target system and the role and competence of the change-agent. Let us close this section by taking a look at some of the strategy questions which arise in connection with the interaction between the two. These can be stated as choice points, questions which ultimately have to be considered in any change endeavor and which can be decided only after a thorough examination of the target system.

1   Who is the client?
2   What is the point of entry?
3   Which systems are involved?
4   To what extent can the change-agent involve the target system in planning and executing Lab Training?

• 1   Who is the client?

This is the first and perhaps the most important strategic question. Is it the organization? A particular T group? The group or person who appointed and pays the change-agent? An individual in stress?

This is a hard question to answer, and we would guess that the *salient* client changes often throughout the course of a Lab Training program. But the question itself should never be too far from the change-agent's mind.

> • 2   *What is the point of entry?*

That is, at what level of the organization should Lab Training be directed first? The top management group? Middle levels? Lower levels? Or where? There are some change-agents, like Argyris[15] and Blansfield,[16] who believe that change can succeed only if it starts at the top and percolates down, that in order for a real change to take place, the highest command must be the primary initiating force.

Others disagree with this strategy. They claim that change programs utilizing Lab Training can start at lower levels of the target system and still be successful. Furthermore, they argue, it is sometimes *preferable* to start the change at lower levels because in some situations—because of a variety of organizational conditions—starting at the top may be too risky.

To some extent, the problem of point of entry can be decided on the basis of the kind of model of change employed. If it is a *line* model, then the consequences of starting at the lower levels may be different from what they would be in a *consultant* or *staff* model.

The kind of model used also pertains to our third question.

> • 3   *Which systems are involved?*

Obviously everyone cannot be trained at once, which raises the question of priorities and choice. Can training be isolated in certain components of the organization, leaving other components without it, or should attempts be made to include segments of all subsystems of the target system in the initial stages of the program? In any case, a careful diagnosis needs to be undertaken in order to trace the most strategic circulation of Lab Training effects throughout the total target system. In our experience, some of the most critical unanticipated consequences arose when a diagnosis of the interdependencies of the subsystems within the target system was not carefully worked out.

How to choose the point of entry and which systems to involve are important *and* related strategic questions. There is no simple guideline to use in making these choices—except an intimate knowledge and diagnosis of the target system, which we outlined above in Table 4, and a consideration of the model of change used.

One final question must be raised now:

> • 4   *To what extent can the change-agent involve the target system in planning and executing Lab Training?*

In order to act in accordance with the values of Lab Training, the change-agent should attempt to involve the target system in planning and goal setting for the change program. Sometimes, though, this is easier said than done because the target system may not have the experience or expertise to collaborate realistically with the change-agent. In any case, the change-agent must attempt to make an adequate diagnosis of the extent to which the target system should be involved in the planning, goal setting, and execution of Lab Training.*

These are some of the main questions which come up and perplex change-agents in initiating Lab Training change programs. They do not, by a long shot, exhaust the endless possibilities of problems. And until we have achieved perfect strategic comprehension of the target system in relation to the change-agent, we will be beset by these and still other unanticipated problems.

III.   Three cases of failure

In medical training, students and physicians are exposed quite regularly to an intriguing ordeal called the "clinical pathology conference," in which a pathologist presents the autopsy of a patient and an expert is called in (in full view of all seated in the amphitheater) to diagnose the precise cause of the fatality. No equivalent teaching device exists in the behavioral sciences, unfortunately, mainly because we are in a relatively early stage of developing a practice.† Yet we

---

* There is a dilemma here often commented upon by change-agents and practitioners. How can systems of collaboration be established if one party to the encounter cannot adequately *choose* because of inexperience or lack of knowledge? Does coercion or faith have to be used during the very first phase of change? Can one start a democratic change program, for example, by ordering people to attend? Can a change-agent insist that his client attend a lab so that collaboration, of a deep and enduring kind, can be achieved?

† There are other reasons as well, for example, the understandable desire for secrecy regarding failures or mixed successes and the difficulty of ascertaining precise causes in these complex social-change ventures.

thought it might be interesting to present several examples of failure or partial failure in order to dramatize and clarify different parts of this chapter.

What we propose to do, then, is to present three brief anecdotes or actual cases that have come to our attention in one way or another. (We have "doctored" and disguised the cases sufficiently so that no confidences will be endangered.) The cases will be presented consecutively and without comment until after the third and last one; then we shall attempt to develop some principles from the case material.

♦ A Case 1: a letter from a government training center

This is a letter which came to one of the authors from a government training officer (Dr. A) attached to a large government training center. Lab Training was started at the center several months ago, and since that time the following things happened: (1) the Director (Mr. Z) went to a two-week lab at Bethel; (2) about 250 government officials had undergone a five-day lab at the center under Dr. A's leadership with other staff drawn from officials Dr. A had personally trained; and (3) Dr. A with Mr. B's support (a strong advocate of Lab Training and second in command of the center) is planning to set up a Lab Training experience for all 2,000 officials stationed there. This letter arrived shortly after plans were laid out to train trainers in order to execute a massive training design.

> I'm still behind on the reports on our Lab Training here, at least on the reports I'd like to get out.
>
> Some of the little things that have cropped up. The director, who went to the two-week lab away from here, feels that those who have only gone through four or five days of training here don't really have the capacity to talk to him.
>
> Those members of the faculty who got the training late wonder why they were left to last. An "in" group and an "out" group developed in the faculty. Some of the outs resented being trained by one of their peers. Some wanted to know: "How did you get to be a trainer?"
>
> The head of our medical department told the director that Lab Training type of training is dangerous.
>
> The chief in Washington (over our director!) asked someone in an aside: "What the hell is Dr. A doing giving that kind of training!"
>
> A grade 15 called in a grade 12 scheduled to attend a five-day lab in April and said, not once but twice: "You don't have to go

to this thing you know. I want you to understand it is entirely voluntary; you don't have to go unless you want to. What are you going to do if some younger official tells you he doesn't like the way you conduct yourself?"

One man comes up to me occasionally, looks around as if to make sure no one is watching, and then makes the sign of T with both hands.

The Director's deputy wrote a letter to headquarters and asked for an evaluation of Lab Training. "If it's good for one, is it good for all?"

I received an informal request from a staff official at headquarters asking me to answer about twelve objections commonly raised to Lab Training.

In short, a considerable number of anxieties have been raised. Some are intrigued; some are scared.

Two weeks elapsed, and another letter arrived from Dr. A:

We have unfortunately hit a snag. How serious it will be remains to be seen. Mr. B (Dr. A's mainline support) has been transferred. This removed our chief advocate suddenly. Within a week the director, Mr. Z, called in the head of curriculum and outlined how he wanted Lab Training put into the curriculum. A meeting was set up with me, the director, and the head of curriculum.

(Up until this time we had been planning, with Mr. B's approval and backing, to put the training into one department and to start in September. We proposed, if we could get the money, to get two outside trainers in for three weeks in August to train this department's staff. Someone from National Training Laboratories had been down and talked this over with the staff, and I had managed to find a friend in Washington who said he would underwrite the program. We had plans for September, but that was the large outline.)

At the May 3 meeting, Mr. Z started out by saying NTL didn't have any final answers to Lab Training and that his trainers at Arden House were quick to admit they didn't know all the answers. Thus, he said, we had a chance to strike out on our own and did not have to be bound by the fixed two-week approach pioneered by the National Training Laboratories. (Up to this time he was the only one who had been insisting on two weeks—we had been talking in terms of four or five days.) Furthermore, we could not have officials forgoing their vacations in August, so any ideas about giving them three weeks of training couldn't be considered. Anyway, it didn't take much training because all his trainers did was sit there—they hardly opened their mouths during the two weeks. He would train the officials himself, and he thought possibly one afternoon would be enough. What he proposed then was that after about six or seven weeks, all the students be given one or two days to give each other feedback. This would be preceded by four or five lectures during the first week or so which would tell them what to be watching for. They could then tell each other after the sixth week what they had observed. At the end of school, the students would be given another day or two to give each other feedback. And so on. One or two of us tried to offer some comments or observations and were either cut off or ignored. As a consultant of sorts, I didn't feel quite up to exploring all the implications of his plan in front of the staff because I felt it was his prerogative to run the school as he wanted to.

Since that time various staff sections have been busy trying to pass on to other staff sections the job of trying to figure out what Mr. Z wants and making plans for his wishes. I've been invited to a meeting in the morning and will see what develops. I intend to talk to Mr. Z by himself after this if I can.

I'm curious to find out whether he will tell me why he changed his mind, apparently, so suddenly and why he chose not to build on any of the data we had so painstakingly gathered. All this he just threw out of the window. And either just before or just after the May 3 meeting, he forwarded to headquarters a report of the school activities in which he asked for funds for the August training I described.

We are unable to figure out whether Mr. B's leaving triggered the change, whether he is scared to try a four-day lab with students, whether he balks at paying the training price, whether he is irked at me, or just what the score is. But what makes it so hard to figure is that all the reports, letters, plans, etc., that he has seen and signed have nothing to do with what he has proposed. Some of what he says might be worked out into something quite useful, but in the meeting he brooked no comment—all he wanted was a rubber stamp.

I am not ready at this point to say the effort has failed because a lot of pressure has been building up in the past ten days. How much it will mean has yet to be disclosed. Certainly, at this moment the plans for the August training seem dead, although we may yet get the test in one department rather than among 800 students. This really bugged me, trying something completely unknown and untested on 800 men.

Several weeks after this letter was written, Dr. A called to say that the government training center had stopped its Lab Training and "had gone back to more traditional training methods."

♦ B   Case 2: a letter from medical services

This letter was sent as a confidential memorandum from the chief medical officer of a large manufacturing company to the vice-president of personnel. A copy of this memo was sent to Dr. A, chief training officer for the company. Dr. A had been hiring consultants who use Lab Training quite regularly in their work for this company.

> The medical division is concerned about the possibility of medical casualties from the T-group type of training program.
> Dr. Jones says that T-group programs have a greater likelihood of producing a higher percentage of disabling mental disturbances than ordinary work situations.
> The purpose of the training division is training.
> The purpose of the medical division is the prevention of illness and disability.
> We feel the purpose of our division warrants our scrutiny of any company activity likely to be related to disabilities.
> We recommended several months ago that the list of candidates for training sessions be passed before the local company medical officer for his approval or comment regarding the names thereon. The suggestion is held impractical by some on the basis that the company medical officers are not psychologically or psychiatrically oriented, have little knowledge or comprehension concerning the nature of the sessions, and are not qualified to determine who are high-risk candidates. It is my conviction that something along the following lines should be required by the company, if for no other reason than the doubt surrounding the advisability of having therapy for medical conditions unsupervised by medical people:
> 1. Collaboration should start immediately to arrange a long weekend session in a suitable place, to be attended by the senior medical representative from each of our plants. Dr. A should prepare a clear statement of the purpose of these T sessions, a clear statement of the procedure used in attempting to achieve the purpose, a clear statement of what these procedures demand from the individual, and a clear statement of the signs which the trainers use as indicators of impending disability, no matter how temporary. In addition, this working session should provide a sample experience for the doctors attending. The purpose of this session would be to take away any feeling that the local doctor was completely "clueless" regarding what is appearing to take on the shadowy form of a mystic cult. . . .

This case had a reasonably successful outcome. The chief medical officer himself attended a two-week lab at Bethel and shortly after his return organized a long weekend session for all his doctors, other key personnel, and line officials, led by two lab trainers. This three-day weekend session was designed as a modified lab, and according to the participants and the trainers, it accomplished its purposes: a better understanding of Lab Training by the doctors and an improvement in the collaboration between medical and training divisions.

♦ C   *Case 3: the undercover change-agent*

The following anecdote is based on interviews conducted with members of an organization in which Lab Training has been tried and failed. In fact, the training endeavor was almost totally disastrous: the staff member conducting the Lab Training was fired, his colleague was transferred, the director of training was ordered to stop all training connected with management development and to provide only technical training, and the vice-president of personnel resigned.

The company itself is a large retailing combine operating about fifteen department stores in the Middle West. The headquarters is located in Milwaukee, and many of the branch stores are located in the conservative German farming centers throughout Wisconsin and Minnesota. The company is family-owned and is operated by the son of the founder, Mr. Hess.

The company had committed itself to a considerable amount of executive training through its personnel department. Each year most of its managerial staff attended a one-week course at a small hotel in the lake country near Milwaukee. For the most part, the human relations training was based on cases very like those collected and used at the Harvard Business School. These case courses had been deemed very successful by management and by the participants.

Last year the company hired a new trainer (Mr. Jones) for their one-week human relations training program. Before taking the job, Jones asked his boss, the director of training, whether they could try some lab training. The director of training didn't understand it completely but said he would take it up with his boss, the vice-president of personnel. The latter had only a dim inkling of what Lab Training was all about but passed on whatever he did know to the president. It wasn't at all clear about who "cleared what with whom" or how much anyone understood about the idea of Lab Training, but in any case, nine weeks of Lab Training had taken place with nine different groups, all at the lower echelons of management. During the ninth week, unannounced and on a surprise visit, the president arrived at the training site and demanded to be given entry into the T groups. Jones refused at first but finally gave in to the president's orders.

Shortly after the president's return to Milwaukee, the training ceased, and Jones was fired, etc. What had happened?

Leading up to the president's visit to the lab, culminating in his storming into the resort hotel during the breakfast hour demanding entrance into the T group, was a whole series of events. First of all, the president had heard about some "interesting" training going on, to his mind, quite unlike what he had come to expect from case-study discussions. He knew nothing about this "group dynamics" business and became angry for not being told about it. Second, rumors had come to his attention that some "hanky-panky" was going on there. In fact, his vice-president of buying had overheard a conversation between two of his assistant buyers which was reported to him. One of the buyers had just returned from a one-week lab, and the other buyer was quizzing her about it. The conversation the vice-president reported to the president went something like this:

BUYER A: Oh, you just came back from Marlboro [the training site]?
BUYER B: Yes.
BUYER A: How was it?
BUYER B: This course was the deepest experience I have had in my life so far. Can you imagine, there was one man who took off his clothes completely!
BUYER A: A striptease?
BUYER B: Uh-huh.

Apparently, Buyer B was attempting to indicate to Buyer A the depth of the experience, the emotional revelations. In fact, what Buyer A passed on to her boss was that a literal striptease took place at Marlboro. Apparently, to this day there are some places in the company where this story is still believed.

Then, there had been an attempted suicide by one of the participants in the training shortly after his return from the week at Marlboro.

Finally, whenever the president asked his vice-president of personnel whether he had visited Marlboro and whether he was aware of what was going on there, the vice-president said he didn't really know what was going on and that he was advised by Mr. Jones to stay away. These events led to the president's surprise visit to Marlboro.

He arrived at Marlboro at breakfast on the third day of a week's program and demanded his entrance into the T group. According to Jones:

> I tried to dissuade him but to no avail. He insisted that he had the right. "If you have nothing to hide," he said, "then let me in. If you have something to hide, then I must find out." So he observed us for a two-hour T session. After the meeting I told him that it was hard to get a realistic picture of what goes on in T groups. He noted this and smiled at my remarks and expressed astonishment about the lack of structure in the group.
>
> After the meeting, while having coffee, he voiced a little surprise about my passive attitude and my not exercising leadership at all. I tried to explain to him how important this is, but I felt that there was an enormous wall of prejudice which I could not get behind.
>
> Then I gave a lecture to the group on leadership, drawing most of my material from McGregor's *Human Side of Enterprise.* Then I asked the participants to organize the last day's training activities.
>
> In the afternoon, right after their second T group of the day, when people were on their feet, the president rose and told everyone to remain in their seats and then delivered a twenty-minute speech. He first said that supervisory training was an important thing and that the company had already spent a lot of money on it. He thought the participants were getting something from the company which they could not reasonably expect to get. Then he went on to say that these are critical times, that the competitive situation was worsening, and that success would require the greatest effort of everybody. This could be achieved, he said, by working hard and by following the given orders without question—all the requisites, I thought, of a paternalistic management. He went on speaking then like a military leader. Then he referred to my short lecture on leadership and said that there was one point he did not agree with at all. (One of the participants had asked whether a subordinate always has to follow orders to the word. I gave a very qualified answer, trying to show that there are times when a superior could be questioned.) The president said that he most strongly wanted to emphasize that a subordinate had better follow orders—there was no question about that! Then he went into a monologue about leadership philosophy, all of which ended up as a flat contradiction of the whole philosophy of the course. People were baffled by this sudden outbreak by the president, and there was a certain amount of confusion about it. The participants realized that here were two exponents of two different philosophies. . . .

Here is the president's version of that fateful day:

> They were discussing group relations, I guess. They were sitting in a circle; they would be silent for awhile, and then they would

ask: "What is your impression of me, and what do others make of me? And I'd like to tell you what I think of you, Jane, or you, Jim." Then there would be silence, long silence, and the pressure and tension would steadily mount; then it would explode and everyone would start talking at once about impressions people had of each other. They would "give feedback," they said. I don't know, I suppose that one can learn a lot about how one feels and sees, but I did not think that this kind of discussion was crucial for management training. Matter of fact, some of it seemed like communism to me; they've gone too far for me, too revolutionary!

IV.   Propositions about the uses of Lab Training in effecting social change

We have attempted to present the risks and promises of engineering social change in target systems via Lab Training. The three cases of "failure," because of their dramatic aspects, should not blind us to the fact that these are the exception, not the rule. On the other hand, abnormal as these three cases may be, it would be a mistake to regard them only for their pathological interest. In fact, what we would like to do now is consider both the successes and the failures and develop propositions about social change which are related to, and clearly built upon, Section II of the chapter.*

1   *In undertaking any planned social change using Lab Training, the core of the target system's values must not be too discrepant with the Lab Training values*   Every target system has a core of values which characterizes it and which determines a good deal of its decisions. Lab Training, also, implies a system of core values. We discussed these earlier in terms of legitimacy of interpersonal phenomena, concepts of control, etc. We stated then that the target system's values should be somewhat in accord, or *potentially* congruent, with Lab Training values. Where the two systems of values are widely discrepant and rigid, and where the value system of the target cannot yield without vitally endangering the target system's core values, then change induced by Lab Training will probably not succeed.

Let us be specific. In the case of the government training center and the department store, it is obvious that the institutional base was perceived—by men in power—as seriously threatened. The values, the

---

* Please bear in mind that these principles can encompass *any* planned social change, not only changes directed by Lab Training.

normative patterns, and the set of shared expectations were all in flux because of the training endeavors of Dr. A and Mr. Jones.

Perhaps the central issue here concerns the definition of "training." Webster defines it as follows: "1. To subject oneself or to be subjected to instruction, drilling, regular exercise, dieting, etc. 2. To form habits or impart proficiency by teaching, drilling, etc." Most "training" affirms these definitions; that is, training is a process whereby individuals learn the skills, attitudes, and orientation congruent to a particular role. Training, viewed in this way, has a conservative connotation. It takes organizations as they are and attempts to shape individuals to them.

What we have been calling "training" is probably misnamed. For certainly a program which aims to change the very structure of the organization through modifying a role orientation* is not training in the usual sense of the word. This is not only a semantic issue. Training, in its dictionary sense and in the sense in which most personnel managers use it and in which top management construes it, is viewed conservatively: fitting people to roles. Training in the sense in which it was employed in these cases signifies a *fundamental* change: an alteration of the values, norms, and patterns of expectations. In this sense President Hess was completely correct in viewing Lab Training as "revolutionary," and Mr. Z was perfectly justified in going slow on Lab Training at the military base. Lab training was revolutionary to the extent that the core of institutional values they (the leaders) were striving to preserve was basically threatened by the Lab Training change programs.

Putting it a bit differently, most organizations agree to various training and development programs insofar as they strengthen the core of institutional values and insofar as they facilitate the functioning of the organization. When programs are seen as imperiling the institutional base, we can expect the strong resistance evinced in these cases.

But most social-change programs, certainly Lab Training, attempt to alter institutional values. How, then, can the inevitable and powerful resistance be reduced?

2 *In undertaking any planned social change, legitimacy for the*

---

* The values of Lab Training we outlined earlier such as "openness," "authenticity," and "collaboration" signify certain orientations toward role; contrast these role expectations with President Hess's expectations.

change must be gained through obtaining the support of the key people This is not to say that Lab Training should start at the top; it does mean that a careful and deliberate effort must be made to gain acceptance by the top management group. Without this, Lab Training is constantly in peril. Notice what happened when Mr. B (the top line official in the government center supporting Lab Training) was transferred: the program came apart at the seams. If Mr. B's successor had been well briefed and oriented and if Mr. Z had been briefed and oriented, then the program may have had more resilience to shock. The same is true regarding the department store case: nobody really seemed to know "what was up" except possibly Jones. And if the vice-president of personnel had been able to tell President Hess what was really going on at Marlboro, it might not have been necessary for him to make the surprise trip.

In any case, efforts must be made to provide top management with as clear and realistic picture of Lab Training as possible. This is done not only as an acquaintance process but also to test top management's commitment to the potential changes. If the commitment is weak at the top level, then a total reevaluation of the strategy is required. It is far better to discover this early, rather than late. In the case of the department store, partly out of fear and mostly from futility, the training staff worked surreptitiously, with the faint hope that the training effects would be accepted. The outcome produced an unstable situation where the lowest levels of management maintained values that were in conflict with those of top management. The tension created by this value conflict was reduced by removing its source, Jones, and restoring the old orientation.

Obtaining hierarchical acceptance, no matter how painstaking and difficult, provides at least some guarantee that management can understand, and hence manage, the change without undue tension.

3 *In undertaking any planned social change, the process of installing the change programs must be congruent with the process and goals of such programs* We are talking here of a fairly simple, but crucial, matter. The change-agent should know what he is doing and should act congruently and authentically. While we are not absolutely confident of this proposition holding in every situation (installing a totalitarian system, for example), we are sure that this is essential for a democratic change program. For reasons that appeared sensible at the time, Jones operated more as an "undercover" agent than as

an agent of change. It is doubtful that he understood the consequences of his decisions: the fact that he viewed Lab Training as a simple substitute for the case method gives rise to this question: Were the goals and meta-goals of Lab Training clearly understood by the change-agents?

It is not obvious that they were understood. Jones, in particular, violated to some degree the *meta*-goals: authenticity was abandoned by the underground methods used to start the program; action was taken without a "spirit of inquiry"; and the nature of the change program was far from a collaborative one. The way Dr. A dealt with Mr. Z and the way Mr. Jones dealt with President Hess were not examples of "authentic and collaborative" relationships.

Unanticipated consequences can jeopardize any change program—only the omniscient can be blamed for those. But in the case of the department store, many of the consequences could have been foreseen and avoided—if Jones himself had used the processes of Lab Training in installing the change program. What we observed instead was the blind use of a "tool" in a way which contradicted its essence.

4 *In undertaking any planned social change, the employment security of the change-agent must be guaranteed* Blau[17] points out that one of the prerequisites for adaptation in bureaucracy is the minimum employment security of the personnel. In terms of the brute reality of existence, this means that most people would not risk their jobs in order to create change. Given the Lab Training approach to organizational change, minimum employment security is essential for the change-agent, particularly if he is a member of the organization. The training staff must maintain their separateness from other company employees and must develop some discretion and autonomy insofar as training functions are concerned.

For Jones there was no real alternative but to let the president "sit in"; it was either that or dismissal. If a situation similar to that one occurred where the trainer had maximum employment security or was an outside consultant, employed temporarily by the company, possibly there would have been a different outcome.

5 *In undertaking any planned social change utilizing Lab Training, the voluntary commitment of the participants may be a crucial factor in the success of the program* We have discussed this at some length earlier. But for emphasis we repeat that the difficulty of de-

scribing Lab Training through verbal orientation, plus the problematical aspects of organizational legitimacy to influence interpersonal behavior, leads to only one conclusion with respect to participant attend-
ance at labs. This is that all delegates must undertake Lab Training
in a completely voluntary spirit. It is highly doubtful that they will
learn if this condition does not prevail.

6 *In undertaking any planned social change utilizing Lab Training, the legitimacy of interpersonal influence must be potentially acceptable* The spread and belief of the "striptease" rumor shows,
if anything, the desirability of an orientation for prospective
participants. But it shows more than that. We must ask: How much
and in what way can (should?) an organization influence the personalities of its employees? It is not exactly obvious that interpersonal
competence is correlated with effective role functioning; in fact, in
some specific situations, there may be no, or an inverse, correlation.
Indeed, the theoretical foundations of bureaucracy are based on *impersonality.* And even with the modern role conception of the modern
manager—which includes social-system management and responsibility—the prevailing norms of legitimacy of organizational influence
must be explored and understood fully by the target system.

7 *In undertaking any planned social change, the effects on the
adjacent and interdependent subsystems relating to the target system
must be carefully considered* All three cases demonstrate this principle, but perhaps none so dramatically as the letter from medical
services. Here we see so clearly how the reverberations and repercussions of Lab Training come back to haunt its creators unless the
shock can be absorbed by their neighboring units. In this case, the
company doctors could have easily absorbed the shock (as they later
did, after an orientation session) if they had been simply informed
about, and involved in, Lab Training. They were irked by being ignored and were disturbed by perceived encroachment of their authority.

But whether it is "doctors" or "headquarters" or "colleagues" or
"bosses," a complete diagnosis of the total effects—on all relevant
parts—must be made before—not after—the training starts.

8 *In undertaking any planned social change, the state of cultural
readiness must be assessed* We emphasized this in the preceding section in terms of the internal state of the target system. Here we mean
more than that. We have in mind the relationship between the organ-

ization and the wider society within which the target system is embedded. It would appear that Mr. Jones (and Dr. A, to some extent) failed to comprehend completely the normative structure he was attempting to alter. The values of President Hess were known well in advance of the training failure, and he reflected the German populist values of the farming communities his stores prospered in.

Cultural readiness, then, depends to some degree on the normative structure of the wider society; a clear diagnosis cannot be made without understanding these forces.

The preceding eight principles provide only a partial view of the complex elements that enter into social change. This complexity, along with the drama of the failures, probably tends to make social change seem more hazardous than it need be. If we have tended to highlight the dilemmas and risks, we do this with the hope that the recognition of these choice points in installing and maintaining similar change programs will enhance their effectiveness.

Ultimately, we believe, the forces for change in the direction of Lab Training's stated goals will gather more and more momentum in our society. There is some evidence for this already. But there are other environmental forces at work as well which portend even further acceleration of democratic processes. First there is a rapid rate of technological change, and second there is a rapid infusion of professionals into organizations. These circumstances represent two of the most important factors in the outlook for change. And Lab Training, with its particular set of change goals, may provide an important instrument for building organizations where effective collaboration and adaptation can take place.

NOTES

1. Schein, E. H., and W. G. Bennis, *Personal and Organizational Change through Group Methods,* John Wiley & Sons, Inc., New York, 1965.
2. Bradford, L. P., J. R. Gibb, and K. D. Benne, *T-group Theory and Laboratory Method,* John Wiley & Sons, Inc., New York, 1964.
3. *An Action Research Program for Organization Improvement,* Foundation for Research on Human Behavior, Ann Arbor, Mich., 1960.
4. Bennis, W. G., "A New Role for the Behavioral Sciences: Effecting Organizational Change," *Administrative Science Quarterly,* vol. 8, no. 2, pp. 125–165, 1963.
5. Likert, R., *New Patterns of Management,* McGraw-Hill Book Company, New York, 1961.

6. McGregor, D., *The Human Side of Enterprise,* McGraw-Hill Book Company, New York, 1960.

7. Lewin, K., "Group Decision and Social Change," in T. Newcomb, and E. Hartley (eds.), *Readings in Social Psychology,* Holt, Rinehart and Winston, Inc., New York, 1947.

8. Allport, G., "The Psychology of Participation," in G. Allport, *Personality and Social Encounter,* Beacon Press, Boston, 1960.

9. Argyris, C., *Interpersonal Competence and Organizational Effectiveness,* Dorsey Press, Homewood, Ill., 1962.

10. Bennis, *op. cit.*

11. Lippitt, R., J. Watson, and B. Westley, *Dynamics of Planned Change,* Harcourt, Brace & World, Inc., New York, 1961.

12. Seashore, C., and E. Van Egmond, "The Consultant-Trainer Role in Working Directly with a Total Staff," *The Journal of Social Issues,* vol. 15, pp. 36–42, 1959.

13. Argyris, *op. cit.*

14. Bavelas, A., and G. Strauss, "Group Dynamics and Intergroup Relations," in W. F. Whyte et al. (eds.), *Money and Motivation,* Harper & Row, Publishers, Incorporated, New York, 1955, pp. 90–96.

15. Argyris, *op. cit.*

16. Blansfield, M. G., "Depth Analysis of Organizational Life," *California Management Review,* pp. 29–42, Winter, 1962.

17. Blau, P., "The Dynamics of Bureaucracy," in A. Etzioni (ed.), *Complex Organizations,* Holt, Rinehart and Winston, Inc., New York, 1961, pp. 343–355.

9

*some questions and
generalizations about
planned organizational change*

POWER AND THE ROLE OF THE CHANGE-AGENT

I have been interested for some time in the age-old question of how and why people are influenced. In the various planned-change programs discussed, the question becomes even more intriguing: How and why do people and organizations change in the direction prescribed? Assuming for the moment that they do improve—change—let us try to examine the role of the change-agent in exerting this influence.

Most behavioral scientists agree that power is the ability to influence; so, in effect, power is an independent variable which leads to *influence*, the dependent variable. There is still further agreement and happily some evidence, that power consists of at least five components; that is, if these components are held by A, they can lead to the influence of B, other things being equal. They are:

1   *Coercive power,* or the ability of A to reward and/or punish B
2   *Referent, or, identification power,* or the influence which accrues
    to A because he (or the group) is attractive, a person whom B
    wants to like and be liked by—in short, a role model
3   *Expert power,* or the power that we associate with science and
    "truth"
4   *Legitimate* or *traditional* power, or, power which stems from insti-
    tutional norms and practices and from historical-legal traditions
5   *Value power,* or influence which is gained on the basis of attraction
    to the values of A

Which of these five sources of power does the change-agent
possess? In fact, this is a question we have to guess at and make
some inferences about because the change-agents themselves tend to
ignore (or are silent about) the sources of their own influence. It
is not coercive power, for we can guess with some confidence that
unless the change-agent is himself a manager or an influential member
of the organization, he does not possess the means to exert coercive
power. In fact, most change-agents are external to the organization
and do not hold any formal title. More to the point, the change-agents
discussed in this chapter would prefer, at least intellectually, not to
wield coercive power, whether or not they in fact possessed it. This
is true for at least two reasons. First, coercive power appears to be
at variance with their normative goals and values, and second, there
is some evidence that coercive power is not as durable as others except
under conditions of vigilant surveillance over the influenced.[1]

Traditional power? Almost certainly not. The change-agents are,
in fact, continually working without legitimization.* Quite often, they
are perceived as odd men out, as strangers, as quite marginal to the
enterprise (or as "committed nuts," according to one manager). So
little influence redounds to them on the basis of traditional norms
and precedent.

Expert power? Possibly some, but it is not obvious that the
change-agent is perceived as a source of really "useful" knowledge.
True, in varying degrees, he does possess useful information about
the human side of the enterprise and about methods of investigating
these phenomena. But it is doubtful that this type of knowledge is

---

* There are exceptions to this, when line managers act as change-agents.
See Chap. 8 for instances of this.

considered "expert" enough—in the sense that an engineer or doctor or lawyer is seen as a source of expertise.

Referent or identification power? Apparently so. Some change-agents, like Sofer, talk directly to the point and attribute some indefinite amount of their influence to the client-system's ability and desire to emulate the change-agent. Still, members will probably identify with the change-agent in different degrees; some, perhaps, will not identify at all. By itself, it would appear that identification or referent power would have to work in concert with another source of power.

So that leaves us with value power, and while I cannot prove it, the most likely candidate, it seems, of the possible sources of power would be this one, the ability to influence through representing and transmitting values which are admired and desired by the client-system. Most of the change-agents in their work do embody a set of values which are certainly communicated to the client-system verbally or otherwise. Argyris makes his own value position very clear, and most of the other change-agents tend to emit cues of one kind or another which provide a consistent value system. These values are based on Western civilization's notion of a scientific humanism: concern for our fellow man, experimentalism, openness and honesty, flexibility, cooperation, and democracy.

If what I have said about power is correct, it is significant (at least in the United States) that this set of values seems to be extremely potent in influencing top management circles.

CHARACTERISTICS OF CLIENT-SYSTEMS

Are there any particular characteristics of client-systems which seek planned change? Mostly, they appear to be subsystems of relatively large-scale international operations in increasingly competitive situations. Also, they are almost always found in rapidly changing environments. They are subjected to what Johnson called "galloping variables," not comfortable and stable conditions. Quite often, it appears the enterprise was founded, developed, and succeeded through a particular innovation or monopolistic advantage which is thought to be in jeopardy. In any case, the type of client-system most typically looking for organizational change programs seems to be eminently suited for an organic form of organization *à la* Burns and Stalker.[2]

Third, there is always some exigency, dissatisfaction, tension, dilemma, or crisis—some discrepancy between the ideal and actual—confronting the organization, which seems to activate the program. It may emanate from the rapidly changing environment or from the internal processes within the system. Fear of survival or problems connected with growth may force change upon management. Some of the exigency states which have initiated planned-change programs were discussed in a recent seminar on organizational improvement sponsored in July, 1964, by the Foundation for Research on Human Behavior. Seen as causing the change programs were the following: employee cutbacks and various retrenchment measures, a merger, significant growth and high rates of change, worsening of the competitive situation, new departures, union-management conflicts and strikes, leadership succession, lack of sufficient management personnel, and a failing product. These problems give some idea of the general range of problems confronting client-systems.

One last characteristic of client-systems should be mentioned: all of them put some faith in the idea that an intermediate proportion of their effectiveness is determined by social and psychological factors. Improvements in this sphere of action, they reason, no matter how vague or immeasurable, may be able to bring about an increment of organizational effectiveness.

THE MEASUREMENT OF EFFECTS

Until very recently change-agents, if they did any evaluation research at all, concentrated almost exclusively on attitudinal and subjective factors. Even so-called hard behavioral variables, such as absentee rates, sickness and accident rates, personnel turnover, etc., were rarely investigated. Relating change programs to harder criteria, such as productivity and economic and cost factors, was rarely attempted and was never, to my knowledge, successful.

And again, the research that was conducted—even on the attitudinal measures—was far from conclusive. Roger Harrison attempted an evaluation study of Argyris's work and found that while there was a significant improvement in the individual executive's interpersonal ability compared with that of a control group, there was no significant "transfer" of this acuity to the real-life organizational setting. In short, there was a fairly rapid "fade-out" of effects obtained in T-group training upon return to the organization.[3] This study also shows that new tensions were generated between those individuals who attended the training program and those who did not, an example of the lack of a *systems* approach, which I mentioned early in the chapter. Shepard's evaluation of the Esso organization shows that the impact of laboratory training was greatest on personal and interpersonal learnings but that it was "slightly more helpful than useless" in changing the organization.[4]

More recently, though some studies have been undertaken which measure more meaningful, less subjective criterion variables of organizational effectiveness. Blake, Mouton, Barnes, and Greiner conducted an evaluation study of their work in a very large (4,000 employees) petrochemical plant. They found not only significant changes in the values, morale, and interpersonal behavior of the employees but also significant improvements in productivity, profits, and cost reduction.[5] David, a change-agent working on a program that attempts to facilitate a large and complicated merger, attributed the following effects to the programs: increased productivity, reduced turnover and absenteeism, and a significant improvement in the area of attitudes and subjective feelings.[6,*]

While these new research approaches show genuine promise, much more has to be done. The research effort has somehow to equal all the energy that goes into developing the planned-change programs themselves.

SOME CRITICISMS AND QUALIFICATIONS OF PLANNED ORGANIZATIONAL CHANGE

The work and direction of the change-agents reported here are new and occur, for better or worse, without the benefit of methodological and strategic precedents. The role of the change-agent is also new and still settling; its final shape has not fully emerged. So it has the advantage of freedom from the constraints and pressures facing most men of knowledge, and at the same time, it suffers from lack of guidelines and structure. With this as a background, let us touch quickly on some problems and criticisms which I see as facing the change-agents in the years to come.

* A staff from the University of Michigan, including Dr. S. Seashore and D. Bowers, conducted the research and operated independently of the change-agent.

Relationship to Other Social Theories of Change

The closest approximation to a theory of change is the systems model of Blake and Mouton. And again, this is a theory of change, not a theory of changing. Their methods of change seem to be largely—and justifiably—engineering models, heavy on techniques and methods of change, but less strong on a theory of change. Though they cite esteemed sources, such as Freud and Lewin, they do not really figure in their models of change. Blake states this most forcibly: "The behavioral sciences have accomplished little of systematic character in the direction of achieving change in situations of organized human activity."[7]

So they write, perhaps inevitably, as "theoretical orphans" developing, on occasion, some autonomous verbalizations and rarely linking their ideas with theories of personal and social change.

Neglect of Problem-solving Models

All the approaches mentioned here tend to emphasize interpersonal and group factors as causal variables in blocking problem-solving activities and tend to deemphasize the cognitive processes of problem solving.

Planned Change and Organizational Effectiveness

What criteria of organizational effectiveness are change-agents attempting to optimize? I can identify six dimensions of organizational effectiveness: legal, political, economic, technological, social, and personal. Which of these do change-agents hope to affect? There is a good deal of fuzziness on this issue, and the data are inconclusive. Argyris, who is the most explicit about the relationship between performance and interpersonal competence, is still hoping to develop good measures to establish a positive relationship. The connection has to be made, or the field will have to change its normative goal, which is to construct not only a *better* world but a more *effective* one.

A Question of Values

It is not all obvious to me that the types of changes induced by the change-agents are (1) compatible with "human nature" or in accord with "findings from the behavioral sciences," as some change-agents assert; (2) desirable, even if they are in tune with man's need structure; or (3) functional.

These new values which are espoused indicate a certain way of *behaving* and *feeling;* for example, they emphasize openness rather than secrecy, superior-subordinate collaboration rather than dependence or rebellion, cooperation rather than competition, consensus rather than individual rule, rewards based on self-control rather than externally induced rewards, team leadership rather than a one-to-one relationship with the boss, authentic relationships rather than those based on political maneuverings, and so on.

Are they natural, desirable, or functional? What then happens to status or power drives? What about those individuals who have a low need for participation and/or a high need for structure and dependence?[8] And what about those personal needs which seem to be incompatible with these images of man, such as a high need for aggression and a low need for affiliation? In short, what about those needs which can be expressed and best realized through bureaucratic systems or benevolent autocracies? Are these individuals expected to be changed through some transformation of needs, or are they expected to yield and comply to a concept of human nature incompatible with their own needs?

This problem of values is an important one and deserves thorough discussion. One of the problems in holding such a discussion is the emotional and value overtones which interfere with rational dialogue. This is exacerbated by a particularly unfortunate way advocates and antagonists phrase the argument. More often than not, one is plunged into a polarized, black-and-white debate which converts ideas into ideology and inquiry into dogma. So we hear of "theory X versus theory Y," personality versus organization, people versus pyramids, participation versus great men, democratic versus autocratic, task versus maintenance, achievement versus socialization, hard versus soft, human relations versus scientific management, external versus internal, and on and on.

Surely life is more complicated than these paired dualities suggest, and surely these dualities must imply a *continuum*—not only extremes—along which different points seem appropriate, given certain criteria to be optimized.*

---

* Burns and Stalker deserve my gratitude for stressing over and over again the importance of appropriateness of management work systems under differing conditions.

Lack of Systems Approach

Up to this point, I have used the phrase "organizational change" rather loosely. In Argyris's case, for example, organizational change refers to a change in values of eleven top executives, a change which was not necessarily of an enduring kind and which apparently brought about some conflict with other interfaces. In most other cases of planned organizational change, the change induction was limited to a small, elite group. Only in the work of Blake is organizational change discussed confidently—in a systems way; his program includes the training of the entire management organization, and at several locations he has carried this step to include wage earners.

Sometimes the change brought about simply "fade out" because there are no carefully worked out procedures to ensure coordination with other interacting parts of the system. In other cases, the changes have "backfired" and have had to be terminated because of their conflict with interface units.[9] In any case, a good deal more has to be learned about the interlocking and stabilizing changes so that the total system is affected.

PLANNED ORGANIZATIONAL CHANGE: IN CONCLUSION

Now that I have discussed in some detail the background, elements, and processes of planned organizational change and placed it in its perspective as a special case of the utilization of social knowledge, it may be useful, both as peroration and conclusion, to make, in the most tentative manner, some generalizations. For the most part they are derived from, or implied in, the foregoing discussion and are anchored in experience and, wherever possible, in research and theory.

First, as I said in Chapter 1, I suspect that we shall see an increase in the number of planned-change programs along the lines discussed in this chapter: toward *less* bureaucratic and *more* participative, "open-system," and adaptive structures. This prophecy is based on a number of factors, the most important of which is the *rate* of change confronting organizations today. Given that pronounced rate of change, the growing reliance on science for the success of the industrial enterprise, the growing number of professionals joining these enterprises, and the "turbulent contextual environment" facing the firm, we can expect more and more demand for social inventions to supplement and revise significantly our traditional notions of organized effort.

As far as adoption and acceptance are concerned, we already know a good deal.* Before any change of a consequential human kind can be accepted and adopted, the *type* of change should be of proved quality, easily demonstrable in its effects, and with information easily available. Its cost and accessibility to control by the client-system as well as its value accord have to be carefully considered.

Acceptance also depends on the relationship between the change-agent and the client-system: the more profound and anxiety-producing the change, the more a collaborative and closer relationship is required. In addition, we can predict that an anticipated change will be resisted to the degree that the client-system possesses little or incorrect knowledge about the change, has relatively little trust in the source of the change, and has relatively low influence in controlling the nature and direction of the change.

What we know least about—and what continually vexes those of us who are vitally concerned with the effective utilization of knowledge—is *implementation*.[12] As I use the term, "implementation" encompasses a process which includes the creation in a client-system of understanding of, and commitment to, a particular change which can solve problems, and devices whereby it can become integral to the client-system's operations. It bears to organizational theory the same relationship that the term "internalization" does to personality theory; i.e., it is a process which leads to automatic self-generation and integral functioning.

When it comes to implementation of organizational changes, most practitioners seem to overemphasize the importance of intellectual *understanding* or the *informational* status of the intended change. Now, as I have said, information and understanding are necessary but not sufficient components for inducing change. More is required *if* the change is to affect important human responses. For human changes are bound up in self-image and its maintenance and the complicated context of the social life and groupings which help to define and give meaning to the individual's existence. If intended change is perceived to threaten (or enhance) the self-image, then we can expect differential effects. If an intended change is perceived as threatening the

* See, in particular, Rogers[10] and Miles[11]

social life space of the individual, then safeguards must be undertaken which ensure new forms of gratification and evaluation.

In short, I am saying that human changes affect not only the individual but also the social fabric and norms from which he gains his evaluation and definition of self. It means, quite probably, that thinking solely about the *individual's understanding* of the change and its consequences is not enough.

From this vantage point, I shall try to summarize the necessary elements in implementation:

1 The *client-system* should have as much understanding of the change and its consequences, as much influence in developing and controlling the fate of the change, and as much trust in the initiator of the change as possible.

2 The *change effort* should be perceived as being as self-motivated and voluntary as possible. This can be done through the legitimization and reinforcement of the change by the top management group as well as by the significant reference groups adjacent to the client-system. This can also be done by providing as much true volition as possible.

3 The *change program* must include emotional and value as well as cognitive (informational) elements for successful implementation. It is doubtful that relying solely on rational persuasion (expert power) is sufficient. Too often, rational elements are denied or rendered impotent because they conflict with a strongly ingrained belief, consciously or unconsciously held. Intellectual commitment is a first step, but not a guarantee to action. Most organizations know what ails them or what could help them; the problem is utilization.

4 The *change-agent* can be crucial in reducing the resistance to change by providing consultation and psychological support during the transitional phase of the change. As I have stressed over and over again, the quality of the relationship is pivotal to the success of the change program. As long as the change-agent acts congruently with the principles of the program and as long as the client-system has a chance to test his competence and motives (his own and the change-agent's), he should be able to provide the support so necessary during the risky phases of change.

As I stated in the Introduction, the forces for change in democratic and scientific directions (and implemented via Lab Training) will gather more and more momentum. There is growing evidence for this already. In addition, there are some powerful environmental forces at work which will accelerate these tendencies. The impact of science and technology; a population of educated, urban adults; the speed of modern communication media; and all those factors associated with the modernization of society are challenging our accepted patterns of life. New methodologies and rules will have to be invented to cope with these changes, not the least of which will be some creative systems of collaboration. As I said in Chapter 1, it will not necessarily be a happy life for those caught up in these changes. But it should be exciting, at least for those who can feel exuberant about the abrasive challenge of the adaptive process and a creative joy from inventing new ways to deal with the constant image of social change.

NOTES

1. French, J. R. P., and B. Raven, "The Bases of Social Power," in D. Cartwright (ed.), *Studies in Social Power,* University of Michigan Press, Ann Arbor, Mich., 1959, pp. 150–167; Kelman, H. C., "Compliance, Identification and Internalization: Three Processes of Attitude Change," *Journal of Conflict Resolution,* vol. 2, pp. 51–60, 1958.

2. Burns, T., and G. M. Stalker, *The Management of Innovation,* Quadrangle, Chicago, 1962.

3. Harrison, R., in C. Argyris, *Interpersonal Competence and Organizational Effectiveness,* Dorsey Press, Homewood, Ill., 1962, chap. 11.

4. *An Action Research Program for Organization Development,* Foundation for Research on Human Behavior, Ann Arbor, Mich., p. 31.

5. Blake, R. R., J. S. Mouton, L. B. Barnes, and L. E. Greiner, "A Managerial Grid Approach to Organization Development: The Theory and Some Research Findings," *Harvard Business Review,* vol. 42, 1964.

6. David, G., "The Weldon Study: An Organization Change Program Based upon Change in Management Philosophy," in D. Zand and P. Buchanan (eds.), *Organization Development: Theory and Practice,* in press.

7. Blake, R. R., and J. S. Mouton, *The Induction of Change in Industrial Organizations,* Scientific Methods, Inc., Austin, Tex., 1962.

8. Vroom, V., *Some Personality Determinants of the Effects of Participation,* Prentice-Hall, Inc., Englewood Cliffs, N.J., 1960.

9. Jenks, R. S., "The Business-within-a-Business," in Zand and Buchanan, *op. cit.;* Schein, E. H., and W. G. Bennis, *Personal and Organization Change*

through Group Methods, John Wiley & Sons, Inc., New York, 1965, and Chapters 8 and 10 of this book.

10. Rogers, E. M., *Diffusion of Innovations*, The Free Press of Glencoe, New York, 1962.

11. Miles, M. B. (ed.), *Innovation in Education*, Bureau of Publications, Teachers College, Columbia University, New York, 1964.

12. Churchman, C. W., and P. Ratoosh, *Innovation in Group Behavior*, Institute of Industrial Relations, University of California, Berkeley, Calif., 1960; Churchman, C. W., and A. H. Schainblatt, "The Researcher and the Manager: A Dialectic of Implementation," Center for Research in Management Science, Working Paper 102, University of California, Berkeley, Calif., October, 1964.

epilogue

In this last essay, I trace the parallel developments of the behavioral sciences and their role in changing organizations. I try to show how organizations of the future will demand greater resources on the part of management and deeper understanding on the part of the behavioral sciences if the enterprise is to cope effectively with its turbulent internal and external environments. Twentieth-century tasks cannot be managed with a nineteenth-century social organization; and the tasks ahead for modern management are formidable. The manager of the future will have to develop extraordinary interpersonal and technical skills, positive attitudes toward change and inquiry, and, most of all, a deep sense of integrity in order for him to deal effectively with the staggering demands of the enterprise.

I have identified the major tasks in this essay and have pinpointed certain research areas and developmental programs that seem necessary to help the manager in a changing world.

behavioral sciences perspective in organizational studies*

The behavioral sciences have made stunning progress in management education. In less than one decade, they have not only infiltrated the field, they have secured a firm foothold in all the leading centers of management studies. Along with two other intellectual developments, economics and the newer quantitative methods, the behavioral sciences have literally transformed management education and research, and they are currently challenging management's natural and penultimate target, management practice.

No boast is intended—for you will see later on that there is a wide gap between present achievement and potential significance—but I wish to point out that blazing advances have been made in the areas of management education and research during the last ten years. In the mid-1950s, before the influential Ford and Car-

* Presented at the Seminar on Behavioral Sciences in Management Education, Indian Institute of Management, Calcutta, August 2–5, 1965.

negie reports on the state of management education were published, management education was in the same state or "fix" as medical education was at the time of the Flexner report in 1910—that is to say, deplorable. In American universities—the less said about European universities, the better—business education, where it did exist, was disreputable, non- or antiscientific. It provided a haven for fools, adventurers, and anemic heirs of industrialists who needed a college degree on the minimum of brains and the maximum of tuition, and it was taught as conventional wisdom cum moral uplift by successful, and hopefully, inspirational practitioners. Business education ranked in the academic hierarchy somewhere between football and a curiously indigenous American course known colloquially as "home economics," a curriculum cocktail of cooking, etiquette, and good housekeeping.

Outside of the United States, the status of management education was even more disreputable, if possible. It was unknown to or snubbed by the academic establishment. It was at best regarded with dark suspicion, as if contact with the world of reality, particularly monetary realities, was equivalent to a dreadful form of pollution. The university seemed intent to preserve the monastic ethos of its medieval origins, offering a false but lulling security to its inmates and stripping the curriculum of virility and relevance. Max Beerbohm's whimsical and idyllic fantasy of Oxford, *Zuleika Dobson*, dramatizes this:

> It is this mild, miasmal air, not less than the grey beauty and the gravity of the buildings that has helped Oxford to produce, and foster, eternally, her peculiar race of artist-scholars, scholars-artists . . . The buildings and their traditions keep astir in his mind whatsoever is gracious; the climate enfolding and enfeebling him, lulling him, keeps him careless of the sharp, harsh exigent realities of the outer world. These realities may be seen by him . . . But they cannot fire him. Oxford is too damp for that . . . Oxford, that lotus land, saps the will-power, the power of action. But in doing so, it clarifies the mind, makes larger the vision, gives, above all, that playful and caressing suavity of manner which comes from the conviction that nothing matters, except ideas.

"Adorable dreamer," said Matthew Arnold, in his valedictory to Oxford: "Adorable dreamer, whose heart has been so romantic! who has given thyself so prodigally, given thyself to sides and to heroes not mine, only never to the Philistine! . . . What teacher could ever so save us from that bondage to which we are all prone . . . the bondage of what binds us all, the narrow, the mundane, the merely practical."

So as the university withdrew behind its comforting walls and aristocratic stuffiness, narrowed its vision and widened its endowment, a parochial form of vocationalism did develop, *outside* the university compound, to handle the needs of the Industrial Revolution and the "merely practical." These were the jerry-built schools of bookkeeping, stenography, and office management, relics of which can still be seen in dark and deserted city streets, atop shabby second-story office buildings, adjacent to the Salvation Army and other symbols of poverty and destitution.

If I dramatize, I do not mean to exaggerate. The intellectual and the practitioner have only recently come out of purdah and recognized the enormous possibilities of joint ventures. Remember that the idea of the professional school is new, even in the case of the venerable threesome: law, medicine, and engineering, to say nothing of the recent upstarts, management, public administration, social service. The professional school is as new as the institutionalization of science itself, say around fifty years old at the most. And even today, it is not greeted with unmixed joy. Colin Clark, writing in a recent issue of *Encounter*,[1] referred to "the dreadful suggestion that Oxford ought to have a 'Business School.'" And yet this newness and lack of tradition is not an altogether bad thing, for in most of the world, excluding the United States, there is no tradition of shoddy management education to live down.

Today the situation is so different from the past that management school faculties can blush, like some modern Icarus, not because they can fly so much higher than their predecessors, but because they sprang from such humble origins. Today management education is respectable, rigorous, and rich, and even the stodgy and the traditional are less wistful and restive for conventional disciplines and scholarship. Aside from the Harvard Business School and the Wharton School, which for many years were the two lonely bastions of respectability in management education, most first-rate universities today include a strong, growing, and vital school or department of management. In a number of universities, such as M.I.T., Yale, Carnegie Tech, Chicago, Purdue, UCLA, Stanford and Columbia, to mention some of the leading institutions, not only is the Ph.D. awarded in management, but the research activity is vigorous and the students and faculty are as creative and bold as are found anywhere in the academy.

Today, there is an economic entity called by Fritz Machlup the "knowledge industry," which accounts, he claims, for over 29 per cent of the GNP. Clark Kerr, in his now famous Godkin lectures, said: "What the railroads did for the second half of the last century and the automobile did for the first half of this century may be done for the second half of this century by the knowledge industry: that is, to serve as the focal point of national growth. And the university is at the centre of the knowledge process."[2]

FACTORS BEHIND THE GROWTH OF THE BEHAVIORAL SCIENCES IN ORGANIZATIONAL STUDIES

Most behavioral scientists start off their careers demanding checks against abuses of Ford and Rockefeller power but secure their careers drawing checks on Ford and Rockefeller Foundations. I am haunted by the fantasy of Henry, John D., and Russell Sage, regarding with horror the new look in management education for which they are to such a large extent responsible.

But behavioral science does not live on bread alone, and these financial infusions, while necessary, have not been conclusive. The behavioral sciences gathered momentum for the reason any science does: because conventional wisdom and practice failed to work. And conventional wisdom began faltering when a number of changes in our society began to affect the basic character of human organization. I am referring here to changes in scale and complexity in modern organizations, to the rate of technological change, the rise of trade-unionism, the growth of the human sciences, the separation of property from power, the influx of professionals into large-scale organizations, the increase of the general educational level and aspirations of workers, and a shift in the value-systems of the world community toward humanitarianism, science, and democracy. These changes, un-reflected in the traditional form of organization known as bureaucracy, were reflected nevertheless in the palpable inadequacy of leadership styles and managerial assumptions about human behavior. In short, the men conducting the enterprise, the managers, were basing their predictions on incomplete and skewed data, a mechanistic and de-personalized view of man, and late Victorian cum Darwinian ideals of Empire. The last three decades of research and practice in the behavioral sciences have been one long casualty list of threatened assumptions and myopic practices on the human side of the enterprise.

For example, the following ideas, no longer startling, perhaps too obvious have toppled the foundations of theory and practice:

• Man does not react solely on the basis of economic gain.

• Man has a hierarchy of needs which change over time toward social and self-actualization and away from basic physical-economic needs. Quite often, management does not recognize this and hence incentives may be off-target and/or inappropriate.

• Man reacts in unanticipated ways to different forms of leadership.

• Man's interpersonal relationships are important, have regularities, are real in their effects, and cannot be subsumed or understood through conventional theory.

• Interpersonal relationships affect organizational effectiveness.

• Interpersonal relationships cannot be outlawed or ignored. If they are, they go underground and turn up in the damnedest places.

• Groups can establish and enforce norms on their membership. These norms may or may not be congruent with management goals.

• Morale is a complex of variables and not necessarily correlated to productivity.

• Communication gets distorted, particularly as it goes up the hierarchy. Subordinates who hold views at variance with their superiors tend to withdraw or suppress their point of view, allowing their superiors to make mistakes even when they "know better."

• The validity and frequency of upward communication appears to be dependent upon the degree of interpersonal trust between superior and subordinate, the degree of power held by the subordinate, and the degree of the subordinate's ambition. None of these factors is taken into account explicitly in the theory and practice of bureaucracy.

• The formal organizational chart only rarely, if ever, resembles the power structure.

• Bureaucratic theory and practice do not possess adequate means for resolving conflict between ranks and between functional groups.

• Bureaucracy has no adequate juridicial process to protect its incumbents.

• The control and authority systems of bureaucracy do not work.

• Bureaucracy cannot assimilate the influx of new technology or new professionals entering the organization.

• Bureaucracy does not adequately account or allow for personal growth of mature personalities.

• Bureaucracy seems unable to cope with rapid, unprogrammed changes.

SUBSTANTIVE STATUS OF THE BEHAVIORAL SCIENCES IN MANAGEMENT

These exigencies have brought about a concern for revitalizing organizational theory and practice. The behavioral sciences have grown out of a response to this need. The array of problems listed earlier suggest the five main substantive areas where the behavioral sciences have contributed most: (1) personality theory, (2) interpersonal dynamics, (3) group behavior, (4) intergroup behavior, and (5) organizational behavior. Less clearly, they also point to the main streams of current theory.

• Argyris[3] extended the earlier work of Mayo and Roethlisberger and sharpened the idea of a basic incongruity between the needs of the employee and the demands of the organization.

• McGregor[4] focused primarily on how the authority system affected motivation and warned that unless other forms of social influence were developed, management would be unable to provide appropriate leadership.

• Likert,[5] working out of the Michigan empirical tradition, applied Lewin's field and group theories to industrial organizations, demonstrating the importance of affiliation and group belonging as motivators and highlighting the pivotal role of the person who can enjoy multiple memberships and serve as a "linking pin" between groups.

• Shepard,[6] Burns and Stalker,[7] deriving their ideas from European sociology, mainly Durkheim and Weber, developed the idea of an "organic" organization as a counterpose to what they call the mechanistic, bureaucratic model.

• March and Simon[8] were able to develop a propositional inventory based primarily on a cognitive psychology and providing behavioral hypotheses related to their main interests, choice, motivation, conflict, and power.

• Trist and Emery, et al.,[9] Rice,[10] and Sofer[11] at the Tavistock Institute brought to bear a fascinating combination of psychoanalytic and open-systems theory in order to focus on the integration between the technological and social requirements of work.

• Tannenbaum and his associates,[12] Blake and Shepard,[13] and others began to apply T groups and sensitivity training directly to the organization in order to change its fundamental value structure. More recently, Schein and Bennis summarized and conceptualized this process.[14]

There are others who deserve mention, but these should provide a representative sample sufficient to indicate the variety and range of methods and ideas:

• From psychology we have psychoanalytic, role, and cognitive theories.

• From sociology there are bureaucratic, social-system, symbolic-interactionism, and role theories.

• From anthropology have sprung the central ideas of norms, sentiments, cohesion, and interaction.

• From political science has come the recent work on conflict theory.

• From economics the decision processes and choice mechanisms have been elucidated.

• From the historical approach have come mainly case studies which have helped to clarify the role of key decision makers.

The methods are equally rich and varied, ranging all the way from anthropological techniques of participant-observation and interviewing to survey research, from rigorous experimental studies to case reports and library studies, from controlled field experiments to computer simulation.

It might be useful to summarize at this point. My contention is that the behavioral sciences are becoming more attached to various spheres of action, to a variety of institutional realities. Management education and practice has proved to be particularly receptive to the behavioral sciences. In my own area, social psychology, we have witnessed a spirited advance resulting from two parallel developments:

1   The general failure of the bureaucratic model to realize its capacities* and to cope effectively with contemporary realities.
2   A growth in empirical organization studies, accelerated by the aforementioned crises confronting organizations. Several theoretical and research traditions have already emerged, for the most part eclectic, empirical, young, and evolving.

Considering their youth and inchoate state, these new behavioral science researchers and theories have made a solid impact on management thinking, particularly upon the moral imperatives which guide managerial action. I shall be deliberately sweeping in summarizing these changes as much to hide my surprise as to cover a lot of ground quickly. It seems to me that we have seen over the past decade a fundamental change in the basic philosophy which underlies managerial behavior, reflected most of all in the following three areas:

1   A new concept of *man*, based on increased knowledge of his complex and shifting needs, which replaces the oversimplified, innocent push-button or inert idea of man.
2   A new concept of *power*, based on collaboration and reason, which replaces a model of power based on coercion and fear.
3   A new concept of *organizational values*, based on an humanistic existential orientation, which replaces the depersonalized, mechanistic value system.

Please do not misunderstand. The last thing I want to do is overstate the case, trapping us all in a false dream. I do not mean that these transformations of man, power, and organizational values are fully accepted, or even understood, to say nothing of implemented in day-to-day organizational affairs. These changes may be light-years away from actual adoption. I do mean that they have gained wide *intellectual* acceptance in enlightened management quarters, that they have caused a terrific amount of rethinking and search behavior on the part of many organizational planners, and that they have been used as a basis for policy fomulation by certain large organizations,

* According to Philip Slater, one must be careful to differentiate those areas where bureaucracy has been inadequate and those where particularistic contamination has crept in. In the first instance, bureaucracy requires modification; in the second instance, it is not bureaucracy which is at fault, say, in its emphasis on rationality and predictability, but role incumbents unable to cope with the system's imperatives and to realize its design.

mainly industrial leviathans, but also by many other nonindustrial institutions.

BEHAVIORAL SCIENCES PERSPECTIVE IN ORGANIZATIONAL STUDIES

I now return to the title of this essay and my earlier remark about the gap between the present status of the behavioral sciences and their potential realization and significance. Though I have been generally satisfied by their total impact on managerial values and thinking, I have wondered if our research output warrants this degree of influence. I have the impression that our real scientific contribution has still to come and that our ideological appeal has surpassed and even masked our scientific appeal—a point which, if true, deserves some study. With this in mind, I should like to emphasize the *future* connotation of the word "perspective" in the title of the essay, rather than dwell on the present or tidy-up the past. Many good and recent books do a thorough job of those formidable tasks.[15] What I prefer to do is look at the future, assess our research and developmental tasks, and outline an agenda for future work.

In order to organize this agenda, I propose to group the problems referred to earlier as stemming from the major predicaments facing modern organizations. These predicaments emerge basically from twentieth century changes, primarily the growth of science and education, the separation of property from power, and other profound changes still reverberating in our society. The bureaucratic mechanism, so capable in coordinating men and power in a stable society of routine tasks, cannot cope with contemporary realities. As Table 1 shows, five major categories of research and theory emerge from these realities. In fact, they can also be viewed as the core tasks confronting the manager in coordinating the human side of enterprise.

Some research progress has been made on the first three, integration, social influence, and collaboration. Much less effort is visible on the problem of adaption. "Revitalization," which I shall discuss later on in detail, has never been explicitly recognized as a problem in organizational behavior. Let us take up each of these in order.

Integration

Integrating man's individual needs with organizational demands is not only a chronic and vexing practical problem, it turns out to

TABLE 1 Human problems confronting contemporary organizations

Problem	Bureaucratic solutions	New twentieth century conditions
Integration The problem of how to integrate individual needs and management goals.	No solution because of no problem. Individual vastly oversimplified, regarded as passive instrument or disregarded.	Emergence of human sciences and understanding of man's complexity. Rising aspirations. Humanistic-democratic ethos.
Social influence The problem of the distribution of power and sources of power and authority.	An explicit reliance on legal-rational power, but an implicit usage of coercive power. In any case, a confused, ambiguous, shifting complex of competence, coercion, and legal code.	Separation of management from ownership. Rise of trade unions and general education. Negative and unintended effects of authoritarian rule.
Collaboration The problem of managing and resolving conflicts.	The "rule of hierarchy" to resolve conflicts between ranks and the "rule of coordination" to resolve conflict between horizontal groups. "Loyalty."	Specialization and professionalization and increased need for interdependence. Leadership too complex for one-man rule or omniscience.

TABLE 1 Human problems confronting contemporary organizations

Problem	Bureaucratic solutions	New twentieth century conditions
Adaptation The problem of responding appropriately to changes induced by the environment of the firm.	Environment stable, simple, and predictable; tasks routine. Adapting to change occurs in haphazard and adventitious ways. Unanticipated consequences abound.	External environment of firm more "turbulent," less predictable. Unprecedented rate of technological change.
"Revitalization" The problem of growth and decay.	?	Rapid changes in technologies, tasks, manpower, raw materials, norms and values of society, goals of enterprise and society all make constant attention to process of firm and revision imperative.

be almost insurmountable conceptually. Its practical side is reflected on the work of two subareas of industrial psychology, personnel psychology, and human engineering.* The first attempts to reduce the tension between individual needs and organizational demands by finding the right man for the right organizational slot. The human engineer, on the other hand, works from exactly the opposite point of view. He tries to construct organizational slots that any man can fit. If each could perfect their work, there would be no need for the other. That is, if the human engineers could, to quote T. S. Eliot, "design systems so perfect, that no man needs to be good . . . ," then personnel psychology, with its emphasis on individual differences and matching people to roles, would be unnecessary. By the same token, if personnel psychology became foolproof, then there would be need for changing the environmental-technical factors. There is no clear and present danger of either of these advances taking place in our lifetime.

In the field of organizational behavior, a number of students and practitioners have tried to promote such changes in the organizational system to reduce the tension between the individual and the organization as "job enlargement," "reality-centered leadership," work-group organization, and improved collaboration between superior and subordinates. More recently, many others have been working more ambitiously to transform the basic value system of the enterprise so that humanistic and democratic values are infused and related to policy.[17]

While these new developments hold genuine promise, and there is no question of their momentum in the United States and Western Europe, they have not demonstrated, as yet, their appropriateness for the so-called "emerging nations."†

Quite apart from these practical problems, the conceptual fusion of personality and organization seems a long way off. There was a flurry of promise, shortly after the heady days following World War II, when the search for over-arching concepts and the unification of science were avant-garde pursuits. A number of attempts were made by intrepid scholars and numerous *ad hoc* committees on interdisci-

* According to Mason Haire, to whom I am indebted for the ideas in this paragraph, the third subarea is the "social psychology of industry," of which this essay is an example.[16]

† Though based only on short experience in India, I would say that there is reason to believe that these newer programs would be particularly suitable for Indian conditions.

plinary studies to establish integrative courses under one or another theoretical guise. The "fall-out" from these attempts can still be observed in old catalogues and remanded textbooks still emanating a charm and magnetism, like a once glamorous, but fading movie queen; it goes under the titles of "culture and personality," "psychological anthropology," "character and society," and other earnest phrases which tried to hold culture and personality together.

Alas, the integration was more verbal than real, and we are left with the same prewar duality of personality and organization which are poles apart, without common concepts or measurements, aching for union, but hardly on speaking terms, as it were.

There is one theoretical and practical ray of hope suggested in the recent work of Robert Kahn and his associates.[18] Taking role as the unifying concept and Merton's idea of role set as meaning the cluster of significant others who transmit expectations to the role

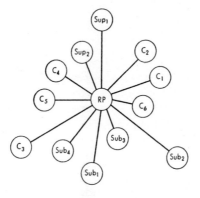

FIG. 5   Illustration of role set

RP = Pivotal role player
Sub = Subordinates reporting to RP
C = Colleagues in RP's role set
Sup = RP's superiors

The role set is developed through an interview with the pivotal role player. *Role conflict* is a function of discrepant expectations among role senders (Sub, Sup, C). *Overload* is a function of a number of role senders and expectations, and *role ambiguity* is derived from unclear and/or uncertain expectations.

player, Kahn is able to identify and measure a number of important dimensions affecting a person in relation to the organizational forces. He operationalizes the constructs of role, role set, role senders, and derives from these empirical referents for role conflict, role ambiguity, and role overload, and he shows how these affect personality functioning and job-related attitudes. Kahn brings the venerable concept of role squarely back into the center of organizational behavior (see Figure 5). Through sophisticated measurement and shrewd usage, he demonstrates, at least to my satisfaction, that role is a crucial unifying idea, one which may bring about a conceptual *rapprochement* between personality and organization, and more surely, will yield important practical returns.

With the foregoing in mind, let us elucidate the integration problem through a more complete study of role set and how it serves as a mediator between personality and organization. We can identify and measure the social ecology of role, in terms of Kahn's dimensions of conflict, ambiguity, and overload, but also in Lewinian terms. For example, role set can be analyzed in the following ways:

- number of role senders transmitting expectations to role player (pivotal role)
- distance between and degree of permeability among various role senders and in relation to role player
- ratio of superiors/subordinates/peers in role player's role set
- compartmentalization and continuity in interrole sets; that is, between role sets apart from workplace, such as family, friends, other reference groups.

From these and other measurements, it would be possible to give numerical meaning to the valence and salience of the complex of forces in the role set. All of these topological and quantitative relationships can be thought of as a *role space*.

A number of researchable questions follow from this basic idea:

1 Can we identify personalities more or less capable of operating effectively within different role spaces? I would wager that paranoids would have a very difficult time with role conflict and that psychopaths would move easily through a highly compartmentalized and conflicting role space.

2 The complexity of a role space, both in numbers of role senders and degree of conflict or ambiguity, could be measured. Would

the role incumbent's ability to manage complexity and simplicity of role space be related to his personality in terms of defense mechanisms? or ego strength? or anxiety areas? or character types? I would predict, for example, that the narcissistic character type would have a more complex, differentiated, but less compartmentalized role space contrasted to the obsessive type.

3   What about the relationship between role suction and self-determination? The subjects in Kahn's research (role players) appeared to be imprisoned by their role sets; at least, they came to take their role senders and their expectations as "givens." To use Redl's graphic term, they were "sucked" into role, enplaced there, and sealed, as it were, by their role senders. But surely, some role players are more active than others in shaping their own role space. How do role players change their role space? What personality variables are associated with role players who are proactive, who maintain a high degree of autonomy and self-determination compared to those role players who are reactive?

4   What effect does a highly complicated and conflicted role space have on the role player? Can one change his behaviors, as one is expected to do, under differing role conditions without depersonalization? To what extent is psychopathy induced in this way? As role players climb higher in the organizational hierarchy, there is evidence that their role space becomes more intense, differentiated, and complex. What effects does this have?

5   To what extent does consciousness of the role space reduce spontaneity of behavior? People occasionally ask about the loss of spontaneity through a heightened degree of consciousness and study. My usual response is that one is always awkward with new knowledge until it becomes internalized and natural. Is that answer complete, or valid? I wonder what would happen, for example, if we trained people to understand their role space more fully so that they could gain clarity in their work relationships through reducing excess conflict or ambiguity. This is a tempting idea. Would it also reduce the grace and spontaneity in one's social relationships? Are psychoanalysts and behavioral scientists as immediate and innocent as they can be or are they inhibited by their own understanding? Does the mover remain unmoved, trapped by inescapable calculations that pass for thoughtfulness?

6   Would it be possible to devise role-space interviews and question-

naires, to augment personality tests, to improve selection procedures? Personality tests used for selection purposes must successfully translate intrapsychic functioning into interpersonal terms.
This is difficult to achieve. One's basic fears and anxieties may
not be correlated to the interpersonal and social behavior necessary to work relationships. But if one can discover the preferred
role space of the job applicant, his reactions to conflict, overload,
and ambiguity, then one could use this knowledge for placement.

The above questions link personality to organization through the
concepts of role and role space. They also betray my bias about the
current state of organizational theory and research; namely, that with
few exceptions, we have not come to terms with useful dimensions
of personality. We have contented ourselves with superficial traits
under the name of rigor and "scientific exactitude." I think it's about
time we began to trade off some rigor for vigor.

One last point in this admonishing mood. Most contemporary
organizational theory, when it does deal with personality, bases its
view of man on Maslow's "hierarchy of needs" theory.[19] I am baffled
to discover that little has been done to test the validity of this
theory. That there is a hierarchy of needs, that the hierarchy is scaled
from physical-economic to social and self-actualization needs, that
once a need is satisfied, it is no longer a motivator, that one climbs
the hierarchy only when the previous level of needs is satisfied, are assumptions upon which a good deal of the newer organizational theory
is based. It would not only be useful, but crucial, to devise more
empirical validation of these ideas.

Social Influence

Of the five themes, this one has developed the richest research
tradition. Starting with the pioneering research on democratic, autocratic, and laissez-faire styles of leadership, Lewin, his associates, and
those influenced by them, have cultivated this field assiduously. What
they say about social influence, they can say with confidence. Their
conclusions spring from a vast number of rigorous field and experimental studies which have systematically varied a continuum of leadership styles, and their effects were observed on a wide range of dependent variables, such as productivity, group cohesion, morale, hostility, and levels of anxiety. Their overall finding is that the more influence a follower has over his own decision and the more committed

he is to the decision, the more likely he is to implement the decision and the more intrinsic satisfaction he will derive from the decision process. But this omnibus proposition must be qualified by a number of modifying factors, such as (1) the personality, values, experience, and background of the follower, (2) the personality, etc., of the leader, and (3) factors in the situation itself. For example, so far as followers go, it was found that the individual's desire for decision-making responsibility was negatively correlated with dependency. Similarly, the higher the need for autonomy, the more he desired and acted effectively under conditions of high initiative.

The history of the theory and practice of leadership since the Industrial Revolution reveals an unmistakeable tendency toward those democratic-humanitarian values exemplified by McGregor's Theory Y. However untested these new theories are, there is no doubt of the swing *away* from coercive, autocratic, and arbitrary forms of power. Even since the early researches of Mayo and Roethlisberger, about thirty years ago, this tendency can be observed. For example, an outcome of the Western Electric studies was a counseling program for employees (totally independent of Roger's, but remarkably close in practice) designed to *listen* to and *accept* their views without necessarily doing anything about them. Then the work of Lewin and his associates led to certain conclusions regarding the importance of *participation* in decision making. This led to the participative management demonstrated in the Scanlon Plan. Following that, the tradition of Argyris, McGregor, and Maslow asserted itself and the notion of *self-control* took hold; that is to say, power should reside ultimately in the individual, not in his boss or work group. More recently, the idea of *mutual influence* between leaders and followers has been advanced, addressing itself to ways and means by which superiors and subordinates can develop a consensus.

This brief review of leadership studies and practices reveals not only its ethical direction—toward shared influence—but implies as well the idea that different patterns of leadership may be more appropriate at one time than at another. This promises one general research area: a set of cross-cultural studies, made under widely different cultural, economic, political conditions (probably using factor analytic techniques) which would measure (1) characteristics of leaders, (2) characteristics of followers, (3) factors in the situation and which would compare their relative effectiveness. Only some ambitious, comparative management study such as this will sort out the issues which concern international management: How exportable are these American ideas? What generalizations, principles, theorems can be made about the phases of organizational development? What are appropriate leadership styles in underdeveloped countries and emergent industrial cultures? For example, I would like to respond with some certainty to these questions which I often hear from businessmen and more often from academic colleagues:*

• Can Indian management utilize the new theories of power and motivation (Theory Y) when the Indian worker presumably is low on the need hierarchy? Before self-control can become relevant does not man have to satisfy his basic economic, physiological, and safety needs?

• Is not the Indian worker far too dependent to accept more autonomy and responsibility on the job?

• Do not Hindu values (reflected in the joint family system and authoritarian values) weaken the probability of authentic collaboration at work?

• Can the Indian leader, with his strong authoritarian background, relinquish absolute command?

• Does not the Indian require a charismatic leader more than his American or Western European counterpart does? Is charisma compatible with democracy?

• Do Hindu beliefs, with their emphasis on self-realization and *dharma* make the ethic of mutual influence and collaboration impossible?

• Do hierarchical relationships between the Indian worker and superior in fact stifle "openness" and true dialogue as they do in our culture?

These are some of the questions which require research and which, I think, it is possible to answer with our present methods and theory.

* I use India here only as an example. The same questions can be raised in revised form about any developing nation. There is a growing literature in this area, but more empirical work is needed. I have found the work of Harbison and Myers,[20] Farmer and Richman[21] particularly useful and rich in this respect.

Collaboration

In modern organizations we observe many of the same social processes of conflict, stereotypy, and centrifugal forces which inhere in and divide nations and communities. They also employ the same furtive, often fruitless, always enervating mechanisms of conflict resolution: avoidance or suppression, annihiliation of the weaker party by the stronger, sterile compromises, and unstable collusions and coalitions. In fact, the analogy between organizations and nations is not a bad one for understanding conflict management and resolution. Particularly as organizations become more complex they fragment and divide, building tribal patterns and symbolic codes which often work to exclude others (secrets and noxious jargon, for example) and on occasion to exploit differences for inward (and always, fragile) harmony. Some large organizations, in fact, can be understood only through an analysis of their suzerainties and satellites, their tactics resembling a sophisticated form of guerrilla warfare, and a venture into adjacent spheres of interest is taken under cover of darkness and fear of ambush.

Basically, conflict originates from two structural sources: (1) vertical, between ranks; (2) horizontal or between various groups and departments. Bureaucratic strategy for resolving vertical conflicts depends solely on a vague "law of hierarchy," and an unvague implication: when in doubt, the boss decides. The bureaucratic strategy for horizontal disputes depends on the equally vague "law of coordination," with an assist from the "rule of hierarchy" when the former fails. In other words, the boss arbitrates and then rules. There is a third, more informal, rule that is typically practiced as a last resort. The boss calls the disputants together and invokes the "rule of loyalty" for the general good. The "rule of loyalty" is a curious one, for more often than not its effects are undesirable and tensions are aggravated, rather than relieved. One of the basic, but often unrecognized, paradoxes of organizational life is that its chief device of integration tends to induce excessive in-group cohesiveness at the price of intergroup cooperation.

Americans, in general, pay fulsome lip service to all forms of cooperation, teamwork, togetherness, etc. The problem is that there is no social translation of this ethic. Indeed, many observers of the American cultural scene point to the discrepancy between individualism, as expressed in Jeffersonian democracy, and cooperation, as expressed in the original confederation of states. The resultant dilution of both ethics is what David Reisman calls "antagonistic cooperation": we feign harmony and act autonomy.

This is no easy conflict to resolve. There is a necessary dialectic between the individual and the group, identity and community. Marxism, which elevates the group and mutes the individual, polarizes the issue. Almost the entire intellectual history of the last 100 years is a monumental footnote to this polarity: on the one hand the theories of Darwin and Freud, and on the other, of Marx and Weber.

The problem of collaboration presses. As professional workers join large-scale organizations in increasing numbers, as tasks become more complex and interdependent, as diverse specialists come together for relatively short periods of time to solve problems, as responsibilities become too complex for one man's comprehension, new social inventions of collaboration are imperative.

With this in mind, let us turn directly to some possible research and development areas: [*]

Intergroup-horizontal collaboration   Likert recognized the presence of "linking pins" who affect the problem of intergroup collaboration. These individuals, on the basis of enjoying membership (or psychological affinity) in overlapping groups, and through their ability to articulate orientations from differing or competing groups and their skill in translating and articulating diverse languages, can perform an important integrative function in complex organizations.

We need to know more specifically how these individuals emerge, what their behaviors are, how they come to be accepted as "friendly, but different," how they manage to transcend and overcome their parochial interests or what Mannheim called "perspectivistic orientation." We also need to know about their social and psychological background. Do they have more in common with each other than they have with their "constituencies"? Do their family background and biographical data turn up any uniformities? Is their creativity and

---

[*] Blake and Mouton have clearly demonstrated through ingeniously controlled and natural experiments, that intergroup therapy is possible and that other forms of social negotiation can be developed. Their work in conflict management is extraordinary and deserves wide readership and implementation.[22]

intelligence more developed? Can they be understood through theories of deviance or marginality?

After these data are marshalled, we shall see whether or not "linking pins" are identical to "emergent leaders." We will also be in a better position to identify and train them.

We need more studies of *temporary systems*—groups which have a beginning, a destiny, and a finite "death." Through a natural history of these groups, we may learn more about the development of collaboration, of the emergence of linking pins, of cliques and cabals, of conflict and its resolution. T groups, widely used as a training technique in the United States and Western Europe, fulfill these requirements but are almost unexploited as a microcosm of social evolution. Also there are numerous groups which meet for fixed periods of time from different nations, with individuals holding different orientations, representing disparate disciplines, engaged in some form of joint ventures. Some examples include the fifty executives at IMEDE in Lausanne, Switzerland, representing twenty to twenty-five countries; the fifty professors from almost as many nations in the Afro-Asian sphere who come for advanced training at ICAME in Stanford University; and the twenty-five economists in public service, from all over the world, who meet for three months at the World Bank Institute in Washington. All of these groups develop mechanisms of collaboration and conflict resolution and would make splendid crucibles for understanding the emergence and maintenance of community.

We need more empirical, longitudinal studies on the emergence of role-related attitudes and their vicissitudes throughout the course of socialization.* This way we can enrich our understanding of "perspectivistic orientation" or the way in which role furthers as well as narrows perspective through the process of role taking and concomitant pressures toward conformity. One would like to see included in this research a sample of scientists at different stages of their career (cross-sectional as well as longitudinal) and observe how their training and socialization shape their perception of reality.

Vertical collaboration The problems of vertical collaboration stem from qualitatively different stresses than the horizontal type. Predominantly, a superior controls the means to the need satisfaction of his subordinates. From this basic structural fact springs all the difficul-

---

* Lieberman's study, reported almost ten years ago, remains one of the few research efforts on the effect of role status on attitudes.[23]

ties which separate bosses from employees, fathers from sons. Experience and research demonstrate conclusively that subordinates tend to withdraw and/or suppress views that are at variance with those of the boss, invent political solutions rather than engage in joint problem solving, allow their superiors to make mistakes, even when they, the subordinates, know better. For their part, superiors desire an atmosphere of trust in order to encourage authentic communication, but they rarely understand how to create and maintain—or even trust—this atmosphere. Read's[24] research demonstrates that upward communication depends on three factors: (1) trust between superior and subordinate, (2) the perceived power of the superior from the point of view of the subordinate, and (3) the ambition of the subordinate. To the extent that the superior and subordinate do not trust each other, to the extent that the subordinate sees the superior as having high power, and to the extent that the subordinate is highly ambitious, upward communication is restricted. In short, power without trust is the main condition of poor communication between ranks.

Read's studies can be elaborated and expanded:

1 How do superiors and subordinates develop trusting relationships? What communication patterns express and develop trust and what communication patterns do the opposite?

2 It is commonly taken for granted that the power differential between boss and subordinate is always tilted in favor of the boss. But we know that bosses are influenced by their subordinates. How does this process work? In what ways do subordinates influence bosses? What sources of power do they rely on, lacking the manifest power of rewards and punishments? Do subordinates control the power to confirm or disconfirm the boss' leadership (i.e. his self-esteem) or his overall effectiveness? If so, how does this manifest itself?

3 Can we use the methods and theory of the new practice of family psychiatry to enhance our understanding of the formation and maintenance of trust? Can we identify and measure "double-bind" situations and observe their effects? Can we extrapolate Erikson's theory of human growth ("basic trust" is the first and most important phase) to the organization?

4 Can we better train leaders and followers to collaborate and work toward atmospheres of authenticity, where valid communication is the norm, not the exception?

Adaptation

In an earlier paper, I remarked that the real *coup de grâce* to bureaucracy has come, not from its ethical-moral posture and social fabric, but from a totally unexpected direction, from the environment:

> The pyramidal structure of bureaucracy, where power was concentrated at the top—perhaps by one person or a group who had the knowledge and resources to control the entire enterprise—seemed perfect to "run a railroad." And undoubtedly for tasks like building railroads, for the routinized tasks of the Nineteenth and early Twentieth Centuries, bureaucracy was and is an eminently suitable social arrangement.[25]

Nowadays, primarily resulting from the growth of science, technology, and research and development activities, the organizational environment of the firm is rapidly changing. As A. T. M. Wilson has pointed out, the number and pattern of relations between managers and eight areas of relevant social activity have become more active and complicated.[26] The eight areas are: government, distributors and consumers, shareholders, competitors, raw material and power suppliers, sources of employees, particularly managers, trade unions, and groups within the firm. Over the last twenty-five years, the rate of transactions with these eight social institutions has increased and their importance in conducting the enterprise has grown.

Emery and Trist, in an important paper, have conceptualized the field of forces surrounding the firm as a *turbulent environment* which contains the following characteristics:[27]

• The environment is a field of forces which contains *causal* mechanisms and poses important choices for the firm.

• The field is dynamic with increasing interdependencies among and between the eight social institutions specified above.

• There is, among the institutions relating to the firm, a deepening interdependence between the economic and other facets of society. This means that economic organizations are increasingly enmeshed in legislation and public regulation.

• There is increasing reliance on research and development to achieve competitive advantage and a concomitant change gradient which is continuously felt in the environmental field.

• Finally, maximizing cooperation, rather than competition between firms, appears desirable (and even necessary) because their fates may become basically correlated.

The upshot of all this is that the environmental texture of the firm, shaped by the growth of science and technology, has changed in just those ways which make the bureaucratic mechanism most problematical. Bureaucracy thrives under conditions of competition and certainty, where the environment is stable and steady and above all, predictable. The texture of the environment now holds in its turbulent and emergent field of forces casual mechanisms so rapidly changing and unpredictable that it both imperils (and implies the end of) bureaucracy.°

Growing out of bureaucracy's inability to respond appropriately to a turbulent environment are two concerns, a research problem called, for convenience, "knowledge utilization," and a training problem.

Studies in knowledge utilization   Essentially the problem of adaptation is one of responding appropriately to new information. "Appropriately" can best be expressed and identified by its obverse, an extreme and naïve susceptibility often seen in spastic states and by its debilitating opposite, a guarded and rigid response. Both will, by avoiding realities and in different ways, lead to maladaptive search behavior, ultimately reflected in lowered efficiency.

The problem can be viewed as essentially one of the sensitivity and receptivity of the organization to new information and ideas and how it processes and implements this "intelligence." Some of the questions this problem suggests are:

1 How does the organization get its information? from its staff? outside consultants? specialized sources? other firms?
2 How does the organization store and retrieve information?
3 What social processes inhibit implementation of valid ideas and what social processes facilitate implementation? For example, the *relationship* between staff and line is probably significant in understanding the process of knowledge utilization within the firm. Similarly, the relationships between external consultants and mem-

---

° Examples of causal mechanisms stemming from the environment are: antidiscrimination laws, development of nuclear power, common market, Sputnik, etc.

bers of the firm are equally crucial. Can we identify and understand the qualities of an effective "helping relationships"? What modes of collaboration have been developed which lead to achievement of goals?

4 I am particularly interested in understanding how ideas are transmitted across political and academic frontiers, another variant of the knowledge-utilization process. John Thomas and I are presently working out a research design which aims to illuminate the problems of cross-national aid projects through focusing on the kinds of relationships which lead to successful implementation and those which fail to effect change.*

Training for change On the training side, the problems of adaptation raise some fascinating questions: Can we train and recruit people alert and sensitive to new ideas, who are not threatened by the prevalence of newness, and who identify with the adaptive process? Putting it differently, can we train people to be more tolerant of ambiguity, less frozen in response to change, more flexible in their approach to problems, more able to develop "poise," and capable of moving quickly and with high commitment to ever-changing problems and conditions?

Revitalization

Alfred North Whitehead sets the problem before us:

The art of free society consists first in the maintenance of the symbolic code, and secondly, in the fearlessness of revision . . . Those societies which cannot combine reverence to their symbols with freedom of revision must ultimately decay . . .

Organizations, as well as societies, must be concerned with those social conditions that engender a buoyancy, resilience, and a "fearlessness of revision." Growth and decay emerge as the penultimate problem in contemporary society where the environment is turbulent and uncertain.

---

* We work under the assumption that the more an intended change involves human values and deeply ingrained habits, the more crucial the relationship is for success. If the relationship is trusting, authentic, where the agreement and contract are entered into for nonthreatening reasons and under other specifiable conditions, having to do with the relationship, the change program has a higher probability of success.

I introduce the term "revitalization" to embrace all the social mechanisms that regenerate and stagnate and with the trajectory of this cycle. As I see it, the properties that lead to a functional autonomy for growth and development are:

1 An ability to learn from experience, to codify, and to store the learning;
2 An ability to "learn how to learn," that is, to develop methodologies for improving the learning process;
3 An ability to acquire and use feedback on its own performance, to develop a "process orientation," in short, to be self-analytical;
4 An ability to direct one's own destiny.*

I mentioned in the Introduction to Part 1 of this book that man is the animal that can shape his own evolution. Through the values (idenes) that infuse and shape human organizations, social evolution is either advanced or retarded. The value system presented here, an amalgam of democracy, collaboration, and science, represents the most civilized and advanced system available. It is a system with no visible alternatives (save that of absolutism or anarchy) and one which, I believe, is not only most suited to our times but captivating as well.

For the manager, revitalization means that the organization has to take a conscious responsibility for its own evolution; that, without a planned methodology and explicit direction, the enterprise will not realize its potential. For the manager, the issue of revitalization confronts him with the penultimate challenge: growth or decay.

What implications does the idea of revitalization hold for the student of organizational behavior? First of all, we need theories of *changing*, not simply change. In other words, theories of organizational change must be developed which embrace variables accessible to control, variables which are congruent to the value system of the organization; in short, *manipulable* variables. What we need, for example, is a theory of democratization, not a theory of democracy. Most theories of social change, at best, resemble astronomy: observation without control. Viable theories of changing require not only scientific verification; they must include as well, strategic variables, accessible to the policy makers.

---

* If these qualities sound identical to those of the mature individual or what Gardner calls the "self-renewal" process, I mean it just that way.[28]

Secondly, we need more and better studies of social evolution. If only we had available in the behavioral sciences an equivalent to the "fruit fly" where we could cheaply and quickly reproduce "instant cultures." We do have, as I said earlier, many potential research sites of "temporary systems"[29] where useful studies could be undertaken. And these are turning up in the most unusual places: new organizations, new cities, new groups emerging—and dying—where methodologies and theories of social evolution could be worked out.

One unexploited research site for studies in social evolution grows out of the contemporary world situation, the so-called developed and underdeveloped countries. We live in a world stratified according to degree of modernization. The future (say, of India) is present; that is, the consequences of modernization are foreshadowed, in America and Europe. Cross-cultural studies encompassing a wide range of technological, political, social, economic, and legal variables on the one side, and covering a continuum of traditionalism-modernism may throw some light on the trajectory and vicissitudes of social evolution, its phases, preemptive threats, functional imperatives, etc. It may be possible, for example, to predict the course of democratization and whether or not authoritarianism, bureaucracy, or charismatic leadership are its necessary precursors.

CONCLUDING REMARKS

Can we look back, at this point, over the range of issues covered, their implications for action, and their basic orientation to the study of organizations? For convenience I shall state these in a more or less axiomatic way:

1 *Organizations are microcosms* Their study reveals the social processes inherent in all social systems at all levels, from small groups to communities. Though organizations differ in purpose and in design, their basic tasks are similar: to achieve effective means of integration, social influence, collaboration, adaptation, and revitalization.

2 *Behavioral scientists have become more committed to the problem of application of their knowledge* They are taking as much direction from contemporary crises as they are from the convenience of known variables. The improvement of practice is regarded as a respectable scientific pursuit.

3 *The utilization of knowledge, its implementation, is a key problem facing the behavioral sciences* The growth of the behavioral sciences has been remarkable, but slightly lopsided. We keep producing new knowledge and ideas, but little work goes into understanding the social processes that stifle or facilitate the diffusion, acquisition, understanding, ingestion, and implementation of the new ideas. It is difficult to be concerned about becoming a "servant of power" when one observes so many good ideas going astray, when the studies of behavioral scientists mildew in inaccessible journals, when policy makers not only disregard relevant information concerning new legislation, but appear to hold attitudes toward behavioral scientists which people usually reserve for undesirable outcasts.*

4 *The key to the problem of knowledge utilization is collaboration between the producers and users of the knowledge* The chief obstacle to effective knowledge utilization is resistance to change. When new ideas affect attitudes and beliefs, the man producing the knowledge (or some middle man or "linking pin") must work with the users of knowledge to disarm their defensiveness to change. As yet there is no institutionalized role to perform this function. Scientists must either take on this responsibility or train others to do so (just as "science writing" has developed as a communication link between a lay public and the scientific community.)

5 *The value systems of the scientific community and the practitioner must be enriched to include the idea of "revitalization"* This means that scientists must take moral and practical responsibility for their findings and that men of action must be receptive to analysis of their own and their organization's behavior and development. Often scientists, radical in their discoveries, hesitate when it comes to the truly radical opportunity of applying them.† For their part, practi-

---

* I am referring to the recent study of California state legislators responsible for a new bill on the control and rehabilitation of drug addicts. Only a handful of the representatives gained any of their ideas from the massive studies of psychiatrists and behavioral scientists. Typically, they were more receptive to cronies, the druggist, the family doctor, and the lobbies.[30]

† In Sir George Thomson's book, *The Foreseeable Future*, he demonstrates the extraordinary power of the new biology, helped by the electron microscope, to affect the genic organization. When he was asked about its obvious applications for controlling genic structure, he replied: "We might as well try to talk of improving a statue by spraying it with machine gun bullets." This reply might be interpreted as revealing not only a disbelief in applied science but also through its imagery, a certain hostility to it.[31]

tioners who cooly engage in risky ventures, are threatened by the risks of self-analysis.

If we grant these generalizations, other questions follow: How do we best educate the manager and the behavioral scientist to work effectively in a world of change? How can the manager develop sensitivity to the discrepancy between individual needs and organizational demands, interpersonal competence to employ appropriate influence, the vision to scan a turbulent environment, the abilty to develop methodologies of collaboration, and the courage to take an active part in social evolution? How do we train the scientist to understand his moral, emotional, and practical commitments to truth? Can the educational system of the scientist include a commitment to knowledge utilization? In what ways can we further collaboration between men of knowledge and men of action?

The remarkable aspect of our generation is its commitment to change, in thought and action. Our educational system should (1) help us to identify with this adaptive process without fear of losing our identity, (2) increase our tolerance of ambiguity without the fear of losing intellectual mastery, (3) increase our ability to collaborate without fear of losing individuality, (4) develop a willingness to participate in social evolution while recognizing implacable forces. In short, we need an educational system which can help us make a virtue out of contingency rather than one which induces hesitancy and its reckless companion, expedience.

NOTES

1. Clark, C., "Oxford Reformed," *Encounter,* pp. 44–52, January, 1965.
2. Kerr, C., *The Uses of the University,* Harvard University Press, Cambridge, Mass., 1963.
3. Argyris, C., *Personality and Organization,* Harper and Row, Publishers, Incorporated, New York, 1957. *Integrating the Individual and the Organization,* John Wiley & Sons, Inc., New York, 1964.
4. McGregor, D. M., *The Human Side of Enterprise,* McGraw-Hill Book Company, New York, 1960.
5. Likert, R., *New Patterns in Management,* McGraw-Hill Book Company, New York, 1961.
6. Shepard, H. A., "Changing Interpersonal and Intergroup Relationships in Organizations," in J. G. March (ed.), *Handbook of Organizations,* Rand McNally & Company, Chicago, 1965.

7. Burns, T., and G. W. Stalker, *The Management of Innovation,* Quadrangle, Chicago, 1961.

8. March, J. G., and H. A. Simon, *Organizations,* John Wiley & Sons, Inc., New York, 1958.

9. Emery, F. E., and E. Trist, "Socio-technical Systems," Paper presented at the 6th Annual International Meeting of the Institute of Management Sciences, Paris, France, September, 1959. E. Trist, G. Higgin, H. Murray, and A. Pollock, *Organizational Choice,* London: Tavistock, 1963.

10. Rice, A. K., *The Enterprise and Its Environment.* Tavistock, London, 1963.

11. Sofer, C., *The Organization from Within,* Tavistock, London, 1961.

12. Tannenbaum, R., I. Weschler, and F. Massarik, *Leadership and Organization.* McGraw-Hill Book Company, New York, 1961.

13. *An Action Research Program for Organization Improvement,* Foundation for Research on Human Behavior, Ann Arbor, 1960.

14. Schein, E. H., and W. G. Bennis, *Personal and Organizational Change through Group Methods,* John Wiley & Sons, Inc., New York, 1965.

15. Schein, E. H., *Organizational Psychology,* Prentice-Hall, Inc., Englewood Cliffs, N.J., 1965.

16. Haire, M., "Psychology and the Study of Business: Joint Behavioral Sciences," in R. A. Dahl, M. Haire, and P. F. Lazarsfeld (eds.), *Social Science Research on Business: Product and Potential,* Columbia University Press, New York, 1959, pp. 45–98.

17. Schein and Bennis, *op. cit.*

18. Kahn, R., D. Wolfe, R. Quinn, J. D. Snoek, and R. Rosenthal, *Organizational Stress,* John Wiley & Sons, Inc., New York, 1964.

19. Maslow, A., *Motivation and Personality,* Harper and Row, Publishers, Incorporated, New York, 1964.

20. Harbison, F., and C. A. Myers, *Management in the Industrial World,* McGraw-Hill Book Company, New York, 1959, especially chaps. 7, 13, and 18.

21. Farmer, R. N., and Richman, B. M., *Comparative Management and Economic Progress,* Richard D. Irwin, Inc., Homewood, Ill., 1965.

22. Blake, R. R., J. S. Mouton, and R. L. Sloma, "The Union-Management Intergroup Laboratory: Strategy for Resolving Intergroup Conflict," *Journal of Applied Behavioral Science,* vol. 1, 1965, pp. 25–57.

23. Lieberman, S., "The Effects of Changes in Roles on the Attitudes of Role Occupants," *Human Relations,* vol. 9, 1956, pp. 385–402.

24. Read, W. H., "Upward Communication in Industrial Hierarchies," *Human Relations,* vol. 15, pp. 3–15, 1962.

25. Bennis, W. G., "Organizational Developments and the Fate of Bureaucracy," invited address, Division of Industrial and Business Psychology, American Psychological Association, Sept. 5, 1964, pp. 6–7.

26. Wilson, A. T. M., "The Manager and His World," *Industrial Management Review,* 1961.

27. Emery, F. E., and E. Trist, "The Causal Texture of Organizational Environments," Paper presented at the International Congress of Psychology, Washington, September, 1963.

28. Gardner, J. W., *Self-Renewal*, Harper and Row, Publishers, Incorporated, New York, 1964.

29. Miles, M. B., "On Temporary Systems," in M. B. Miles (ed.), *Innovation in Education*, Teachers College, Columbia University Press, New York, 1964, pp. 437–490.

30. Blum, R. H., and M. L. Funkhouser, "Legislators on Social Scientists and a Social Issue," *Journal of Applied Behavioral Science*, vol. 1, 1965, pp. 84–112.

31. Thomson, G., *The Forseeable Future*, Cambridge University Press, London, 1955, cited in G. Murphy, "Toward a Science of Individuality," in A. Abrams, H. H. Garner, and J. E. P. Toman (eds.), *Unfinished Tasks in the Behavioral Sciences*, The Williams & Wilkins Company, Baltimore, 1964, p. 202.

index

Catalog

If you are interested in a list of fine Paperback
books, covering a wide range of subjects
and interests, send your name and address,
requesting your free catalog, to:

McGraw-Hill Paperbacks
1221 Avenue of Americas
New York, N.Y. 10020